Cosmopolitics:

The Collected Papers of the Open Anthropology Cooperative, Volume I

Edited by

Justin Shaffner

and Huon Wardle

OPEN ANTHROPOLOGY COOPERATIVE PRESS

Open Anthropology Cooperative Press

Centre for Cosmopolitan Studies, 71 North Street, St Andrews, Fife KY16 9AL Scotland, U.K.

http://openanthcoop.net/press/

First published in January 2017 by

Open Anthropology Cooperative Press

ISBN-10: 1541348214

ISBN-13: 978-1541348219

Cover image by Max Wardle

DEDICATION

To Sidney Mintz (1922 – 2015)

CONTENTS

CONTENTS

ACKNOWLEDGMENTS

The OAC Press is an offshoot of an experiment begun early in 2009 by Keith Hart and a handful of collaborators. This group conjoined around the project of bringing anthropology to people, and into the internet era, via the communications technology of the moment. So, they set about creating a social networking site for the purpose, the *Open Anthropology Cooperative* (OAC). Numerous academic anthropologists were attracted to the scheme, and the formation of the OAC Press came about in order to allow open access discussion of their ideas via regularly held seminars. Since 2009 this body of work has amassed on the press website as a sequence of working papers,[1] and on the OAC main website[2] where a record of the related seminar discussions may be found.

In 2015 the editorial team – Keith Hart, Justin Shaffner and Huon Wardle – began to consider how to publish them in book form. We aimed to do this in the same spirit as the OAC itself – open access, open comment, free use. We had always made these papers individually downloadable; but thought that some readers would value owning a hard copy of a collection of them. This is why we are publishing this edition via one of the most accessible and wide-reaching publication formats available at present, Amazon.com's CreateSpace. Finally, the OAC has been forced to make its readers pay for something, but we hope that this combined record of some of its intellectually plural lines of conversation will make its own way.

The theme for the first collection, on Cosmopolitics, takes this plurality as its starting point. A second collection, on Political Economy, is in the pipeline. We wish to acknowledge here with hearty thanks the generosity of all those who have given time to this enterprise and particularly to those who have generously offered papers for discussion and publication here— Thomas Sturm, Martin Holbraad, Sidney Mintz, Philip

Swift, John McCreery, Alberto Corsin-Jimenez, Joanna Overing, Lee Drummond, Jean La Fontaine, Daniel Miller and Liria de la Cruz & Paloma Gay y Blasco.

Sadly one name on this list, Sidney Mintz, stands out. Sid's life spanned almost all the history of modern academic anthropology: he was a student of Ruth Benedict, colleague of Eric Wolf and many others, and a towering figure in the American anthropological scene. Already approaching 90 by the time we contacted him, Sid became a firm supporter of the OAC Press's efforts. In a final email to Huon Wardle in July 2015, on rereading his own paper 'Devouring Objects of Study', he noted with characteristic good humour that:

> I thought it was quite interesting and even well written, something I rarely am confident enough to say about anything I write. You've made my day... Do let me know when/if the book becomes a reality. I'll want to show it proudly to friends, if I have not yet gone to my reward!
>
> Our best wishes,
>
> Sid

It was not to be and Sid's style will be greatly missed. The editors are now able to say that the book has become a reality.

Notes

1. http://openanthcoop.net/press/publications/

2. http://openanthcoop.ning.com/

FOREWORD

The digital revolution[1]

Michael Wesch, then an assistant professor of cultural anthropology at Kansas State University, is well-known for his inspiring YouTube lectures and documentary shorts. In 2009 he received over a hundred applications for his graduate course in 'digital ethnography' from around the world. The only problem: no such course existed. Wesch teaches undergraduates and had organized a 'digital ethnography working group' for them; and that was it, so far. But millions have seen his creations on YouTube and people want more of it. The world is changing all around us and anthropology must try to keep up, not just because we study this world as anthropologists, but because our students live in it and they are rapidly leaving their teachers behind.

The new communications technologies are blurring the boundaries of disciplines, transforming the content of education, spawning new genres and sites of research, demanding fresh intellectual strategies. And academic institutions act as a brake on our ability to engage with all this. Anthropology as a discipline has not yet grasped the potential of this new world. When we contemplate its future, we need to think again about its scope, reach and impact, about the audiences we wish to address and how.

We are living through the first stages of a world revolution as significant for humanity as the invention of agriculture. It is a machine revolution, of course: the convergence of telephones, television and computers in a digital system whose most visible symbol is the internet. It is a social revolution, the formation of a world society with means of communication adequate at last to expressing universal ideas. It is a financial revolution, the detachment of the virtual money circuit from production, linked to the West's loss of control over the world economy. It is an existential revolution, transforming what it means to be human and how each of us relates to the rest of humanity. It is therefore also a revolution in anthropology that will make everything we have done so far seem like the prehistory of our discipline, whatever its name becomes.

Oswald Spengler observed in *The Decline of the West* (1918) that the world historical moment you are born into does not need you; it will carry on with or without you. But he offered a challenge to his readers "Do you have the courage to embrace it?" So too with this revolution: you can engage with it or you can hide from it. And every person's trajectory is particular to them, even if some common outlines can be glimpsed as the revolution unfolds. The revolution is based on social networking: Google, Facebook, Flickr, Twitter, Stumbleupon, Academia.edu, Instagram and all the rest. Social bookmarking is especially important. Classification of knowledge was hitherto done by experts and every piece of information had its unique place in a folder somewhere. Now tagging makes it possible for anyone to leave a mark on something they like or consider useful and you can find their guidance with increasingly sophisticated software. The people are now generating the categories. Even Google is becoming obsolete because its millions of hits are impersonal, less attuned to the user's own profile.

Participation in all this has sharpened my appreciation of the sociology involved. Twitter divides people into followers and followed. For those of us brought up on Fascism and Stalinism, the talk of leaders and followers that animates Web 2.0 is something of a turn off. But when the Latins invented 'society' to describe their aspirations for collective order, the word they used had as its root 'to follow'. If anyone was attacked, the others agreed to support them in battle. The hierarchy was temporary; so too on Twitter. The idea of society as a state with fixed boundaries came much later. The new social networks are personal and unequal; they often have a commercial feel that puts off many intellectuals.

But there is something exciting going on that it would pay us to understand and use.

In May 2009, an unanticipated chain of events led to the launch of the *Open Anthropology Cooperative*. Some Twitter friends began discussing the possibilities for an online anthropology network. Someone suggested trying Ning and I jumped in. An administrative team drawn from the launching group supervised its explosive growth in the first few months. In less than a year we had 2,000 members from an amazing diversity of backgrounds. Our visitors settled down at around 500 a day; the largest group came from the US, Britain and Canada (in a ratio of 4:2:1), but the next batch made interesting reading, in order: France, Portugal, Germany, Brazil, Georgia, Italy, Greece, Australia, Switzerland, India, Netherlands, Sweden, Turkey, Norway, Mexico, Spain, New Zealand.

We soon set up over a hundred discussion groups (some of them in Spanish, Portuguese, German, Italian, Russian, Norwegian, Turkish and Georgian), blogs, a forum, a wiki repository, the OAC Press, a seminar series and personal pages in all their multimedia variety. Anyone can start anything on the OAC; some of them do, many more stay quiet. The administrators got some minimal rules generally accepted. In time, however, the Ning platform became less heterogeneous (despite having over 8,000 members today); the active users now come mainly from the US and Britain; linguistic diversity has vanished, participation rates are lower. This pattern is not unusual in web networks. We later started an OAC page on Facebook which is livelier, with 12,000 members who keep up a daily flow of announcements, links to pages elsewhere, short posts and personal updates.

We already know that fieldwork will never be the same again because of the digital revolution. It will be less lonely for one thing. But what can anthropologists, with our supposed expertise in social relations, do more generally to help shape the future of our institutions? Our students, readers and those we study expect to be engaged through these new media. For some this will be an uphill struggle. We must move from monologue to conversation, from guild disciplines to the lifetime self-learning that the internet affords. The universities now lag behind the students in terms of media literacy. The 'edupunk' movement, armed with user-friendly digital technologies, rejects the forced imposition of costly out-dated software systems that universities have bought. The latter face a threat to their monopolies when teachers extend their classrooms to non-university students. Anthropology has always been something of an anti-discipline, sitting uneasily with academic bureaucracy. We have a lot to gain, professionally and as human beings, from joining this revolution.

What have I learned from all this? The two great memory banks are language and money.[2] Exchanges of meanings through language and of goods through money are now converging in a single network of communications, the internet. We must discover how to use this digital revolution to advance the human conversation about a better world. Our common task is to make a world society fit for all humanity. And anthropology is indispensable to such a project.

The digital revolution is driven by a desire to replicate at a distance or by means of computers experiences that we normally associate with face-to-face human encounters. All communication, whether the exchange of words or money, has a virtual aspect in that symbols and their media of circulation stand for what people really do for each other. It usually involves the exercise of imagination, an ability to construct meanings across the gap between symbol and reality. The power of the book depended on sustaining that leap of faith in the possibility of human communication. The virtual is abstract, but reliance on more abstract forms of communication carries with it the potential for real persons to be involved with each other at a distance in concrete ways. The idea of 'virtual reality' expresses this double movement: on the one hand machines whose complexity their users cannot possibly understand, on the other live experiences 'as good as' real.

If we would make a better world, rather than just contemplate it, we must learn to think in terms that reflect reality and reach out for imagined possibilities. This entails capturing what is essential about the world we live in, its movement and direction, not just its stable forms. The idea of *virtual reality* expresses this form of movement — *extension from the actual to the possible*. 'Virtual' means existing in the mind, but not in fact. When combined with 'reality', it means something that is almost but not quite real. In technical terms, 'virtual reality' is a computer simulation that enables the effects of operations to be shown in real time. 'Reality' is present in time and space ('seeing is believing'); and its opposite is imagined connection at a distance, something as old as story-telling, but given new impetus by the internet. Already experience of near synchrony at a distance, the compression of time and space, is altering our perception of social relations, of place and movement.

How might offline activities influence what we do online and vice versa? I have been influenced by Martin Heidegger's *The Fundamental Concepts of Metaphysics: World, Finitude, Solitude* (1929). For Heidegger, 'world' as something whole is an abstract metaphysical category and its dialectical counterpart is 'solitude', the idea of the isolated individual. Every human subject makes a world whose centre is the self. This opens up only when we recognize ourselves as finite, as individual; and this leads us to 'finitude', the concrete specifics of time and place in which we live. So 'world' is relative both to an abstract version of subjectivity and, more important, to our particularity in the world (seen as position and movement in time and space).

Living alone in our own world seems more real when we go online. But the two are imagined and reciprocal; neither is a suitable object of inquiry. We experience them from a relative location in society. Thus it is unsatisfactory to study the social forms of the internet without considering what people bring to them from elsewhere. This off-line social life is an invisible presence when people are online. We should not deny some autonomy to 'virtual reality'. Would we dream of reducing literature to the circumstances of readers? And this is Heidegger's point. 'World' and 'solitude' may be artificial abstractions, but they do affect how we behave in 'finitude'. The dialectical triad forms an interactive set.

Anthropology for the internet age

Like the editors, I start from Immanuel Kant's (1795) argument that the basic right of all world citizens should rest on universal hospitality. We should be free to go anywhere, since the world belongs to us all equally. We are highly mobile today, but most human beings are more restricted in their movement than ever. Kant's confidence in an emergent world order, when launching 'anthropology' as a modern academic discipline, was the high point of the liberal revolution, before it was overwhelmed by its twin offspring, industrial capitalism and the nation-state.

The world is much more socially integrated now than two centuries ago and its economy is palpably unjust. We have barely survived three world wars (two hot, one cold) and brutality provokes fear everywhere. Moreover, the natural consequences of human actions are severely disruptive, if left unchecked. Kant (1784) held that "In man (as the only rational creature on earth) those natural faculties which aim at the use of reason shall be fully developed in the species, not in the individual." He meant through libraries or the means of communication that we have today. The anthropologist, Roy Rappaport (1999) recently wrote that "Humanity is that part of the world through which the world as a whole can think about itself". Or, in C.L.R. James' (1938) words, "The distinctive feature of our age is that mankind as a whole is on the way to becoming fully conscious of itself". The task of building a global civil society for the 21st century is urgent and anthropological visions must play their part in this.

Copernicus solved the problem of the movement of the

heavenly bodies by having the spectator revolve while they were at rest, instead of them revolve around the spectator. Kant extended this achievement into metaphysics. In *The Critique of Pure Reason* (1781) he wrote, "Hitherto it has been assumed that all our knowledge must conform to objects...(but what) if we suppose that objects must conform to our knowledge?" In order to understand the world, we begin not with the empirical existence of objects, but with the reasoning embedded in that experience as all the judgments we have made. The world is inside each of us as much as out there. We must bring the two poles together as subjective individuals who share the object world with the rest of humanity.

The cheapening of information transfers thanks to the digital revolution makes it possible for much more information about individuals to enter into commercial transactions at a distance. This trend to customize economic relations has its counterpart in many aspects of contemporary social life. It involves a new idea of the person, one based on digital abstractions as much as on new forms of individuality. Academics' dealings with Amazon are at once remote and personal.

The use of new technologies means that learning can now be more individualized and ecumenical at the same time; and this poses a threat to the academic guild's traditions. Teachers must live with this radical revision of subject-object relations. Learning anthropology would be impossible if we were not human beings in the first place. Anthropologists must also cope with mass mobility and media. What can we offer that is not delivered more effectively through novels and movies, journalism and tourism? The rhetoric and reality of markets today encourage individuals to choose the means of their own enlightenment. Anthropological teaching must reflect all this; any new paradigm for the discipline must reflect the social and technological implications of the internet age.

The *Open Anthropology Cooperative*: between social movement and the academy

Ever since the internet went public and the World Wide Web was invented, I have made online self-publishing and interaction the core of my anthropological practice. The OAC promised to be the most powerful vehicle for this project yet. The predominance of academics there is reflected in this collection. The chapters show that anthropologists are often idiosyncratic individuals with an extraordinary range of interests. But as a collective we are extremely conservative. It is unsurprising then that publishing papers for discussion in seminars was the OAC's most prominent achievement. Our network has not moved with the times, as we once hoped. Nevertheless, the OAC has been and still is a great leap towards bringing anthropology into the 21st century. This book and its subsequent companion volume on economy serve as eloquent testimony to its hybrid originality.

In practical terms, the OAC is a place of online interaction. It is also an archive where each member can store photos, videos, music and texts on their home page and post similar material around the site. The language issue, however, is crucial. Despite the OAC's worldwide reach and initial linguistic variety, the trend has been inexorably towards the dominance of a few native Anglophones. Our inability to sustain a multilingual community is particularly troubling given anthropology's global aspirations and the public impact the network could have had. The OAC's founders believed we were launching a social movement; and the heady first weeks reinforced that feeling. But the network was born in reaction to academic bureaucracy and its leadership has since been trying to catch up with events.

The most useful lessons from the OAC experiment for other online organizations (including public anthropology web projects) are pragmatic. The social web offers an ever-evolving selection of sites, apps and services, many of which are free or relatively low-cost. Innovation is rapid and open source is increasingly common. On the other hand, the speed of application launches and failures means that free sites are often not stable for long. Most anthropologists feel powerless in the face of technological change. New software and web applications (increasingly for mobile phones) are not usually tailored to academic needs; but they are often flexible enough, given basic technical knowledge; and willingness to endure many bouts of trial and error helps. You have to invest time and energy to find out what works and what does not.

The OAC opposed elitism, bureaucracy and academic hierarchy; so we tried to avoid centralized leadership and control. But what kind of leadership replaces hierarchy? In a context of calls for less bureaucracy among academic anthropologists, the site's laissez-faire policy privileged self-regulation over firm rules. But this is like promoting the free market without rules of oversight. No-one would try to build a community on free market principles; but in retrospect it seems that we did.

The OAC shows that anthropologists may be adaptable bricoleurs online, piecing together communication technologies for chatting, learning, teaching and sharing. But it remains problematic to break with academic prejudices about online publication and interaction. To attract participants, we reproduced the very academic values that we founded the OAC to escape from. The network thus offers an anomalous commentary on how anthropology treats online and academic conversation as being mutually exclusive. The OAC became a compromised public island avoiding academic bureaucracy, yet populated by its denizens.

Social and academic networks are significantly different in their need for time investment, volunteer labor and long-term objectives, not to mention power relations and status hierarchies. Much social web activity does not concern itself with aims, intentions or long-term goals. It's easy and can keep ticking over until boredom or newness force change. Academic networks do not work like that. The OAC mixes them together. Dabbling on Twitter or Facebook is not analogous to what goes on at the OAC. Being an active member there takes more time commitment, at least some critical thought and the shared expectation of pointed exchange or response.

The ethnographic model was never intended to inform a movement to change the world. Contemporary anthropology and social science reflect the world and are not designed to improve it. The internet's growth has generated a strong counter-movement to the status quo. Anthropologists spent the last century – a time of urbanization, war and the break-up of empires – seeking out isolated places that we could study as if they were outside modern history. Having realized at last that we live in a world unified by capitalism, we now spend our time bemoaning the fate of the universities and our own irrelevance to public discourse.

The OAC was born as a reaction more than a movement. Its slogan of being 'open' turned out to be contradictory. The leadership, who abstractly rejected hierarchy, became managerial and half-hearted. We preferred to maximize membership at the expense of making rules that might exclude people. They left anyway. We were always catching up, never ahead of the game.

The OAC's instigators, members and critics never used anthropology or social theory to address the problems we faced. Anthropologists, it seems, cannot catch up with a changing world while they meticulously document it. We are losing control of our master-concepts like culture to other disciplines and even to web moguls who are not afraid to engage with the popular media. Anthropologists do have something to offer the general public. It is just that we are terrible at communicating it. More often than not, anthropologists are confounded when interacting with the world outside academia.

The OAC struggled to reverse this trend and reinforces

it by producing little to attract a general audience. Fear of marketing our expertise, of 'branding' anthropology or seeking out media attention undermined an innovative project that once promised so much. Our web-based activities closely resemble office politics. So a public-facing anthropological experiment became inward-looking, being by and for academics and subject to prejudices and hierarchies similar to those in the universities. Like academic anthropology, the OAC is better at describing what happened than explaining it. The social media have undoubtedly shaped the OAC's attempt to expand anthropology's horizons to a global level. Worse, we have not yet been able to draw on our own discipline to help fulfil its promise.

'Anthropology' and the new human universal

By 'anthropology' I mean a human teleology in the sense of Kant, Rappaport and James above. We must develop self-knowledge as individuals and as a species, especially the relationship between the two. This relationship is mediated by a bewildering range of associations and identities which have been the prime focus of anthropology conceived of as a social science. The vast bulk of humanity is more interested in how each of us relates to the whole.

For Kant a 'cosmopolitan' approach to world society would lead us to the exercise of human reason at the species level. For him, humanity's last and hardest task would be the administration of justice worldwide. Meanwhile, anthropology explores the cognitive, aesthetic and ethical universals on which human unity might be founded. The categorical imperative to be good provides a moral link between individuals and this inclusive order.

Kant published *Anthropology from a Pragmatic Point of View* in 1798. It was based on lectures he had given for a quarter-century. He wanted to attract the general public to his subject. Histories of anthropology rarely mention this work, perhaps because anthropologists have since moved far away from Kant's original premises. He summarized "philosophy in the cosmopolitan sense of the word" as four questions: What can I know? What should I do? What may I hope for? What is a human being? The first question is answered in *metaphysics*, the second in *morals*, the third in *religion* and the fourth in *anthropology*. But the first three questions "relate to anthropology" and might be subsumed under it.

Kant conceived of anthropology as an empirical discipline, but also as a means of moral and cultural improvement. It was an investigation into human nature and into how to modify it. He aimed to provide his students with practical guidance and knowledge of the world. His lectures were to be "popular" and of value in later life. Above all, the *Anthropology* contributed to the task of uniting world citizens by identifying the source of their "cosmopolitan bonds". The book moves between vivid anecdotes and Kant's sublime vision as a bridge from everyday life to horizon thinking. Kant concentrated on "what the human being as a free actor can and should make of himself". This is based on observation, but also involves the construction of moral rules. Anthropology is the practical arm of moral philosophy. It does not explain the metaphysics of morals which are categorical and transcendent; but it is indispensable to understanding interaction between human agents. It is thus 'pragmatic' – "everything that pertains to the practical" – popular and moral, being concerned with people's motives for action. His book's value lay in its systematic organization, so that readers could insert their experience and develop new themes appropriate to their own lives.

Academic anthropology is not equipped to inform participation in the world today because its cultural relativism reflects the dominant nation-state structures of the twentieth century. How might people find a more secure foundation for self-knowledge as individuals and as a species? Anthropology for Kant reflected both his idea of a just world society and his vision of individual subjectivity as a means to that end, as a branch of humanist education. Twentieth-century civilization placed barriers between each of us as a subjective personality and society as an impersonal object. Its anonymous institutions – states, capitalist markets, science – left little room for personal agency, beyond spending the money we had.

We all embark on a journey outward into the world and inward to the self. Society is mysterious to us because we have lived in it and it now dwells inside us where it is ordinarily invisible from everyday life. Wherever we have lived becomes a source of introspection regarding our relationship to society; memory allows us to synthesize these varied experiences of the world. If a person would have an identity, this requires making out of fragmented social experience a more coherent whole, a world as singular as the self.

Emergent world society is the new human universal – not an idea, but the fact of our shared occupation of the planet crying out for new principles of association. This entails making a world where all people can live together, not the imposition of principles that suit some powerful interests at the expense of the rest. The next universal will be unlike its predecessors, the Christian, bourgeois and imperialist versions through which the West sought to dominate or replace the cultural particulars that organize people's lives everywhere. We discover our common humanity in great literature which aims for universality by going deeply into particular personalities, places and events. Good ethnography does the same. So does case law at its best. The new universal will not just tolerate cultural particulars, but will recognize that true human community can only be realized through them.

There are two prerequisites for being human: we must each learn to be self-reliant to a high degree and to belong to others, merging our identities in a bewildering variety of social relations. Western cultures emphasize how problematic it is to be both self-interested and mutual. When conflict between the two is expected, it is hard to be both. Yet the two sides are often inseparable in practice and some societies, by encouraging private and public interests to merge, have integrated them more effectively than ours. One premise of the new human universal will thus be the unity of self and society.

It is now harder for self-appointed guilds to control access to professional knowledge. People have other ways of finding out for themselves, rather than submit to academic hierarchy. Many agencies out there compete to give them what they want, including the self-learning possibilities afforded by the internet. Popular resistance to the power of experts is moral – most people want to restore a personal dimension to knowledge. Anthropologists' dependence on academic bureaucracy leaves us highly vulnerable and the OAC's aspiration to liberate anthropological discourse through online media foundered because academic norms took it over.

'Anthropology' is indispensable to the formation of world society. The prospects for the academic discipline to contribute to this process are poor, given its prevalent localism and anti-universalism. Kant's vision of anthropology as humanist education contrasts starkly with the emphasis on scientific research outputs in today's universities. We should emulate his program of personal life-long learning to develop practical knowledge of the world. Kant recommended both systematic observation of life around us and that we study "world history, biographies and even plays and novels". He aimed to integrate individual subjectivity with the moral construction of world society.

The rapid development of telecommunications networks today contains a far-reaching transformation of world society. Anthropology is one way of making sense of it. The academic seclusion of the discipline, however, its passive acquiescence to bureaucracy, prevents us from grasping this historical opportunity. We rightly cling to our commitment to joining the people where they live, but have forgotten what this move was for or what else is needed if humanity can build a universal society. The internet offers a wonderful chance to open up the flow of knowledge and information, already partly realised.

It matters less that an academic guild should retain its monopoly of access to knowledge than that 'anthropology' should be taken up by a broad intellectual coalition for whom the realization of a new human universal – a world society fit for humanity as a whole – is an urgent personal concern. Rather than obsessing over how we can control access to what we write, which means cutting off the mass of humanity from our efforts, we must figure out new interactive forms of engagement that span the globe and make the results available to everyone.

Keith Hart
Paris, 2016

Notes

1. I want to thank Fran Barone for writing Barone and Hart (2015) together; Huon Wardle for providing the opportunity to publish Hart (2010a); Justin Shaffner for the help he has given me in navigating the internet; and all three for their companionship and work at the *Open Anthropology Cooperative* and its Press. This essay also draws on Hart (2009, 2010b).

2. The motto of my website, http://thememorybank.co.uk.

References

Barone, F. and K. Hart (2015), The Open Anthropology Cooperative: Towards an online public anthropology, in S. Pink and S. Abram (eds) *Media, Anthropology and Public Engagement*. New York: Berghahn, 198-222.

Hart, K. (2009), An anthropologist in the world revolution. A*nthropology Today* 25.6: 24-25.

Hart, K. (2010a), Kant, 'anthropology' and the new human universal. *Social Anthropology*, 18: 441–447.

Hart, K. (2010b), An Anthropology of the Internet, http://thememorybank.co.uk/2010/02/06/an-anthropology-of-the-internet-2/.

Heidegger, M. (2008 [1929]). *The Fundamental Concepts of Metaphysics: World, Finitude, Solitude*. Bloomington: Indiana University Press.

James, C.L.R. (1989 [1938]). *The Black Jacobins: Toussaint L'Ouverture and the San Domingo revolution*. New York: Vintage Books.

Kant, I. (2008 [1781]). *Critique of Pure Reason* (Norman Kemp Smith). Google Books.

Kant, I. (1993[1784]). Idea for a universal history with cosmopolitan intent, in C. Friedrich (ed) *The Philosophy of Kant*. New York: Modern Library.

Kant, I. (1795). P*erpetual Peace: A philosophical sketch* (various editions).

Kant, I. (2006 [1798]). *Anthropology from a Pragmatic Point of View*. Cambridge: Cambridge University Press.

Rappaport, R. (1999). *Ritual and Religion in the Making of Humanity*. Cambridge: Cambridge University Press.

Spengler, O. (1962 [1918]). *The Decline of the West* (abridged). New York: Alfred Knopf.

Chapter 1

INTRODUCTION:
COSMOPOLITICS AS A WAY OF THINKING

Huon Wardle and Justin Shaffner

From its launch in 2009, the *Open Anthropology Cooperative* (OAC) and its publications series were shaped by what we can reasonably call cosmopolitical concerns. Weeks after its creation, the OAC gathered hundreds, then thousands, of visitors and members from every region of the world — everywhere there is a networked computer at least. A flurry of discussion immediately took place on the OAC forum around what to make of the fact that within a few months an unprecedented global assembly of anthropologists had sprung into being. The whole world of anthropology seemed to have arrived at one virtual site, and the question was what to do with this singularity. From this point of view, the numbers proved illusory — perhaps a disappointment - if the expectation was that, like Venus on her seashell, a new kind of global anthropological politics would also spring up out of the waves. Many people visited, read what was offered, and left comments - perhaps modeling their behaviour on how they used other social network sites – but, for most, the OAC was simply a launch pad to "go" somewhere else. (It is worth remembering that like other websites the OAC is only metaphorically "a place", but then it is not "just a place" either). The OAC had proved its global reach, sure enough, but this did not initiate any definable architecture of social change itself. Thus, arguably the OAC has not built on its initial promise of creating a globally articulated forum, and in that sense, the ideas fomented by this venue for openness and cooperation have been more a sign of the times than an expression of a realizable social future (Barone and Hart 2015).

One of the acknowledged successes of the OAC, though, has been its open access publication series.[1] From the beginning, the aim was to make anthropological work available online without copyright restriction and to use the social media platform to open these essays (and now books) to discussion by anyone who wants to participate. In principle at least, from the start, this was anthropology for, and open to, the "people"; the idea being that, since anthropology is the study of humanity, anyone who is human would have an interest in what that fact implies. Again, of course, the results were more limited than the hubristic expectation. The papers and surrounding dialogue that the OAC has gathered together are nonetheless fascinatingly diverse, all of them offer at least a sideways (and often a front on) view on the stroboscopic display of global humanity that, in just a few decades, the new digital technologies of mass communication have set in motion.

So, when the time came to put some of the OAC papers together in edited form, this awareness of the shifting meaning of the words "cosmos" and "politics" immediately emerged as a key theme shaping our editorial perspective. It is for this reason that with our first volume of collected papers we have brought together work by Alberto Corsin Jimenez, Daniel Miller, Huon Wardle, Jean La Fontaine, Joanna Overing, John McCreery, Lee Drummond, Liria de la Cruz, Martin Holbraad, Paloma Gay y Blasco, Philip Swift, Sidney

Mintz and Thomas Sturm, that foregrounds the "cosmopolitical" dimension of contemporary experience. But what does this venerable compound word signify? In contemporary social science we find that at least two distinct uses of the word are in play.

Kant and the cosmopolitical

The initial sense of the word is Kantian. It is fair to say that from its beginnings the aims of the OAC were imbued with a Kantian spirit. Thomas Sturm in this volume explores Kant's cosmopolitanism and his anthropology in detail ("What Did Kant Mean..."). Nonetheless, even now, Kant's ideas on anthropology and cosmopolitanism are not widely known (or understood) within contemporary social science, so it is worth giving a brief light-and-shade sketch of the Kantian position and its contemporary relevance before entering more complicated terrains of debate.

For Kant cosmopolitanism, and the cosmopolitics that goes with it, delineates a firmly anthropocentric set of problems ([1795]1988). First, at issue are the political struggles of human beings who, whatever their differences (and also because of them), must inevitably come to recognise themselves as occupying a common world. Secondly, there is the historical awareness that an already existing global community is ever more integrated in politically complex ways; perhaps primarily due to war, conquest and human displacement, but also through mutually beneficial commerce and peaceful movement. So, thirdly, questions arise about the transformation in the thought and practice of individual human beings as they become aware that, whatever local communities they feel they belong to, whatever local *common sense* they may adhere to, whether they wish it or not, they are part of a human community at large. The cosmopolitical sphere is, then, a scene of emergent mutual recognition of this interconnection. In turn, the cosmopolitical describes an arena for debating and contracting certain general principles – rights, freedoms – that should apply to all humans as such. Hence Kant's *ius cosmopoliticum* postulating a basic extension of hospitality to all humans as citizens of a common humanity in-the-making ([1795]1988:112fn).

The role of anthropology in this Kantian picture is to discuss the pragmatics of what it means to be human in the light of the cosmopolitical framework; in particular to find out what humans can make of themselves as "free acting" beings who are nonetheless destined to share the same world for better or worse with others akin to themselves. Anthropology offers a guide both to the meaning of the diversity involved in this cosmopolitics but also, crucially, regarding what humans have in common, including their "unsocial sociability" — their tendencies toward both love and violence. As Thomas Sturm summarises Kant here:

> We are citizens of the world in the sense that our nature is partly plastic, and more specifically that we ourselves produce our rules of action and, thereby, our social world. This is a fact that holds, in principle, for each of us, and which each of us better recognizes in social interaction (Sturm, "What Did Kant Mean...").

Kant's sphere of cosmopolitical debate and action, and the anthropology that goes with it, are, of course, emblematic of an enlightenment view. Humans, belonging as they do to one species, have an obligation to care for their own kind. Recognising myself as an instance of humanity becomes a duty toward human beings at large. At the same time, by universalising the significance of my individual life, this recognition offers a kind of personal liberation of my individuality from pure historical contingency, while giving onto a genuinely informed politics. Incorporating the cosmopolitan project as a dimension of personal world-knowledge (*weltkenntnis*) is, meanwhile, a matter of developing one's own schemas and ideas for life and in this way arriving at "maturity" (acquiring a "character" is another way Kant puts it [1798]2006). What Kant opens for the kind of study we call anthropology, then, is the realisation that the human being is a self-interpreting, self-conceptualising, hence a self-making, creature.[2] How this human comes to interpret its own life – creating schemas, analogies, symbols and concepts for it – is inextricable from how its politics grow and take shape.

Because human nature is partly plastic, and the ideas people live by are significantly an expression of their freedom from natural constraints, anthropology is not a natural, but rather a moral, science (an argument developed by Dilthey). By reflecting on their own ideas people can change them. This, in turn, means that human thought is not susceptible to the same kind of analysis that natural objects are. Anthropology is itself an extension of the desire and freedom people have to understand and change themselves. This reflexive insight, in turn, gives the ground from which Kant argues that, as they strive to define who they are, humans must sooner or later arrive at an awareness that they are citizens of a common cosmos since this is the necessary horizon for defining their own humanity. This rethinking takes place in the midst of fundamental uncertainty about the nature of the world as it is outside the conventions of human perception and conceptualisation. Hence, for Kant, anthropology has as its central concern the creation of a cosmopolitan conceptual toolkit that can be put to use to rethink the pragmatics of our everyday individual experience. To adapt a phrase, whether we are consciously aware of it or not, "the personal is cosmopolitical".

The utopianism in Kant's account – a peaceful world society is possible – is justified by his awareness that this ever-intensifying social interdependence of human beings globally – the inevitably inter-indemnifying struggles of hospitality and hostility that humans engage in – has the potential to lead toward moral institutions with greater and greater inclusivity. From this stance, cosmopolitan interaction (reasoned or unreasoned) is unavoidable, as is the cosmopolitical debate that travels with it ([1795]1988). Hence, Kant gives the possibility of peaceful cosmopolitan co-dwelling, within diverse ways of life and out of particular conceptions of freedom, as the widest ethical frame for his anthropology ([1798]2006). Living "wisely, agreeably and well" (as Keynes would later put it) at a global level is not only conceivable, there are some existing facts in favour of its achievability.

In this way, cosmopolitanism is not just a provocation constantly to review the global anthropological situation: more than this, the as-if utopia offered by a cosmopolitan end-state provides anthropology with its outer meaning as a type of knowledge and inquiry (*wissenschaft*) directed actively at the self-making of world citizens. It should be noted that the ethical framings of the kind Kant gave to anthropology were for the most part deemed irrelevant or anathema (if they were noticed at all) by the logical-positivist social science established in the Twentieth century with its unrecognised outer stabilising frame – nationalism. They were periodically picked up by anthropologists, notably Malinowski in his last manuscript, *Freedom and Civilization*. However, this short nationalist Century – 1918-1989 – is long gone and with it the implicit idea that the national boundary is also a boundary on morality and truth, albeit recent global events have again foregrounded a politics of isolationism or 'nativism' as it is now sometimes termed.

Acquiring a cosmopolitan orientation becomes the guiding ethical principle through which anthropology as a search for knowledge gains meaning, as opposed to being simply a pursuit of the Machiavellian or meaningless in human experience. At the same time, knowing that it is in the character of human beings to create new distinctive ideas for life, Kant presents anthropology as a quest on the part of humans through which they acquire new understanding of the concepts they are using, thereby gaining new insights and widening the scope their own freedoms. To know or understand something is to gain some autonomy with regard to that thing (cf. Lino e Silva and Wardle 2016). However, significantly, Kant's theory of the human is a theory of the limits on human comprehension: some of these limits are set by the natural human capacity to sense the surrounding world, some by the limited hold humanly created concepts have on reality once human sensations are schematised into thoughts.

Clearly, many of the ideas and freedoms humans create for themselves and live by are delusional judged by their incompatibility with the larger principle of free and peaceful community with others world-wide; but who is to decide which ideas and on what grounds? An intercommunicating world entails a complexly, chaotically interconnected politics whose radical uncertainty threatens the rights and freedoms of all humans in contingent and variable ways. Kant's answer is cosmopolitan (self-)education (Hart 2010): learning to live in the same world. Each individual educates themselves to the best of their capacity in elements of a common ethics for a global type of life in the midst of fundamental mutual human uncertainty.

"A transgression of rights in one place in the world is felt everywhere" states Kant in support of his demand for a constantly re-initiated cosmopolitics ([1795]1988:119). Equally, a growth of freedoms in one place may also herald a like emergence elsewhere. We are wise to be alert to either of those potentials. These are ideas Simmel develops in the early Twentieth Century in his neo-Kantian theory of fission and fusion in social circles and the networks that connect them; and that Ulrich Beck extends in the end of that century with his conception of globally dispersed risks to the individual (Simmel [1922]1955, Beck 1992). For Kant, anthropology and cosmopolitanism answer a demand of rational self-interest; they supply the kind of knowledge individuals need to co-dwell in an increasingly interconnected and politically threatening world. His view is also crucially dialectical: new schemas, symbols and judgements about life appear out of the often hostile interaction between people and peoples. Hostility between ideas and communities is never absolute though; the constant need for re-envisaging humanness within a global frame comes about because there are no absolute boundaries on human interchange and community. Certainly, cultures have some general, but not absolutely defining, characteristics. Likewise historical epochs do not place defining perimeters on human interchange, conceptual elaboration, or on the kinds of relations of ethical answerability that go with these.

Whatever the intensity of local common-sense metaphors, sentiments and aesthetic judgements, the real value of these are as conventional signposts expressing the contingent relationship of the diversely placed individual to their universal situation – the ramifying network that is the human cosmos taken as a whole (Kant [1790]1952, Wardle 1995). In his anthropology and elsewhere Kant makes use of the ethnological evidence provided in his day, but ethnology is not an end in itself. We need to know about the ideas and ways of lives of others, not because of their fascinating linguistic or conceptual differences to us as such (themes developed by Herder and Humboldt for example), but instead because the continuance and development of their distinctive conventions, social rules and freedoms are intrinsically interconnected with the future of our own. Here begins Kant's daunting (some will say impossible) task of cosmopolitan self-education.

Cosmopolitan awareness does not, then, rest in knowledge of sui generis differences, rather it involves an exploration of difference toward a continuous imaginative expansion of the area of our common human truths and common human goods. In this way, the narrower horizon of responsibilities to an immediate circle of relationships widens into a duty to humans in general allowing of highly diverse ways of thinking and acting. Every individual has a stake in this kind of cosmopolitical knowledge whether they realise it yet or not (Wardle 2000, 2010, 2015). Kant would respond to the oft reiterated jibe that cosmopolitanism is merely the language of the elite or the narcissistic by answering that we are all cosmopolitans (Josephides and Hall 2014). Logically, and as a matter of fact, as humans we are all involved in creating the cosmopolitical institutions of the future. What kind of future that will be, what our place in it will be, we cannot yet tell. The common cosmos is always an object of search and variable judgement, but we can assume that our acts of moral imagining and choice now will effect the outcome – the "kingdom of ends" as Kant puts it.

Building a picture of the new cosmopolitics[3] – ontologies, non-human agents and "decolonisation of thought"

Whatever we make of Kant's cosmopolitics, there is, however, a second, newer use of the "cosmopolitical" that builds on a deep-seated modernist sense of anthropocentric uncertainty and anxiety, one that casts doubt on both the perceived unity of the human and also the possibility of a shared common world. Puzzlingly this newer cosmopolitics has tended to deny any relation to the old. Stengers, who coined this newer usage, states that she was unaware of Kant's use when she first developed her own and that her alternative view denies Kant's applicability:

> "I'm very likely to be told that... I shouldn't have taken a Kantian term... I was unaware of Kantian usage... the cosmopolitical proposal, as presented here, denies any relationship with Kant or with the ancient cosmopolitanism" (2005:994)

Given that what she is describing claims no connection to the older significance, what, then, do Stengers and those who draw on her work mean by "cosmopolitics"? As we will see, the question extends to this: is there in fact a connection between these two distinct understandings of cosmos and politics despite the claim to epistemological distinctness; and if there is, what does this relation consist in? What kind of dialogue can be established and on what terms? The question demands a further explication of the newer usage. This will also give us an opportunity to see where the papers for this volume fit into, or offer a perspective on, a revised concept of the cosmopolitical.

If the kind of cosmopolitical awareness described by Kant has been with us for so long, traceable to the Stoics and beyond, why does the goal of intra-species recognition and responsibility still seem so far away? This turns out to be a key implicit quandary for the newer cosmopoliticians. It is one which they answer by pointing to the fact that for humans there is not a single cosmos but rather many cosmologies, multiple changing worldviews, and as such, there is no singular knowable world or humanity. Rather, there are as many ways of knowing what it means to be human as there are projects of knowing. From Stengers viewpoint and those who have expanded it such as Latour, the enlightenment politics of human recognition is founded on a transcendental illusion of foundational common knowledge. The very capacity for self-interpretation that Kant shows is key to understanding what we have in common is also the ground for a fragmented, multi-dimensional, multi-foundational politics. "Perspective" thence acquires the uttermost significance in this approach; diverse perspectives offer up multiplex and chaotically juxtaposed ontologies, but no simple vista onto a common world, nor a simple picture of the human. In this newer view the "cosmos" in cosmopolitics becomes charged in a way not seen since Diogenes and the Cynics in ancient Greece (Turner 2015).

Questions of metaphysics, ontology and cosmology are, indeed, in the air in Twenty First Century philosophy and anthropology. The engagement with the ontic, with what people studied by ethnographers take to exist, amounts to something of a revitalization movement for an ethnographically-driven anthropology if we are to judge by contemporary heated debates (cf. Carrithers, Michael, et al. 2010, Holbraad and Pedersen 2014), or the newly formed journal *Hau*, whose stated aim is "to reinstate ethnographic theorization in contemporary anthropology as a potent alternative to its "explanation" or "contextualization" by philosophical arguments".[4] The literature has grown voluminously in this area, but one symptomatic feature is the heightened awareness of the "other-than-human-agents" active in the ethnographic worlds in which anthropologists travel. We have become attuned to identifying new kinds of entities, in particular, new types of agents in places where they might not have been noticed before; or where, in the past, we might have dismissed their presence as poetry or reification (trying in this way to reduce them to prefigured philosophical "contexts" or "explanations" such as "myth", "belief", or even "representation" itself perhaps). The newer cosmopolitics is above all about rethinking inter-entity relationships. We are no longer guided by looking at how humans live in what we take to be "their" environment, "their" *umwelt*; the other beings and things involved will have their say. Their viewpoint must be taken into account, including on what constitutes an environment or *unwelt* in the first place. Other than human entitites can no longer be thought of as mere supports for "our" world, or as symbols for human thought-consumption in general.

We will recognise too, though, the distinctly human agents whose ideas are feeding these debates, especially Bruno Latour and Eduardo Viveiros de Castro who have become its main figureheads and provocateurs, at least within anthropology. These two have different, but in some areas compatible, theoretical agendas. Latour is working with a theory whereby agency (the capacity to create effects) appears as a facet of participation in a network (originally ethnographically centered on the actor-networks of scientists, e.g. Latour 1988). Some of the agents involved are recognizably human and some are not. One of Latour's points is that the particular capacities of the humans would be impossible without the assistance of the non-human agents and "actants". Having established the great diversity of these networks, he has called on Isabelle Stengers' cosmopolitics to talk about what happens at the boundary between different projects and the cosmoses they bring into being, as well as the work of translation that mediate them (Latour 2005a, 2005b).

Viveiros de Castro takes as his starting point lowland Amazonian societies where human relationships with other animal and spiritual beings are of the essence, and the capacities of humans are again integrated with the capacities of non-human-agents in the task of regenerating society. Crucially, he has repositioned a generic and defining feature of animist worldviews: humans, animals and certain objects, despite their outward appearance (their skins), share soul stuff (and hence a single culture or worldview) and are thus capable of transforming and exchanging their multiple natural outer forms. The particularities of the "human condition" are thus discovered through contrasts (and transformations) with the condition of "beasts" and "gods" (1992:304). This animist insight has a central status in his specialised social theory, "Amerindian perspectivism" (Viveiros de Castro 1998, 2012).

The importance of these ideas for an understanding of cosmopolitics comes from their power *in combination.* Latour's extension of network theory to include non-human-agents gains strength from Viveiros de Castro's revised exploration of an animist worldview. Viveiros de Castro's theory, specific to Amazonian societies, takes on much greater significance as part of Latour's reappraisal of modernity (Latour 2004, 2009), and vice versa. Latour's critique of the moderns (1993) is newly mobilized in Viveiros de Castro's generalized symmetrical perspectival anthropology (see his "Manifesto Abaeté"[5]) and in his emphasis on the "controlled equivocation" needed for conceptual translation and ethnographic description (2004). Of itself, animism is hardly news in the world of anthropology (even taking into account the special turn Viveiros de Castro gives it) but Viveiros de Castro's ideas gain much greater force if it turns out that, in one way or another, *we are all animists*, which is effectively what Latour has been arguing for some years, that "we have never been modern" (1993).

By removing the hierarchical order that makes a singular nature the measure of every subordinate worldview (cf. Wagner 1981), the new cosmopoliticians, in principle, democratize cosmology opening the door to an infinite number of further universes. Rather than trying to eliminate inadequate worldviews in the name of nature, each cosmos is welcomed for the project it describes; there is no best cosmology that all could aim towards partly because there is no "totality", only many transforming networks and communities of actors and entities. Even Hilbert's hotel (Benardette 1964) with its infinite number of rooms is full sometimes, but this can easily be remedied — the guest in room 1 shifts one room down along the corridor ad infinitum. Here, we can knock on the door of Humanity1, H2, H3..., H∞. Thus, theoretically at least, space is made for each new entry in the cosmological encyclopedia – a splendidly baroque scene of endless refractory courtyards, staircases and corridors. At the same time, of course, the cosmopolitical anthropologists present themselves in the special role of describers, translators, negotiators and diplomats (Latour 2005b) when it comes to neighbourly relations between all these "rooms" or cosmoses. This image of infinite space crumpled into the form of rooms is central to Deleuze's account of the Leibnizian fold (1993), whose language Vivieros de Castro transposes to his own theory of "Amerindian" and "anthropological" perspectivism (e.g. 2007:160). It is also the theme that Corsin Jimenez takes as his starting point in understanding anthropological knowledge practices (this volume).

Combined, a central feature of these new perspectives is that they remind us how humans depend on other-than-human agencies for their social projects. These relationships are not peripheral. They are of the essence in understanding how people gain a cosmological perspective. In particular these relationships should be understood as constitutive of what it means to be a human actor because human capacities transform in concert with the changing relationships between human and non-human actors. Taken even further, then, humanness (subjectivity) is relative to whatever particular networks and relationships appear situationally. We are reminded of Wagner's image of the "fractal person" — "never a unit standing in relation to an aggregate, or aggregate standing in relation to a unit, but always an entity with relationship integrally implied" (1991, p. 163). Hence, we may view these new developments as, on the one side, subtracting from the ethics of human recognition and hospitality that guided the older cosmopolitics. However, perhaps we may come to see them as having promethean qualities too. Certainly (some) human voices will lose their right to speak for everyone; but at the same time it may come about that others gain a voice (cf. de la Cadena 2015). And there may be similar losses and gains when we place the two kinds of cosmopolitics in a conversation.

Both Viveiros de Castro and Latour are working out of a structuralist-post-structuralist trajectory which involves decentring and relativizing human subjectivity. Of course, we have known about the relationships between humans and other-than-human entities for a long time in anthropology – as the extensive literature around totemism, taboo animals and liminal objects shows. In his book *The Two Sources of Morality and Religion*, (1935) Bergson indicates that when we stare at the spinning roulette wheel and rotate our hand to "make it" stop where we want, then we are, in a generic way, invoking the same kinds of animistic-magical-pantheistic forces that we humans have always enlisted in pursuing our life projects. Bergson adds that what we call religious experience can lead both to "closed" and to "open" ways of experiencing the material world and its psychic properties. In an ecstatic open mode,

> the soul opens out broadens and raises to pure spirituality a morality enclosed and materialized in ready-made rules: the latter then becomes, in comparison with the other [the open mode of experiencing] something like a snap-shot view of movement … Current morality is not abolished; but it appears like a virtual stop in the course of actual progression (1935:46).

However, leaving the history of thought entailed here

aside, combined, these newer expositions have allowed us to clear some of the intellectual overgrowth; perhaps enabled us to see some new wood beyond.

One key issue is this: as anthropologists our focus often narrows to particular people and their relations with each other, but for the people in question, their world is not made up solely of other people or of human relationships: it is engaged with a panoply of diverse significant entities and relationships between them. In this volume ("An Amazonian Question of Ironies and the Grotesque"), Joanna Overing tells how the Piaroa of the Amazon, must continuously try to clean up the poisons left behind by the gods Wahari and Kuemoi in Mythic Time so that they can live a human life now. The practices of ingestion, excretion and cleansing involved are absolutely of the essence in living a beautiful life of wit and laughter in their present day cosmos. In a different vein, but with a comparable degree of ethical and aesthetic concern, Sidney Mintz' gathers together decades of his own interest in kinds of food and ways of eating ("Devouring Objects of Study: Food and Fieldwork"). All this offers him the ground for a global vision of human beings united in their dependence on foodstuffs (we know ourselves through what we eat); and of the anthropologist as, in turn, a "devourer" of these varying "objects". Humans, we come to see, are unified by their fragile relations with a diversely edible world. And, we may think here of the efforts made by space scientists to domesticate extraterrestrial environments in light of anthropocenic awareness that the earth may soon become too toxic to support human life (Battaglia 2016).

The older cosmopolitics understood that the subject knows itself by way of the objects that preoccupy it – that make up its world. The aim is an "enlarged mind" (to use Kant's phrase; [1790]1952:153) capable of extending the scope of its preoccupations. However, the newer cosmopolitics goes further; subjectivity is co-dependent — it is the kinds of exchanges between humans and other agents and entities that are key to a cosmos: "humans", "beasts", "things", "gods" together compose particular, mutually defining, worlds (collective "nature-cultures").

Some of the entities we encounter in these worlds, as strangers or guests, will feel familiar, others much less so. Adjusting our ethnographic focus can, then, offer rewarding perspectives and remind us to consider, in any given field situation, "for this person, or for those people, how is their community, their cosmos, made up?" And, in talking of a community we will include not just the relationships of human beings, but also all the other agents and crucial objects that are clearly participating and contributing to whatever meaning "society", "community" and "cosmos" comes to encompass.

The basic question that the newer cosmopolitics has revitalized, then, is how do all these beings and things (which were taken to have a merely semiotic status in previous "cultural" accounts) participate actively in the lives of the people anthropologists are studying? For example, if someone says in a tragic tone that "society", "the healthcare system" or "the banks" have failed, then the ontologically-oriented reader will feel entitled to raise the question "what kind of other-than-human-entitites are these that they can 'fail' a given person, shared project or cosmos?" In this vein, Mitt Romney claimed during the 2012 US presidential elections that "Corporations are people too my friend". Corporations do indeed increasingly present themselves as persons politically and economically, but, of course, this is actually not new (see Bashkow n.d. for an anthropological understanding of modern corporations as a transformation of "house societies"): social persons of this kind have long been able to invoke their jural right to freedom of worship, for example. The (quasi-)political claims of "bodies corporate" were a prime object of enlightenment critique, of course, as *The Wealth of Nations* (1776) exemplifies. This was because the political power of the corporations in their day stood directly at odds with how enlightenment thinkers understood individual freedom and human moral agency. Adam Smith exemplifies this stance, but it is integral too to Immanuel Kant's view and hence to his understanding of how a cosmopolitics should proceed. So it seems worth our while (both as anthropologists and as human beings) to treat claims on behalf of corporations very seriously, and to treat the power of other-than-human-agents likewise. Above all, Stengers asks that, as makers of claims about a "good common world" or of one yet to be composed, anthropologists and others should "slow down", and exercise a certain Dostoievskian "idiocy"; we should recognise and pay attention to the many participants and cosmological interests involved in a situation before assuming we can already know "who can be a spokesperson of what, who can represent what" (2005:995).

As ethnographers, if we can shape what is involved in these kinds of concerns and questions into a method, then the answers we uncover are likely to be revealing: we will gain new concepts and frames for anthropological comparison – new accents on what reality can be like for a human being. Even for Viveiros de Castro, this seems to be what is motivating his theory; he is interested in what the world is like for Amazonians precisely because they too are human. Their world is interesting "to think with" precisely because it too is a "human" world, hence his interest as an anthropologist (Viveiros de Castro 2014). As we might expect, this kind of striving curiosity lies behind many of the chapters in our volume: for example John McCreery ("Why Do the Gods Look Like That") asks why, when divinity is known to be immaterial, there are human-like statues of Chinese deities and why do the gods differ as they do in the ways in which they are depicted? Wei-Ping Lin has provided one answer: "statues make the formless omnipresent gods settle down and build a stable connection with the villagers" (2008:460): McCreery tests the implications of this. Again, questions of cosmos are answered by exploring the inter-entity relationships involved, but the knowledge derived is still very much knowledge about a human perspective.

A few years ago, the BBC released a film made by Emad Burnat and Guy Davidi called *The Village that*

Fought Back: Five Broken Cameras (2012). Emad Burnat, a one time Palestinian farmer, is the narrator and the film is made up of video footage edited to show the struggle between people in Bil'in and the Israeli army and Israeli settlers in this part of the West Bank. The film foregrounds the effects this has on the villagers, many of whom are arrested, some shot and one is killed by Israeli soldiers, and on Emad Burnat himself. The "five cameras" of the film are quite explicitly presented as protagonists in Emad's narrative since they are either shot at or otherwise broken. Emad's compulsion to film, and the fact of the camera constantly "filming", become cruxes for understanding the reality of the situation. Other key agents include the Israeli jeeps, the bulldozers and excavators, the wire mesh wall that divides the Palestinians from their former farmland, the newly built high rise settlements that tower over the surrounding landscapes, the olive trees that are torn up at the roots or set alight. In the unfolding visual description we see different objects acquiring prominence as components of the "struggle": the villagers build an "outpost" on what they consider to be their own land and this building then takes on a certain life of its own.

Looking at a situation of this kind, the new ontologists will have us attend to the objects and people that are cooperating (or otherwise) *immediately* in the unfolding of this particular reality, this specific montage of shots. They would have us see all this, not in terms of the mechanisms and structures of a static society, but as elements of a process through which reality is constantly being sutured together. There is clearly value in this way of looking, because it takes us closer, in certain ways, to what the people involved actually perceive. What they envisage acquires greater significance than if we claim that this is a "representation", an "identity" or the expression of a "system of symbols". And, so, anthropologists may be able to jettison some of the heavy machinery of interpretation by which they mediate between "reality" and "ideology" – structure, semiosis, episteme, doxa, whatever. So far so good we may think. This, for example, is a central concern of the chapter

"Can the Thing Speak?" by Martin Holbraad, who has taken a key part in arguing for a revised kind of ontological awareness in anthropology. And here he makes a further step. We should no longer perhaps think of what we do as a study of (or an) "anthropos" — perhaps what we need instead is a deep "thing-ology", one that gives us much more direct access to things as they are, not as they are mediated by human-oriented concerns about belief or representation.

That "things" can act independently of human intentions should hardly come as too much surprise; the question is of course which, when and where and who is in control. In particular how is this awareness operationalized and theorized in an ethnographic account? Daniel Miller gives us one answer in his "Extreme Reading of Facebook" (this volume). Facebook is a body corporate, a "big bang", whose powers of engrossment may seem mind-boggling to anyone (perhaps those very few remaining persons) of a fusty enlightenment mind-set. Miller makes a crucial point when he argues from Nancy Munn that the power of a body like Facebook lies in its command of "negative transformations of spacetime... any cultural form that creates expansion has to have within itself the opposite quality which would destroy and shrink spacetime". Titanic powers of this type may well remind us of Overing's account of the Myth Time struggles of Kuemoi and Wahari strewing behind them a world full of poisons for the people of Today Time to sort out, re-ingest and turn into a beautiful "human life". However, these questions of scalar expansion and contraction are taken up in another register by Alberto Corsin-Jimenez in his chapter ("How Knowledge Grows") to talk about the "optics of volumes" involved in being able to envisage the state as a large body, specifically as "Leviathan". The most individualist of thinkers will accept that the State is "something big", it has "large proportions" thus its effects on humans are large — how has this knowledge of the state body come about? Corsin-Jimenez offers an erudite survey of the intellectual-technical means by which the modern state acquired space and embodiment.

His intervention also reminds us that in the background of the new ontology are "hyperobjects" — objects such as "global warming" or "finance money" that are so large, and whose effects are so ungovernable, that they defeat traditionally "modern" scales of human thought and action (Morton 2013).

The ideas underlying the new cosmopolitics are clearly potent and have reach, but a few initial sounds of caution are warranted. At the ethnographic level, applying the kinds of insights that Latour and others are developing via this programme still presents us with a politics of explanation when we decide to *generalize* – when we make claims at the "cosmological" level. In Ruth Benedict and Margaret Mead's joint research project – *The Study of Culture at a Distance* – there is a case where former Shtetl jews are being interviewed, and one of the lines of inquiry concerns whether women have souls or not. The male interviewees seem unanimously to take the view that women do not have souls. When a woman is interviewed about whether women have souls she replies "certainly, more than men" (Mead et al. 1953:135-137). So immediately we can witness how friction regarding the way the cosmos is constituted is not just friction between different peoples and their cosmologies, but also takes place *within* groupings and it scales down to the level of individual meaning (see Radin's *Crashing Thunder* for more on this, 1926). Joanna Overing, who has worked for many decades with the Amazonian Piaroa, has indicated that Viveiros de Castro's interpretive emphasis on predation and certain kinds of relationship with spirit-beings amongst the Araweté has the effect of giving analytical preeminence to adult men (shamans and warriors) in that world – because prioritizing the significance of certain kinds of ritual exchange with spirit-beings also foregrounds the power of male human beings to *make society* (e.g. Viveiros de Castro 1992:142; note the contrast with Overing 1999, 2004, n.d.). Anyone who has read Evans-Pritchard's The Nuer (1940) carefully will notice that the point of view that predominates is that of a young adult Nuer man. So, again, alongside the issue of subjective change and personal transformation, we are left with dormant questions about how the community or cosmos might be constituted *otherwise* from *other* subject-positions.

In fact, many ethnographic accounts are written out of the experiences of young, often single (or at least alone in the field), graduate students of perceived affluency, already given to occupying certain social categories and networks, both at "home" and in the "field", positions that thus limit their perspectives and understandings. When it comes to a vision of a kind of fieldwork that might collapse these predictable categories of field and home, questioner and questioned, friend and informant, the discussion here ("Friendship, Anthropology") by Liria de la Cruz and Paloma Gay y Blasco precisely helps us reconsider the fieldsite and the ethnography that awaits it as analytical artifacts built out of the experience of particular kinds of human relationship. We are reminded that the notion of "the gypsy woman", the "middle class Spanish woman" are precisely operationalized by the type of intellectual apparatus that is an ethnography. In this way, we come to recognise this artefactual character of the ethnography when it comes to rethinking our individual experiences of friendship, of being categorized, of categorizing; and the part these play in our notion of "our" world.

What is valuable in all this "ontological" discussion, then, is at least twofold: it reminds us of the purpose of ethnographic work as Malinowski described it, which is to understand "their" (the people with whom we as anthropologists work) "vision" of their "world"; and, in addition, when it helps clear out of the way some of the mediating theoretical language. We cannot achieve the basic Malinowskian insight if we have already decided in advance what a "rationally" structured world looks like and what kinds of actors are existent or non-existent and how they really are, or *ought to be*, ordered and interrelated. This is what the newer cosmopolitics is challenging. Arguably, the highpoint of the rationalist stance in anthropology came in the late 70s and early

80s. By then ethnography had become far less engaged with understanding how people in a certain setting viewed their world, and much more concerned with identifying where those people fit in preconceived theoretical templates, whether that be Structuralist, Marxist, Cognitivist, or Semiotic-Interpretive.

In this particular sense, the more rationalistic and linguistically orthodox ethnographic writing became, the more circular it became too; since it ceased to matter how the particular people involved thought about and acted on the questions at issue. The post-modern trend certainly undermined confidence in what theory could do by itself in that respect: but, as has often been noted, post-modern writing, if anything, took us further away from people and instead attended to the life and concerns of the ethnographer, and a lot of what resulted was facile and narcissistic. One positive reaction to this has been to argue much more vigorously for the phenomenological validity of informants' concepts with the aim of "rendering [their] categories analytical" (Toren and Pina Cabral 2009:10). Ethnography thus becomes the apparatus for an analytical "rendering" of local terms – *baloma, baraka, cargo, the corner, crab antics, mana, mayu-dama, moka, naven, offcomers* – concept-words which, for all their specificity in capturing a world outlook and a pattern of action, still yield insights into universal human capabilities for the perspectives they offer on different "spaces of reason". The new cosmopolitics could be described as "neo-rationalist" in this regard, highlighting the creative work that concepts – whether "etic" or "emic" – do in different knowledge practices (Crook and Shaffner 2011). For instance, they can enable us to put in question ideological principles that have a similarly reified status in our outlook (e.g. marriage, productivity, mental illness, and welfare), including those that act as an analogic base for modern anthropology and ethnographic description, such as "kinship" (Schneider 1984), "culture" (Wagner 1981), or the "relation" (Strathern 1995). Cosmopolitics, then, involves putting a more varied, and more jaggedly juxtaposed, range of concepts into play to test out the parameters of our supposedly common world and the experience of being human in it.

Given this awareness of the analytic value of terms like these, what seems to be strikingly absent in the ontological approaches we have discussed so far is a consideration of *imagination*. For an anthropologist, questions of the kind "which agents are participating in the world of the people we work with?" fundamentally comes back to a concern with how those people – individually and in aggregate – *imagine their world*. So, in asking that type of question, we are giving an epistemological value to their ways of imagining and reasoning. We are, after all, hoping to answer why these people do the things they do; not from our preformed theoretical template, but from what we understand to be their pattern of thought and action. There is a problem involved here that philosophers describe in terms of "internalism" versus "externalism" (e.g. Williams 1981). Are people's reasons for action best understood in terms of their motivations (internalism) or by reference to the layout of the field they find themselves in (externalism)? We can cut a long story short here by asking how far we anthropologists will go in crediting our own external gaze, and our capacity to model the given situation (including its ontic properties), with the power to explain the internal motivations and understandings of those we are encountering (Wardle 2014: 280).

Concerns akin to these (and to those described by John McCreery) are explored by Philip Swift (in his chapter on "Cosmetic Cosmologies in Japan"). At Ise, Buddhist and Shinto shrines "[e]verything happens as if the invocation is simulated, seemingly going no further than the curve and contact of surfaces – clapping, bowing, and the pressing of palms together." There is indeed "*something happening here/What it is ain't exactly clear*"[6] since responses to questions are frequently equivocal, but whatever "it" is demands an inspection of our intuitively held topology of internal versus external, motivation versus outcome. This awareness of "something happening" seems, in turn, to depend on a particular understanding of the "surface" which, while it is literally "superficial", its very artificiality is also "efficacious". We are led to ask what notional self or motivational state (for example, what manner of "prayer") is implied by this particular mode of relationship to divine objects whose divinity is often disavowed. A Protestant "man of action" may feel uncomfortable here we guess, but there is nothing inactive about Japanese social life; indeed the gods do not want offerings that have not been "fabricated by means of a device". We are left with a puzzle and a challenge.

We have seen that Latour's interest in ontology has to do with describing what kinds of coalition of human and non-human agents are at work in creating a particular reality – and hence what it is like to be a subject or agent in this or that arrangement or assemblage, which is where "cosmopolitics" has also entered the picture. If particular situations throw up distinct coalitions of subjectivity and agency, then these will show up as a distinct "cosmology". It is not obvious from Latour's description how the transition or translation involved, from network to cosmological gestalt, comes about — how the cosmological boundary is formed. Nonetheless, different coalitions and cosmologies clash where some key feature of their world is at stake. A mining company conflicts with a group of forest users over the capacities, meaning and value of the entities and forces present in that setting. Latour points to the fact that this kind of clash is not just one between Western technological civilization and a "local culture" over the *same* resource; it is a clash between two entirely distinct assemblies of people and things *for whom reality coheres in fundamentally distinct ways*. They cut the network differently (Strathern 1996).

In *Tristes Tropiques*, Levi-Strauss mentions a case where Spanish colonists torture Amerindians to see if they have souls, while Amerindians drown a conquistador to see if he has a body: their worlds and their world-hypotheses – their cosmo-ontologies – are fundamentally distinct. It should be noted though that the logic of the differences involved indicates, for Levi-Strauss at least, a common manner of structuring thought (1973:91). It is a shared logical foundation of this kind that Jean La Fontaine (this volume) draws on in her chapter here when she critically assesses our fear the others are engaged in profane acts of human sacrifice ("Ritual Murder?"). Ironically, inhumanity is ascribed to others according to a universally available human thought-scheme.

The outcome of clashes of understanding like these will be, Latour suggests, that either one of these realities is erased, or there will develop some kind of negotiation and redefinition of terms. Notice that Latour is not an internalist – the reasons the individual gives for whatever is going on are insufficient because the truth of their cosmology is not to be found in what one person thinks about the matter, but is rather distributed across the network, particularly in the co-activities of all the other agents. But, nor is Latour an externalist either – that which is exterior to the actor only makes sense if we take into account what this actor is aiming at, who they are trying to enlist and wherefore. The perspective on reality is itself a fold of reality: what appears to be internal knowledge is external seen from the adjacent position that overlaps and encloses it.[7] A lot of this feels quite paradoxical and we may feel that this adds to its attraction.

In his chapter here ("Cosmopolitics and Common Sense"), Huon Wardle comments on this aspect of the Latourian viewpoint. Indeed the question of "viewpoint" is curious in all this. Latour is always careful to avoid a claim to any special analytical position from which to understand some other person's network or cosmology. He is certainly arguing against the possibility of any type of "externalist" or transcendent stance from where we might judge what is "really" going on. Me (and "my" knowledge) are always inside the "social" according to Latour. In this regard, he likes to use metaphors from computing: as subjects we are always plugging in new connections and downloading new signifiers that will help us extend our network capabilities, nevertheless we cannot reach beyond the horizon of our own particular knowledge state because this knowledge is integrated in a supportive network. We would, so to speak, be tearing our own knowledge out of its own fabric of meaning by doing so. We may add components and programmes to enhance our capacity: either way, there is no view "outside" our networked subjectivity. Following the philosopher Leibniz, Latour thinks that I/we is always already occupying whatever optimal reality it can at any given moment.

This may remind us of Voltaire's satirical creation, Dr Pangloss, who lives "for the best in the best of all possible worlds". And, if we have understood Latour, there really is no universalisable standpoint from which subjectivity can take a view on and then critique its own understanding in any foundational terms; which also means there is no transcendent position from which an anthropologist can critique the conditions of experience of another person or group of people. The role of the anthropologist is rather to describe the enfolding and remaking of reality with certain actors in view. But let us remind ourselves that the politics of cosmology, both *between* cosmologies and *amongst groupings of people* is usually precisely aimed at organizing and ranking certain ways of understanding the world, and, in some cases, at the extreme, this will involve the intentional eclipsing, or erasing, of particular points of view.

Latour does, though, praise the potential in anthropology to show that there are many ways of living a life. This side-by-side diversity seems to offer an opportunity for a kind of critical appraisal; the process of comparison involved might also contribute toward the peaceful negotiation between cosmological views. Sometimes Latour points to a special role for anthropologists in mediating between clashing cosmologies (a kind of disinterested third party?), but it is not clear at what point this mediation might become an externalist view vis-à-vis each side; hence the anthropologist would be making claims to intellectual transcendence which Latour has seemingly already ruled out of bounds within the game of asking and giving of reasons. In what seems like a similar vein, Viveiros de Castro has urged anthropology to be "as the practice of the permanent *decolonization* of thought" (2014).

This, however, taking into account Latour's argument, feels incoherent. Viveiros de Castro appears to be asking that we should relinquish "our" *given* view in favour of its constant variation and transformation through encounters with others', and particularly, that we should halt the colonisation of other people's worlds through the superimposition onto theirs of our own cosmological models and concerns. We may well sympathise with that proposition, but it does not seem compatible with what Latour is telling us. Latour argues that we can negotiate about our mutually incomprehensible cosmologies, but we cannot absolutely "decolonise" our view because this would involve jumping out of our conjunction in the network into some kind of transcendent position. At best we can adapt our view into something else: innovation and transformation necessitate convention as an analogic base, or starting point (Wagner 1981). Perhaps, then, we would colonise in a new way but, it would seem, we do not decolonise, *per se*. Maybe this is what Viveiros de Castro already means by that phrase, one can only guess, since here we are at the outer limits of understanding the programme that they are laying out, sometimes in a shared, sometimes in a distinct, register.

Some final Remarks on subjectivity and imagining; and the beginning of a critical response

There is a lot that is useful food for thought in the approaches that "the ontologists" (Holbraad and Pedersen 2014) are making available. We have mentioned some features; the focus shifts from deploying a heavy theoretical machinery vis-à-vis social reality toward closely observing the kinds of aggregates of people and things that fieldwork affords. All this is grist for the mill of following the lines of interconnection that the people that we are working with in the "field" have themselves established as important. Researching the field from the point of view that *we are all animists* may well yield rewards – though further questioning is necessary when we ask on behalf of a particular situation, "in what way is that true? And how is it important?" Or, how to recompose an understanding of the world or the human in the singular from all of these different multiple perspectives. Do they add up, and if so, how? So, epistemologically, there are other kinds of concern too.

It is striking that, despite Latour's claims, particularly his insistence that subjectivity is always network-specific, there is in fact a universal capacity at stake here (already mentioned) – imagination. Human beings live in distinct worlds, at least in part, because they imagine them distinctly. Some particular human being may recognise agency in a stone or in their i-device; this will change from scene to scene. In contrast, we know that *all human beings imagine things and that this activity is constitutive of what the world is like for any given human being*. Imagining is a universal capacity of humans (distinctive, though, we might add, not exclusive). My empathic ability (or inability) to orient myself in another's world, a world that is foreign to me, is likewise an imaginative capacity and a limiting condition (or an absence of one; see Stein 1989). In contrast, the particular agency of stones or i-phones varies depending on the social set-up. Imagining and reality are sometimes opposed to each other (as are empathy and psychological naturalism), but we should also remind ourselves that imagining is the ground from which reality is constituted via experience – there is no experience that does not involve imagining. To quote Mimica, "What we call "reality" and "rationality" are its works" (2003: 282). They are literally after the fact of the imagination.

If one is not philosophically a Leibnizian, one may find it hard to take Latour's claims that objects have intentionality as seriously as we do the fact that human beings imagine and thence they conjure into being highly diverse human scenarios. The imagination is constitutive of our perception and experience of reality – and often realities clash: we are not calling here on the distinction imagination versus reality, but rather on the synthetic relation imagination-and-reality. However, when considering Leibniz' central place in contemporary "ontological" framings of the project of anthropology, his role as a founder, *arguably the founder*, of ethnology in the Seventeenth Century should also be acknowledged (Vermeulen 2015); likewise the deep-seated differences from the very beginning between the projects of ethnology and anthropology despite their common origins in Enlightenment thought. Here, then, we may note an antithesis: between infinite perspectival extension of intellectuality versus the limits of reason, between ethnology and anthropology, between Leibniz and Kant.

We are all animists, then, in the sense that, in figuring the world, and in living in it, we recognise ourselves as enlisting the assistance of innumerable things, people and non-human-agencies that help us continue the project of a life with others. Our claim then is the capacity for imagination is a human universal; one possessed by anthropologists *in common* with the people they work with. In contrast, the sense in which cockatoos, *khipu* knots, corporations, i-phones, or financial instruments act and have intentionality varies from fieldsite to fieldsite. This is not at all to dictate *what* people *should* imagine, or to prejudge how their worlds *should* look to them, let along why – certainly not to rule out certain worlds or particular formations of reality *a priori*. Nor is it to deny that other animals have their own respective cognitions (e.g. de Waal 2016). There is plenty of room to debate and celebrate *how* the imagination participates in making reality. But it is clear that the fact of imagining does offer a universally available position of (cosmopolitan) critique because all human beings share this faculty. And here one is reminded of a comment by Hannah Arendt:

> Imagination... is the only inner compass we have, we are contemporaries only as far as our imagination reaches. If we want to be at home on

this earth, even at the expense of being at home in this Century, we must try to take part in the interminable dialogue with its essence (1953).

Anthropocentric anxiety is also anthropocenic uncertainty. The older comforting perception of the protecting hand of Leviathan supporting mid-Twentieth Century anthropology's notion of culture has fragmented – with mechanical bits and pieces left in its place. Meanwhile, intensified awareness of being part of the same human species beyond the older circles of sympathy accompanies and triggers contemporary fears that humans have altered the balance between themselves and nature to such a degree as to set off ungovernable ontological effects; perhaps most of all irreversible chaotic environmental change forced forward by the unstoppable financialiation of the common human landscape. Anthropologists were quicker than most to diagnose the "runaway" character of global society and the human as a "fearful god" in the midst of its creations (1968); but in the interim the world ran away even faster leaving the expert and their expert knowledge ever further behind. The individual human, once mechanically severed from those it loves, hates, eats and kills – beasts, plants, things, gods – is also a homeless being, one incapable of hospitality. This modernist insight, accelerated by contemporary facts, surely underlies part of the urgent activity of the newer cosmopoliticians.

What the clash between the old and new cosmopolitics highlights, then, is a central and continuing problem for anthropology — one that is at least as much a matter of epistemology as of ontology: ways of knowing have their own "ontogenesis" (Gow 2011), but our capacity to comprehend this fact is epistemic. How, imaginatively, are anthropologists to localize the places, people, concepts and experiences that compose the intellectual apparatus that is "a fieldsite" within a larger local-global topology, or a common cosmos writ large? What kinds of ideas of cause and effect should ground our accounts — a scientific conception of the cosmos? Our "common sense", folk conceptions? Is it instead the cosmos as expressed in the words and actions of our informants that counts? In a world of massive human movement we can hardly expect ethnographic concepts to stay in place. And if so is the "informant" a specific category of person or can they truly be "anyone" (Rapport 2012)? The motto that Leach adopted for anthropology was "only connect" (1967), but how should we place their cosmology in relation to our own? Should theirs be bridged to ours, and if so, at what point? How to keep one from taking the other hostage? Do we anthropologists have, anyway, anything approximating to a unified cosmology? Ultimately, we may ask, what is cosmology? This renewed problem of localization (cf Fardon 1990, Negarestani 2014), with its concern for how to establish a ground for anthropological understanding, and hence ethnography, in many ways re-plays the inaugural moment of "modern anthropology", which has haunted the history of the discipline ever since, and here we return to Kant and his original grounding of cosmopolitics in universal history.

"Humanness" is both given by nature and also a thing of the human's own making, Kant argues, saying this in an era where other enlightenment thinkers, like Hume took the make up of the human to be universal and given. What we call "culture" is precisely the visible byproduct of this human self-making, for Kant. He thus makes room for freedom in his argument: there is freedom to make different manners of life, distinct kinds of social truths on top of, out of, and in addition to what is naturally given. But his formulation has come back to haunt us in an "anthropocenic" world, as Lee Drummond shows in his chapter for our volume. When it comes to an athlete like Lance Armstrong, whose seemingly "naturally given" athleticism has been enhanced by drug use, the fault-line is laid bare at the tense intersection of what is given and what is plastic: the horizon where, as Kant would have it, what humans may freely "make of themselves" comes up against what nature "makes of them". But to critique Kant via Armstrong is, of course, to read Kant's view of the nature-culture distinction anachronistically. Indeed, the Armstrong case exemplifies a world where new entities and their chaotic effects appear constantly and ideas about how to humanize the conflicts that arise are themselves diverse; branching off toward distinct possibilities for a common human future.

Sturm's chapter ("What did Kant Mean... ") offers a context for Kant's pragmatic and cosmopolitan viewpoint on history, placing it within discussions taking place in the late 18th Century. He points to tensions that existed during the enlightenment concerning the possibilities for a cosmopolitan history. Amongst these were central questions for historical inquiry such as: "what is human nature?" and "how malleable is it?" "What constitutes a cause in history?" "What part do human motives play in historical change?" Figures such as Herder came to the fore at this time to decry an enlightenment tendency to project current values onto the history of other peoples and epochs. Sturm proposes that Kant's cosmopolitan viewpoint simultaneously accepted human plasticity without relinquishing the claim for a universal human nature. He shows how Kant's intervention in debates of his time about what constitutes a rigorous science or discipline of history, precisely problematises the givenness of the "human". In this sense, Kant, by introducing the idea of mediating "categories" and "concepts", inaugurates the possibility of a modern anthropology, one that could take humanity and human society in all of his variability across all time and space as its subject matter.

In that sense, Kant's opening move – his cosmopolitics – is modern anthropology's facilitating and limiting condition. All of the founders – Herder, Alexander and Wilhelm von Humboldt, Durkheim and Mauss, Boas, and Levi-Strauss – wrote in relation to his anthropological concern. Contemporary critiques, even of Kant, are enabled by his intervention. Kantian thought remains the horizon of modern anthropology, even if remain mostly unaware of it (Viveiros de Castro & Goldman 2012: 426), just as we are unaware of Leibniz' role in initiating ethnology (Vermeulen 2015). In this way, one could, to borrow a phrase from Whitehead,[8] say that the safest general characterization of the Euro-American anthropological tradition is that it consists of a series of footnotes to Kant. We may think here of Foucault's comment that while anthropologists may feel that they can "do without the concept of man, they are also unable to pass through it, for they always address themselves to that which constitutes its outer limits" (see Piette 2015). Hence, the necessity to come to terms with our own Kantian heritage, affirming rather than disavowing it, making it explicit.

Modern anthropology works from an implicit assumption of a universal human architectonic, of the constituting role that concepts play in mediating human thought and experience. The assumption of the concept, and of our particular image of it, both facilitate and limit our capacity as anthropologists and ethnographers to orient and navigate what we take to be others' "worlds". "Localization is the constitutive gesture of conception and the first move in navigating spaces of reason" (Negarestani 2014). For anthropology, this concerns the problem of how to locate oneself in the field, and subsequently, the "field" internal to ethnographic description, with the added twist of having to describe others' concepts in terms of our own. It is a topological problem through and through. As Wagner notes, "every understanding of another culture is an experiment with one's own" (1981: 12).

Our accounts of others' "concepts" are only as robust as an anthropological concept of the concept (Viveiros de Castro 2003; cf. Corsin-Jimenez & Willerslev 2007), since the former is invented in terms of the latter (Wagner 1981). Our image of the concept acts as a control on the kinds of concepts we allow ourselves to imagine to exist. The moment we think we know *a priori* what a concept is, ethnographic understanding is forestalled. We do not yet know fully what a concept is, which is why it should be a site of ongoing inquiry, rather than remaining *given* and *implicit*. But what a concept is, is relative to where it is within a general ecology, or space, of concepts (Negarestani 2015). What the Kantian turn does then is make explicit the assumption of the concept as both the facilitating and limiting condition of modern anthropology (Zammito 2002), as both a means to and an object of knowledge.

What is unique about the grand project of ethnography is, hence, that it highlights or foregrounds *other people's* capacities – imaginations, gestures, practices, and ideas – not as sites of intervention, per se, but rather as places, moments or vantage points from which to recursively intervene and transform our own concepts and thinking (Holbraad 2012, Holbraad and Pedersen 2017). The assumption that the other is analogous to us, that their capacities (in particular their capacity for concepts) are not only universal but also contemporaneous and symmetrical with ours (Fabian 1992), rather than subordinate, allows us radically to extend our understanding of concepts as such, and thus to transform our anthropological image of what it is to be human, or of what is possible for humanity.

After Kant ([1798]2006), the hope has been that a distinctively anthropological intervention in knowledge about human nature will allow us not only to better understand the unfolding of human history, but also to make better interventions in it. "Our" here, in Kantian terms, ultimately indexes no particular society, culture or nation state, but rather a cosmopolitical anyone and "all of us". The idea being that by reflecting on human self-knowledge – the limits of humanity's momentary conception of itself and its world – may allow human history to become a site of intervention that opens up pragmatic potentials for further human co-dwelling in a common world: earth. Here the two senses of cosmopolitics, Kant's and Stengers' are not only closer than they originally appeared to be, but also come full circle in the historical moment where the anthropocence and "world society" emerge as new universals (Hart 2010); ones that both implicate but also transcend any given particular locale or region.

Notes

1. For a full list of the OAC series see:
   http://openanthcoop.net/press/publications/

2. See Charles Taylor on the pivotal role of Kant in re-orienting human self-knowledge in this direction (1985: 81-83).

3. Our account of the "new cosmopolitics" intends neither to be comprehensive, nor to imply that it exists as a homogenous approach or field. There are significant differences say between Descola's program and that of the "recursive" anthropologists (e.g. Wagner, Strathern, Viveiros de Castro, etc), or between them and Latourian inspired "science studies", or even object oriented approaches. What we intend instead is an account of the intellectual implications of these positions, exploring what they have in common in relation to the older Kantian sense of the "cosmopolitical", in order to bring them back into dialogue with each other.

4. See http://www.haujournal.org/index.php/hau/index

5. See
   https://sites.google.com/a/abaetenet.net/nansi/abaetextos/m
   anifesto-abaet%C3%A9

6. Lyrics from "For What It's Worth" by Buffalo Springfield

7. 'a subject will be that which comes to a point of view... the transformation of the object refers to a correlative transformation of the subject' (Deleuze 1993:21).

8. "The safest general characterization of the European philosophical tradition is that it consists of a series of footnotes to Plato" (Whitehead 1929).

References

Arendt, H. 1953. 'Understanding and Politics' *Partisan Review* XX(4):377-392

Barone, F. and Hart, K. 'The Open Anthropology Cooperative: Towards an Online Public Anthropology' in Pink, S. and S, Abram (eds) *Media, Anthropology and Public Engagement*. Oxford: Berghahn.

Bashkow, Ira. n.d. "House, Temple, State, Corporation: On the Origins of the Corporate Form." Unpublished manuscript.

Battaglia, D. 2016. 'Aeroponic Gardens and their Magic: Ethics in Suspension'. Keynote lecture given at the conference The Ethics of Energy. Centre for Cosmopolitan Studies, University of St Andrews, 18th March.

Beck, U. 1992. *Risk Society: Towards a New Modernity*. London: Sage.

Benardette 1964. *Infinity: An Essay in Metaphysics*. Oxford: Clarendon Press.

Bergson, H. 1935. *The Two Sources of Morality and Religion*. London: Macmillan

Carrithers, Michael, et al. "Ontology is just another word for culture." *Critique of anthropology* 30.2 (2010): 152-200.

Crook, T. & Shaffner, J. 2011. "Preface: Roy Wagner's "Chess of kinship": An opening gambit" In *HAU: Journal of Ethnographic Theory*. 1, 1, p. 159-164.

Deleuze, G. 1993. *The Fold: Leibniz and the Baroque*, Conley, T. (trans.), Minneapolis: University of Minnesota Press.

De La Cadena, Marisol. 2015. *Earth Beings: Ecologies of Practice across Andean Worlds*. Durham: Duke University Press.

De Waal, F. 2016. 'To Each Animal its Own Cognition' *The Scientist*, May 1st (http://www.the-scientist.com/)

Fabian, J. 1992. *Time and the Work of Anthropology: Critical Essays 1971-1991*. Amsterdam: Harwood.

Fardon, Richard, ed. 1990. *Localizing strategies: regional traditions of ethnographic writing*. Edinburgh : Scottish Academic Press; Washington: Smithsonian Institution Press.

Gow, P. 2011. 'Answering Daimã's Question: The Ontogeny of an Anthropological Epistemology in Eighteenth-Century Scotland' in Toren, C. and J. Pina Cabral. 2011. *The Challenge of Epistemology*. Oxford: Berghahn.

Hallowell, I. 2010. *Contributions to Ojibwe Studies: Essays*, 1934-1972. Lincoln: University of Nebraska.

Hart, K. 2010. Kant, 'anthropology' and the new human universal. *Social Anthropology*, 18: 441–447. doi: 10.1111/j.1469-8676.2010.00128.x

Holbraad, Martin. 2012. *Truth in Motion: The Recursive Anthropology of Cuban Divination*. Chicago: University of Chicago Press.

Holbraad, Martin and Pedersen, Morten Axel. "The Politics of Ontology." *Theorizing the Contemporary*, Cultural Anthropology website, January 13, 2014. http://www.culanth.org/fieldsights/461-the-politics-of-ontology

Holbraad, Martin and Pedersen, Morten Axel. 2017. *The Ontological Turn: An Anthropological Exposition*. Cambridge: Cambridge University Press.

Jiménez, A. C. and Willerslev, R. (2007), 'An

anthropological concept of the concept': reversibility among the Siberian Yukaghirs. *Journal of the Royal Anthropological Institute*, 13: 527–544. doi: 10.1111/j.1467-9655.2007.00441.x

Josephides, L. and Hall (eds). 2014. A. *We the Cosmopolitans*. Oxford: Berghahn.

Kant, I. [1790]1952. *The Critique of Judgement*. Oxford: Clarendon Press.

Kant, I. [1795]1988. *Perpetual Peace and Other Essays*. Indianapolis: Hackett

Kant, I. [1798]2006. *Anthropology from a Pragmatic Point of View*. Cambridge: Cambridge University Press.

Latour, B. 1988. *The Pasteurization of France*. Cambridge MA: Harvard University Press.

Latour, B. 1993. *We Have Never Been Modern*. Cambridge MA: Harvard.

Latour, B. 2004. Whose Cosmos? Which Cosmopolitics? A Commentary on Ulrich Beck's Peace Proposal In *Common Knowledge*, Vo. 10 Issue 3 Fall 2004 pp.450-462.

Latour, B. 2005a. *Reassembling the Social*. Oxford: Oxford University Press.

Latour, B. 2005b. 'From RealPolitik to DingPolitik – or How to Make things Public' in Latour, B. and P. Weibel (eds.) *Making Things Public: Atmospheres of Democracy*. Boston: MIT Press.

Latour, B. 2009. Perspectivism: 'Type' or 'bomb'? *Anthropology Today*, vol 25. no. 2, pp. 1-2.

Leach, E. 1968. *A Runaway World?* New York: Oxford

University Press.

Levi-Strauss, C. 1973. *Tristes Tropiques*. Harmondsworth: Peregrine.

Lin Wei-Ping. 2008. 'Conceptualizing Gods through Statues: A Study of Personification and Localization in Taiwan' *Comparative Studies in Society and History*, Vol. 50(2):454-477.

Lino e Silva, M. and Wardle, H. 2016. *Freedom in Practice: Governance, Autonomy and Liberty in the Everyday*. Oxford: Routledge.

Mead, M. (ed.) 1953. *The Study of Culture at a Distance*. Chicago: Chicago University Press.

Mimica, J. 2003. The Death of a Strong, Great, Bad Man: An Ethnography of Soul Incorporation. *Oceania*, 73(4), 260-286.

Morton, T. 2013 *Hyperobjects: Philosophy and Ecology After the End of the World*. Minneapolis: University of Minnesota Press.

Negarestani, Reza. 2014. "What is philosophy?" https://www.urbanomic.com/philosophy/

Negarestani, Reza. 2015. "Where is the Concept? (Localization, Ramification, Navigation)", in Robin Mackay (ed.), *When Site Lost the Plot*, pp. 225-51. Falmouth: Urbanomic.

Overing, J. 1999. "Puzzles of Alterity in an Amazonian Ontology: How is a God, Spirit or Animal a Human Being from a Piaroa Point of View?" Paper given at the American Association of Anthropologists: November, Chicago IL.

Overing, J. 2004. "The Grotesque Landscape of Mythic 'Before Time'; the Folly of Sociality in 'Today Time'": an Egalitarian Aesthetics of Human Existence', In Mader, E. & E. Halbmayer, (eds.), Kultur, Raum, Landschaft, Frankfurt am Main: Brandes & Apsel/ Südwind.

Overing, J. n.d. "Adiwa! Piaroa Philosophies of Power, Violence, Ingestion, Excretion, Blood and Beauty" Unpublished Paper (https://st-andrews.academia.edu/JoannaOvering)

Piette, A. 2015. "The Volume of Being." Open Anthropology Cooperative Press: Working Paper #19. http://openanthcoop.net/press/2015/12/22/the-volume-of-being/

Radin, P. 1926. *Crashing Thunder: The Autobiography of an American Indian*. New York: Appleton & Co.

Rapport, N. 2012. *Anyone: The Cosmopolitan Subject of Anthropology*. Oxford: Berghahn.

Schneider, David M. 1984. *A Critique of the Study of Kinship*. Ann Arbor: The University of. Michigan Press.

Simmel, G. 1955. 'The Web of Group Affilations' in K. Wolff and R. Bendix (eds) *Conflict and the Web of Group Affiliations*. New York: The Free Press.

Smith, A. 1776. *The Wealth of Nations*. Edinburgh: Strahan & Cadell Publishers.

Stein, E. 1989. *On the Problem of Empathy*. Washington: ICS Publications.

Stengers, I. 2005. 'The Cosmopolitical Proposal' in Latour, B. and P. Weibel (eds.) *Making Things Public: Atmospheres of Democracy*. Boston: MIT Press.

Strathern M. 1995. *The Relation: Issues in Complexity and Scale*. Cambridge: Prickly Pear Press.

Strathern M. 1996. "Cutting the Network." *The Journal of the Royal Anthropological Institute*, Vol. 2, No. 3 (Sep., 1996), pp. 517-535.

Taylor, C. 1985. *Human Agency and Language: Philosophical Papers, Volume I*. Cambridge: Cambridge University Press.

Toren, C. and Pina Cabral J. 2011. *The Challenge of Epistemology*. Oxford: Berghahn.

Turner, C. 2015. 'Cosmopolis: Toward a Positive Conception of Cynic Political Philosophy' *Yearbook in Cosmopolitan Studies*, 1:1-52.

Vermeulen, H. 2015. *Before Boas: The Genesis of Ethnography and Ethnology in the German Enlightenment*. Lincoln: University of Nebraska Press.

Viveiros de Castro, E. 1992. *From the Enemies Point of View*. Chicago: Chicago University Press.

Viveiros de Castro, E. 1998. "Cosmological deixis and Amerindian perspectivism." *JRAI* 4 (3): 469–88.

Viveiros de Castro, E. 2003. And. After-dinner speech given at Anthropology and Science, the 5th Decennial Conference of the Association of Social Anthropologists of the UK and the Commonwealth 2003. Manchester, Department of Social Anthropology, University of Manchester.

Viveiros de Castro, E. 2004. "Perspectival Anthropology and the Method of Controlled Equivocation." *Tipití: Journal of the Society for the Anthropology of Lowland South America* 2, no. 1: 3–22.

Viveiros de Castro, E. 2007. 'The Crystal Forest: Notes on the Ontology of Amazonian Spirits' *Inner Asia* 9(2):153-172.

Viveiros de Castro, E. 2012. *Cosmological Perspectivism in Amazonia and Elsewhere*. Four Lectures given in the Department of Social Anthropology, University of Cambridge, February–March 1998. HAU: Masterclass Series 1:45-168.

Viveiros de Castro, E. 2014. *Cannibal Metaphysics*, trans., ed., and intro. Peter Skafish. Minneapolis, MN: Univocal.

Wagner, R. 1981. *The Invention of Culture*. (2nd ed.). Chicago: University of Chicago Press.

Wagner, R. 1991. The fractal person. In M. Godelier and M. Strathern (eds), *Big Men and Great Men: personifications of power in Melanesia*, pp. 159-173. Cambridge: Cambridge University Press.

Wardle, H. 1995. 'Kingston, Kant and Common Sense', *Cambridge Anthropology* 18(3):40-55.

Wardle, H. 2000. *An Ethnography of Cosmopolitanism in Kingston, Jamaica*. New York: Edwin Mellen.

Wardle, H. 2010. 'Introduction: A Cosmopolitan Anthropology' in Rapport, N. and H. Wardle A Cosmopolitan Anthropology, Special Issue of *Social Anthropology* 18(4).

Wardle, H. 2014. 'An End to Imagining?' in Harris, M. and N. Rapport (eds.) *Reflections on Imagination*. Oxford: Ashgate.

Wardle, H. 2015. 'Cosmopolitanism'. *Elsevier Encylopedia of the Human and Behavioural Sciences*.

Whitehead, Alfred North. 1929. *Process and Reality*. New York: Macmillan.

Williams, B. 1981. 'Internal and External Reasons' chapter 8 in *Moral Luck*. Cambridge: Cambridge University Press.

Zammito, John H. 2002. *Kant, Herder, and the Birth of Anthropology*. Chicago: University of Chicago Press.

Chapter 2

COSMOPOLITICS AND COMMON SENSE

Huon Wardle

> *HORATIO*
> *O day and night, but this is wondrous strange!*
>
> *HAMLET*
> *And therefore as a stranger give it welcome.*
> *There are more things in heaven and earth, Horatio,*
> *Than are dreamt of in your philosophy.*
>
> *(Hamlet, Act 1, Scene 5)*

The paradox of a 'stranger' welcoming something 'strange' was not lost on her Tiv audience when Laura Bohannon recounted Shakespeare's Hamlet to them in 1950s West Africa: without a relevant genealogy how could they assess the meaning of the ghost King's relationship to Hamlet? (Bohannon 1966). The same paradox looms in the idea of a cosmopolitan or world anthropology: who plays host to whom intellectually in a discipline without favoured sites or privileged genealogical matrices? Who will arbitrate which 'spectres' are honoured and which are relegated (Derrida 2006)? If we accept that both the ethnographic field and anthropology as a discipline are now not simply multi-sited but in truth 'unsited', then this paradoxical predicament is already with us (Cook et al. 2009, Lins Ribeiro 2006). Modern anthropological knowledge has always been imagined in a certain way; it comes in emic form from a fieldsite to a centre of knowledge where it is welcomed for its potential to inform etic debates. But who will play host and whom guest in an ethnography and anthropology which does not distinguish fixed intellectual loci or points d'appuis?

In what follows, I argue that pursuing the logic of a cosmopolitan anthropology will inevitably open up a renewed discussion on the meaning of subjectivity vis-à-vis the social. I take as my focus a debate between Ulrich Beck and Bruno Latour over the notion of the cosmopolitan or cosmopolitical. Their contrary positions signal the increasingly strong divergence between a humanist and an organicist answer to the question 'what is a subject'? On the one side, Beck stands for an enduring humanism associated especially with Kant and refracted in latter-day anthropology by diverse figures including Firth, Mintz and Hannerz. For Beck, the human subject is 'a primary substance' (Whitehead 1978:157): in his stance, understanding the current condition of human subjectivity is paramount for social science; other questions are questions only relative to this substantial one. On the other side, Latour ranks with proponents of organicist philosophies and anthropologies including Peirce, James, Whitehead, Bateson and, closer to the present, Strathern. For these thinkers, subjectivity derives its qualities from its distribution across emergent networks: it is not a property solely or necessarily even mainly of human individuals. The important discussion on cosmopolitanism is not, in the first instance, then, about whether this term will replace other terms or even whether cosmopolitanism is a 'good thing'; it rather has to do with the diverging conceptions of subjectivity it engages, and the intellectual and ethical effects of these engagements.

This paper begins with an excursus into the debate in

question, looking first at Beck's cosmopolitanism then at Latour's contrasting cosmopolitics. We will see that Latour's critique revolves around the proposition that Beck's cosmopolitanism is too sociological and not anthropological enough (Latour 2004). My worry is that Latour's comparative anthropology may itself be too purified - insufficiently comparative, plural or subjectivized, but I will leave those concerns until later. However, Latour makes some points that we undoubtedly need to consider in arriving at a distinctly anthropological cosmopolitanism – one that accounts for the common sense of ethnographic knowledge. Against Beck's humanistic cosmopolitanism, Latour posits a cosmopolitics in which people, along with many non-human agents, create conflicting natures which they then fight over. I suggest that the positions of Beck and Latour may usefully be triangulated with a certain type of 19th Century skepticism or ethical egoism. Via a discussion of Kantian common sense I return to the issue in hand – what might be distinctive about an ethnographically informed anthropological cosmopolitanism? What assumptions concerning subjectivity might it presuppose or engage? An initial rapprochement between cosmopolitics in the Latourian sense and cosmopolitanism may involve acknowledging the activity of some of Latour's non-human agents both in the common sense of anthropologists and of their informants.

Zombie categories made visible

Ulrich Beck has described extensively the crisis in 'methodological nationalism' that he sees at the centre of the fragmentation of latter-day social theory – and its cosmopolitanization (2002, 2004, 2006). The roots of this crisis lie in how the state has lost its metaphysical priority as the cause, frame and context for all the social phenomena that constitute it. There is an awareness that most of the stock concepts of Twentieth Century social science; the statistics that give mathematical meaning to state practices; society (understood as a synonym of the 'national fallacy' 2002:29); the family; the household; social class have become what Beck terms 'zombie categories' under current conditions (2002: 24). Taking their meaning each from the other, these concepts continue to do intellectual work even though the lived reality to which they refer no longer exists. The symptom of these developments, and in certain respects the cure, is the 'clash of cultures and rationalities within one's own life' (2002:35). Insofar as the awareness of attachments across these supposedly bounded categories becomes an ethical project, it lends itself to acknowledging a sense of 'global responsibility in a world risk society, in which there are "no others"' (2002:35-36).

> *methodological cosmopolitanism* implies a new politics of comparison... The monologic national imagination of the social sciences assumed that Western modernity is a universal formation and that the modernities of the non-Western others can be understood only in relation to the idealized Western model (2002:22).

In this new field, 'there is not one language of cosmopolitanism, but many languages, tongues, grammars' (2002:35). However, on this point Beck is wary of giving value to culturally relative 'cosmopolitanisms' since with this move we revert to the conspectus of multiculturalism in which each individual becomes 'the product of the language, the traditions, the convictions, the customs and landscapes in which he came into the world' (2002:35). In the specific intervention that becomes the object of Latour's critique (2004), Beck argues that rather than positing multiple and incommensurable forms relative to one another, cosmopolitanism must be based on a type of contextualized universalism.

> The true counterposition to incommensurability is: there are no separate worlds (our misunderstandings take place within a single world). The global context is varied, mixed, and jumbled—in it, mutual interference and dialogue (however problematic, incongruous, and risky) are inevitable and ongoing. The fake joys of

47

incommensurability are escape routes leading nowhere, certainly not away from our intercultural destiny (2004:436).

It is this 'single world' cosmopolitanism that becomes the focus of Latour's criticism. Beck, Latour argues, has taken his cosmopolitanism 'off the shelf, from the stoics and Kant' (2004:453). For Latour, Stoical and Kantian cosmopolitanism both imply an 'already unified cosmos' (Latour 2005:262,fn362). I will dispute this further on, but it is certainly true that this represents Beck's stance – we have each internalized 'jumbled' versions of a single world (Beck 2004:436). Further, in Latour's view, it is no use our continuing to say that if only we could agree about the one world we all inhabit then our problems could be resolved: we do not inhabit one world but instead a pluriverse of divergently mediated worlds ('pluriverse' being an adoption from William James, 1909). In the sense that people will not give up these multiple worlds without a fight, then they are incommensurable. In an ironic echo of Kant's proposal that enlightenment consists in throwing off a 'self-imposed immaturity' (Kant 1983:41), Latour tells us that instead of continuing to appeal to a shared (human) nature, Westerners need to jettison the Eurocentric 'exoticism they have imposed on themselves' (2004b:43); that is to say, they need to join the others in recognising many, variably mediated, natures.

As elsewhere in his writing, on this point Latour is fulsome in his approval of Viveiros de Castro's account of Amerindian multinaturalism (Latour 2009). Unlike Westerners who hold that there is one nature but many cultures, Amerindians entertain many natures and a single anthropomorphic culture. For Amazonian indians the specific natural form of an entity hides its general anthropomorphic meta-structure. Latour presents the parable of a fight between Amerindians and conquistadores: Amerindians debate whether Spaniards have bodies while Spaniards discourse over whether Amerindians have souls – there is no shared nature regarding which their arguments can be resolved. The most important lesson here from Latour's point of view is that the stabilization of any given form of nature involves the mobilization of hosts of non-human agents who intervene, interfere and play diverse negotiative roles; whether as divinities, test tube cells, DNA profiles, or 'non-material couplings' (1996). No purpose, then, in invoking Amerindians as participants in a shared cosmopolitan future: Amazonian Indians 'are already globalized in the sense that they have no difficulty in integrating "us" into "their" cosmologies. It is simply that in their cosmic politics we do not have the place that "we" think we deserve' (2004:457,fn13).

Latour's cosmopolitics is, hence, not simply a struggle between human individuals and their diverse worldviews, it is a fight between human subjects plus all the non-human actors who participate (and can be thought of as having an interest) in the mediation and institutionalisation of specific fields of nature-and-culture. Thus Latour defines subjectivity in the following pragmatic (some might say generous) way: 'every assemblage that pays the price of its existence in the hard currency of recruiting and extending is, or rather has, subjectivity' (2005:218). This formulation has the effect – and this is of course central to Latour's project - of reanimating, repersonalising and resubjectivising numerous inert or 'dead' commodities, categories, symbols, properties and objects, and making their cosmopolitical role visible and analytically crucial.

Subjectivity amidst a multitude of Gods and Demons?

This matter of redefining subjectivity is surely the most fundamental point of divergence between Beck and Latour. In Beck's stance, subjectivity remains without question a property of human individuals. For him, cosmopolitanisation further pushes to the front the only kind of subjectivity that counts – the subjectivity of the thinking and acting human individual. As he states, 'the question "who am I?" is now irrevocably separated from origins and essences' (2004:449): cosmopolitanisation entails intensified individualisation. Without resort to a frictionless ethnic or national mandate, individual human subjects increasingly must answer directly to (and ethically for) the multitude of 'gods and demons' populating their versions of the world (Weber 1948:148). At the same time, despite their divergence, an emphasis on re-envisioning subjectivity is shared by Latour and Beck precisely because both eschew Twentieth Century social constructionism. Beck shows how the category 'society' has crumbled because the 'transnational' has become so irrefutably knotted into every aspect of subjective experience. The 'national fallacy' may, nonetheless, become intensified in these conditions. Even while it has lost its 'institutional or geographical fixity', the state continues to act – individuals are still forced to build their practices around its manifold intrusions (Trouillot 2001:126). But, Beck argues, nationality has at the same time become decreasingly comprehensible in value-rational terms: belonging to a particular nation-state has dwindling value as an explanation of anything else. Latour, in the same vein, indicates the futility of invoking a 'society' that lies behind, and at the same time explains, every political manoeuvre apart from itself:

> To insist that behind all the various issues there exists the overarching presence of the same system, the same empire, the same totality, has always struck me as an extreme case of masochism, a perverted way to look for a sure defeat while enjoying the bittersweet feeling of superior political correctness. Nietzsche traced the immortal portrait of the 'man of resentment', by which he meant a Christian, but a critical sociologist would fit just as well (2005:252).

Latour and Beck share something very significant, then: they reject a cornerstone of classic sociological critique and in so doing they reach back to social philosophies that predate 'society' as an analytical category. For Beck this involves an explicit return to Kant. Meanwhile Latour, as we have seen, calls on the pragmatism of Peirce and James in support of his revised sociology of actors and networks. But this reaching back takes them in distinct directions.

The reversed gaze beyond Twentieth Century social theory is a highly significant facet of the current intellectual dialogues around cosmopolitanism: there is a search for a conceptual language and this can involve either a redefinition of concepts already in play, new coinings, or a return to parallel dialogues from the past. Here I will briefly triangulate the position of Latour and Beck by introducing a relatively unknown mid-Nineteenth Century social philosopher, Max Stirner, into their controversy. Stirner, if not the most subtle of debaters, nonetheless brings some of the relevant issues into strong contrast. 'Saint Max' as Engels and Marx nicknamed him (1963), was one of the Young Hegelians who clustered in Berlin in the 1840s. It seems that he was amongst the quietest of that group (Mackay 2005). He published his only significant book, The Ego and its Own, in 1844. The foundational stance of the Ego and its Own is that the entire array of apparently humanizing institutions – the state, humanity, human rights, man, society, marriage, family and money comprise 'spooks' or 'fixed ideas' not absolutely different to the gods and ghosts of previous eras. The idea of 'man' or humanity is as much a 'spook' as is the 'nation' which it appears to transcend. These concepts stand in an authoritarian relationship to the individual ego which is unable to know itself while they continue to dominate its consciousness. Nationalist, revolutionary and humanist movements evidence in common a generalized respect for Man, or the Citizen, or the Party Member alongside a uniform contempt for the individual as an individual ego.

The inability of the self to distinguish itself from its own fixed ideas is ubiquitous, argues Stirner. 'How ridiculously sentimental', he comments, 'when one German grasps another's hand and presses it with sacred awe because "he too is a German"' (1907:302). Anyone who rejects incorporation into marriage or fatherland or humankind is labeled an 'egoist'; but it is the label that reveals the sanctity of the specific category, the particular 'spook'. As a young Hegelian, Stirner's narrative of how the ego ('I who really am I') comes to know itself vis-à-vis these other lion-skinned 'thistle-eaters' is historical and dialectical:

> What manifold robbery have I not put up with in the history of the world! There I let sun, moon, and stars, cats and crocodiles, receive the honour of ranking as I; there Jehovah, Allah, and Our Father came and were invested with the I; there families and tribes, peoples and at last Mankind, came and were honored as I's; there the Church, the State, came with the pretention to be I, and I gazed calmly on... so I saw I above me, and outside me, and could never really come to myself. (1907:294-295).

To which a latter-day commentator might add: 'here I allowed multinational corporations, private security firms and CCTV cameras to act extraterritorially as 'I'; there supermarkets, university ethics committees, banks and lobby groups, web portals and credit agencies ranked themselves unquestioned as 'I', while I, 'who really am I', continued to draw money from the cash point.

Stirner's ethical egoism demands that any principle or *idée fixe* that I invoke I should appropriate as a principle for myself alone. The 'money' I use is therefore not a metaphysical money somehow independent of myself, but is rather my money - money according to me; likewise any of the other 'spooks' that are important for how I act or think. The others likewise speak, not in the name of some further 'moral, mystical, or political person', but from their own unique ego (1907:294). In response to Fichte's humanistic 'transcendental idealism', Stirner posits a 'transitory egoism' that rejects the assimilation of myself into any other transcendent human 'I' (1907:237). Taking back 'the thoughts [that] had become corporeal on their own account... I destroy their corporeity... and I say "I alone am corporeal"' (1907:16). I will act, then, only in accord with whatever principles guide my action because those ideas alone truly exist for me and I will assume that the others will act with consideration to their fixed ideas and spooks.

Curiously, the more we read about Stirner's 'egoism', the more we may feel there is something self-less about it. If, as Stirner suggests, I accept that my limits are purely of my own subjective making then I relinquish the fundamental egoist's rationale that the remit of my idees fixes should expand where and when I please because my ideas must be true objectively for all. In contrast, Stirnerian skepticism - the extension of an indifference regarding the presuppositions of others into how I consider my own principles - rather than exemplifying egoism, suggests instead a stance that Bakhtin calls 'playing a fool'. In Bakhtin's account, a 'self-consciousness' may emerge for the ego whereby, in its attempts to extricate itself from the rhythm of its relations with others, it 'has passed all bounds and wants to draw an unbreakable circle around itself' (1990:120). Hence, perhaps, the element of holy idiocy suggested in Marx's nickname for Stirner.

However, some important themes emerge here. On the one hand, the strident emphasis on ethical individualization connects closely with Beck, on the other, the recognition of how non-human agents or 'spooks' participate as actors in the lives of individuals is significantly Latourian, albeit that Latour is more generous towards his 'actants' (2005). Speaking teleologically, Stirner occupies a pre-Durkheimian world where individuality can still be thought of without reference to a society that preconditions it. He can nonetheless cognise some of the forces that will coalesce to establish that understanding. We should remind ourselves that Stirner lived in a German milieu that was ideologically but not socially or politically unified – the disparity between the exercise of power, subjective imagining and shared sentiment was all too obvious to him. Either way, Stirner would surely have agreed with Beck about the historical processes leading to individual self-recognition and no doubt he would have approved of Beck's description of 'zombie categories' so close as it is to his own notion of the 'spook'. Stirner would nonetheless have disapproved of the further idealistic step towards a shared cosmopolitan project. With Latour, he would have concurred that we live in many disparate worlds in the company of a multitude of non-human agents, though, again, he would strongly have disavowed the intellectual decentring that enables Latour to equate the subjectivity of these 'spooks' with my own self - 'I who really am I'.

The point in contention is not simply that Nineteenth and Eighteenth Century intellectual conditions seem suddenly more familiar; that these parallel conceptualisations appear more than ever synchronously available and salient as part of our own apprehensions. The problem can be posed another way: what stands between these perspectives and our moment is Twentieth Century mechanistic nationalism and the sociology and anthropology that accompanied it. Perhaps there are ways nonetheless of thinking through, round and beyond that monolith.

To begin with we need to take heed of the conceptual revision that is entering the foreground. The Twentieth Century use of the word 'culture' familiarized us with the idea of a system of signs that could be grammatically ordered and exchanged at the collective and personal levels. One thing that Latour - and Stirner too in retrospect - tells us is that the matter is not so simple at all: the entities we have come to call cultural signifiers or symbols are not inert exchangeables, nor do they fall into place within mechanical systems: instead they act on us and for us; they are, in this sense, agents with subjectivity of their own. And, as Beck indicates, they may well - are likely to - have a life after their own death. Whatever social science now emerges will have to encompass those insights within its own common sense: we need to rethink the common sense of anthropology looking backward and forward.

The common sense of cosmopolitan knowledge and ethics

The loss of interpretive power of social and cultural constructionism is by no means a new predicament; Hannerz has explored extensively the ecumenical situations and orientations that this loss opens up for view (1989, 1997, 2006). As long ago as the 1950s, Firth had indicated how social boundaries are 'in any case arbitrary... [human beings] are continually overcoming barriers to social intercourse' (1951:28). Nevertheless, Beck and Latour combined present us with new challenges for how we rethink both the modes of communication and the models of subjectivity that are now in question. Since I want to bring Kant to my aid in exploring these issues without jettisoning either Beck or Latour, I must first dispute Latour's argument that Kant offers us the cosmopolitanism of an 'already unified cosmos' (Latour 2005:262,fn362). It seems one thing to criticize Kant for his unified architectonics of subjectivity, rather different to suggest that the cosmos that this subjectivity confronts is itself already completed for Kant. My suggestion here, which builds on earlier work, is that Kantian common sense offers a distinctive frame for figuring what is involved in a cosmopolitan imaginary and by extension for understanding the current common sense of anthropology (Wardle 1995, 2000).

Cosmopolitan ethics and knowledge are closely tied in Kant's writings with the capacity for reflective judgement [1. Kant's teleological reflection on world history in Perpetual Peace (1795) pursues his detailed inspection of teleological thinking in the Critique of Judgement (1790).] (Arendt 2003, Kant 1983, 1952:96-97). Reflective Judgement, as Veblen tells us, can be understood as the 'faculty of search... the faculty of adding to our knowledge something which is not and cannot be given in experience' (1884:264). Those who consider Kant to have taken for granted the outcome of this search (a unified cosmos) have in Veblen's words 'taken up the Critique wrong end foremost' (1884:263). Subjectively, cosmopolitanism exemplifies not a world that is already unified but a reflective search for unification which takes place with others in mind. The shifting horizon of our judgement at any given moment is whatever 'everything', whatever 'cosmos' we can summon to encompass what we know. Far from being unified before the event, our cosmopolitanism is fundamentally relative to each situation of subjective judgment.

Hannah Arendt ends her essay 'Some questions of moral philosophy' by drawing on what Kant has to say about common sense in his Critique of Judgement (Kant 1983, Arendt 2003). She argues that what he states there should act as a central point of reference for those who wish to understand ethics after Nazism. In Arendt's view, this final Critique of Kant's, surpasses the rational ethics of the Critique of Practical Reason. The fascist disaster was not caused, Arendt suggests, by a failure of rationality (Nazi functionaries were rational enough; overly capable of applying a purely technical reasoning to human affairs) the failure was rather one of judgement, an incapacity to judge commonsensically that the rational procedures in question were universally monstrous and wrong. She points to Kant's treatment of 'common sense' in aesthetic terms. Kant answers the potential fragmentation and individualization of public knowledge by examining the subjective ability to organize communal knowledge through an aesthetics of common sense judgement.

Arendt argues that each of my common sense judgements, results from an imaginative process that involves me in exploring the field of associations that make up the community to which I understand myself to belong. Community is here radically relative to my own striving and imagining; it could well include known individuals but it might equally involve the heroes of novels or films, dead relatives, figures I know from the pages of wikipedia, people who I observe on the street but whom I never choose to keep actual company with. I am as a result 'considerate in the original sense of the word, [I] consider the existence of [these] others and... try to win their agreement, to "woo their consent," as

Kant puts it' (Arendt 2003:142). I cannot communicate concretely with Elias Canetti or Fellini's filmic hero Guido, but I may well have them in mind in arriving at certain judgements (the sense in which I try to woo their consent is complex, of course). In this regard, when I explored the cosmopolitan imaginings of my Jamaican friends in earlier work, I realize in retrospect that I did not always take full account of how the spirits of the dead and other divinities can be interactively present in how situations are imagined and common sense judgements arrived at (Wardle 2000; I have explored these issues in more recent work 2007). Particularly, given his early flirtation with Swedenborgism (De Beaumont 1919), Kant would have understood the part played by the voices and visions that told Socrates to cross-examine the Athenian pretenders to wisdom (Plato 1997).

Common sense (unlike pragmatic moral reasoning in Kant's view) is, again, an aesthetic faculty not a matter of logic. The common sense of a particular individual includes their distinctive gestus, their tonality, the particular rhythm of that person's modes of expression in arriving at judgement. It describes a style of characterising events and objects imaginatively and applying these patterns judiciously to particular situations. Of course how an individual's common sense expressiveness looks to an observer is incommensurable with how common sense is experienced in the first person. Either way, this judiciousness is not simply a matter of organizing perceptions correctly or not: on this it is worth quoting Arendt at length.

> The point of the matter is that my judgement of a particular instance [depends]... upon my representing to myself something which I do not perceive. Let me illustrate this: suppose I look at a specific slum dwelling and I perceive in this particular building the general notion which it does not exhibit directly, the notion of poverty and misery. I arrive at this notion by representing to myself how I would feel if I had to live there, that is I try to think in the place of the slum dweller. The

> judgement I come up with will by no means
> necessarily be the same as that of the inhabitants...
> but it will become an outstanding example for my
> further judging of these matters. (2003:140)

Common sense is, hence, an active capacity: it entails the ability to search out and organize the examples and exemplars we need in order to form judgements about people and situations.

True to his Copernican turn, for Kant, common sense is hence a subjective faculty, not an objective body of knowledge or a closed set of rules of thumb. And, from the objectivist standpoint of social science, Kantian common sense appears as, once more, radically relative. There is no need to assume that we may be able to map one individual's 'common sense' onto another's even though, subjectively, common sense strives toward universal validity. Common sense judgement may arrive at a moment of objectifiable decisiveness (a box ticked or not, for example) but it has of itself no measurable properties only qualities: our understanding of common sense must take account of the 'very great difference of minds' as Kant puts it (2006:124). Nonetheless, as Arendt argues:

> The validity of my judgements will 'reach as far as
> the community of which my common sense makes
> me a member – Kant who thought of himself as a
> citizen of the world, hoped it would reach to the
> community of mankind (Arendt 2003:140)

The exercise of common sense is, furthermore, reflexive. In his Anthropology, Kant encourages us first, to 'think for oneself'; second, to think oneself 'in the place of every other person' with whom one is communicating; third, to think 'consistently with oneself' (Kant 2006:124, Wardle 2000:130). 'Every other person' surely means here not every person with whom I could communicate in some concrete setting according to some acknowledged standard of measurement, but rather every other person whose personal standpoint I can imaginatively 'bear in mind' in such and such a regard. Hence, Kant construes a triadic process of reflexive refinement which consists in (1) knowing my own mind (2) considering fully (enough) the standpoints of the others (3) bringing this diversity into a kind of judicious consistency (back to 1). Here is Arendt's gloss: 'while I take into account others when judging, this does not mean that I conform in my judgment to theirs. I still speak with my own voice and I do not count noses in order to arrive at what I think is right.' (2003:140-141)

This refinement of common sense is, as Simmel would say, a progressus ad infinitum: newer, more highly differentiated, diversely informed judgements constantly come to mind even while others are forgotten or perhaps remain only half cognized (1978:118). There is no point at which I am able to say 'I now possess as much common sense as I need'. Arendt's argument is that ethics requires the constant intellectual traversing of the community to which I imagine myself to belong. The scope of common sense is a function of the narrowness or broadness of association that I am capable of organizing in this way and the judgements that result. She posits a situation in which someone cites Bluebeard as their moral exemplar – such a person we can try to avoid. The far more dangerous individual is, instead, the one for whom 'any company would be good enough', who is incapable of considering others in the moral-aesthetic frame of judgement. In conclusion, reiterating the well-known phrase, Arendt comments how in 'the unwillingness or inability to relate to others through judgement... lies the banality of evil' (2003:146).

Note how Stirner's ethical egoism observes stages (1) and (2) of the Kantian progressus, but disables him from engaging in (3). Kant saw beyond the predicament that Stirner finds himself in. Stirner conflates thinking for oneself (as a correlate of individualization) with the idea that in my judgments I can only have myself in mind: on the contrary, Kant suggests, I constantly displace myself in favour of the others in order to judge in ways that have the potential to be generally true, not merely true for myself. What Stirner sees as a monstrous relinquishing of the self to fetishes and ghosts, Kant recognizes as a necessary moment in the process of arriving at a moment of judgement - so long as I am indeed thinking individually. It seems unlikely, though, that Kant would have guessed the degree of significance that all-or-nothing decision-making would later take for the existentialists whereby every choice is a test of the self's faith in itself.

How does this subjective picturing of common sense help us to consider the disputed vision of cosmopolitanism versus cosmopolitics? There is already, of course, a historical trajectory in which Kant's subjective sense of community meets and is transformed, on the one side into Weber's 'subjectively believed' ethnic belonging (1978b: 391) and, on the other, into Simmel's subjectively organized 'web of group-affiliations' (1955). The mid-Twentieth century interactionists with their emphasis on subjective choice between cultural-symbolic options are also inheritors of Kant, but they echo only rather distantly the qualities of Kant's original description. Their attempts to find a systematics as rationally convincing as Durkheim's took them further and further away from the aesthetic and imaginative dimensions of the Third Critique. But if the systematism of Durkheimian society is now redundant, then this also throws doubt on the interactionists' answer: interactionism as originally conceived will always be on the look out for social systems to critique in terms of rational subjective choice. Intersystems theory, which starts with a similar problematic, relies, likewise, on a 'system' that is then, so to speak, crossed out (Palmie 2006:441).

A considerate cosmopolitics?

For the task in hand, instead of extending our historical survey further (a useful mission), we need to put some Latourian tests to Kant's common sense. In particular, we need to ask how incorporative can Kantian common sense be of the kinds of non-human subjectivities Latour demands that we include? However, once we have pursued that question, it seems fair to turn the tables and ask in return; how capable are these non-human subjectivities of making common sense judgements? What capacities for moral aesthetic 'consideration' can we expect of these other subjects? Let us remind ourselves of Latour's generous definition of subjectivity. Agents and actants are characterized by their 'subjectivity'; the big issue is that there are many more of these subjects in heaven and earth than were dreamt of by Twentieth Century sociology. Subjectivity is acquired by becoming a gathering point in a network and by demonstrating the further ability to 'recruit others': many, many actants can apply and become qualified on this basis (2005:218). And, whatever subjectivity is, it is certainly not given *a priori*; on the contrary, as Latour puts it, '[y]ou need to subscribe to a lot of subjectifiers to become a subject, and you need to download a lot of individualizers to become an individual' (2005:216).

As Latour observes, non-human agents have always held centre stage in the ethnographic worlds of anthropologists; whether as baloma spirits, patrilineal ancestors, yams or cassowaries. And as Strathern shows, accounting for the relations making up these persons, and the relationships between them, has been integral to social anthropology as a project (1990). In ethnographic accounts, non-human persons quite openly participate in the day to day lives of the humans around them: Tallensi ancestors punish recalcitrant entrepreneurs (Fortes 1959); yams decide to roam across the Dobuan gardens during the night thus threatening the matrilineage (Fortune 1963:108); or, in a case I am more directly familiar with, Saints instruct city dwelling Jamaicans to go out and warn of impending destruction (Wardle 2007). In many respects, as anthropologists, we can agree with Latour that 'humans have always counted less than the vast population of divinities and lesser transcendental entities that give us life' (2004:456). But the question in response might be 'counted' for whom? 'counted' by whom?

First let us consider again some of the ethical dimensions. What Latour is asking of Western cosmology is a repersonalisation of the invisible agents – machines, pandemic diseases, state practices which, while officially inert, act *de facto* as subjects. Would it help our understanding of liberal ethics if we came to recognise how Israel or Iran act not merely as a 'symbols' or even as determining systems, but as subjects instigating and authorising reactions? The anthropomorphism might at least be more honest. None of this is in fact ruled out by how Kant describes the aesthetics of common sense: we consider the examples and exemplars who partake in the community of our imagination and we make our judgements 'without counting noses'. The dilemma derives not from this direction – my human subjectivity – but from the other side: can I expect 'consideration' from these non-human agents; will they consider me as part of their community, a community of humans and non-humans? What kind of ethical behaviour may I expect – the unbending Tallensi ancestor? The humorous and unreliable Jamaican Saint? Certainly if we able to recognize their field of associations as Arendt recognizes Bluebeard, we can at least make some relevant judgements.

However there are anthropological problems too, and they take us back to where we began. Any anthropologist who works closely with Amerindianists must surely view as problematic the amount of weight a strikingly reified Amazonian Indian 'cosmology' bears in Latour's account. Let us consider the five century long process that the term 'Amerindian' represents, that is to say the process by which people recognized as 'Indians' became American Indians. Viveiros de Castro would have us believe that this process has reached a point where Amerindians have 'no difficulty' in integrating 'us' into 'their' cosmology (Latour 2004:457,fn13). Not for 'them', then, the 'self-reflexivity of divergent entangled cosmopolitan Modernities' as Beck puts it (Beck 2004:36). In this vista, the Amerindians exist outside the constant mediations, the typical interchange of personnel, the repeated 'overtaking' that characterizes the actor-network in Paris (Latour 2005). Perhaps more pertinently, the Brazilian nation as an actant, for example, is as utterly invisible in this Amazonian Indian cosmology as is the cosmology's role as an actant in South American national mythology. Does Latour's pluriverse necessitate a purified self-organising cosmology for which Amerindians are the outstanding metonym? These are, surely, ways of thinking that anthropologists have learnt to treat with extreme suspicion. Is it possible then that Latour's pluriverse is insufficiently plural? More consideration seems needed.

Conversing at the edge of time: an ethnographic example by way of conclusion

It is March 2004. I am standing on the edge of the road with Lazarus watching the early morning traffic running into Kingston, Jamaica. Lazarus is an elderly Blue Mountain coffee farmer of Middle Eastern extraction: his parents fled Southern Lebanon to the West Indies in 1948. He owns about 25 acres of hillside crop and, every Friday, brings his workers down to drink white rum in the local bars here. Lazarus and I are talking about the war in Iraq that we have been watching via CNN news broadcasts over the last few days. Our conversation begins with apparently shared common sense assumptions and judgements. We both agree that the invasion was illegal according to international law, it will probably spark a civil war and is certain to breed more violence. When I speak, I draw on the catalogue of ideas and rhetorics that I have gleaned from the news media and hearsay, shaped through previous discussions with those around me. Lazarus concurs with what I say, but his field of examples and exemplars includes a range of distinct elements and his narrative moves toward a quite different, and in effect absolute, endpoint.

> You see, Britain is the lost tribe of Israel: that is why it ever run things in the world. But now America take over. You know about the stone of Scone that was under the throne of England in time past? It hold the power. That stone send to America with the

Mayflower. Now America take over. You see the British must control the Black because once Hannibal have control over the British them. And Black rule hard, man: them make the people bend over and fuck him in the arse; fuck him, man. So that is why the British must ever control the Black. But now that power pass to America. Book of Revelations - America, man, are the lamblike beast come to rule the world in the last days.

For me to understand Lazarus' way of framing these issues requires a complicated exchange of standpoints. For the moment, I am interested primarily in the form or morphology of his discussion rather than its meaning. When I, so to speak, step into my own shoes as a white middle class European I am used to seeing the world perspectivally. In a perspectival image the vista recedes towards an actual-imaginative vanishing point. Things nearer to me are larger, more sharply focused: objects further toward the horizon are decreasingly distinguishable, less fully meaningful and smaller. This is the ordering principle carried into our conversation both by the CNN broadcasts that are its focus and by my own ways of thinking and talking – the assumption of a certain kind of relation between centre and horizon. What, however, if my personhood were defined by being one of those 'distant' subjects/objects nearer the horizon? It is not that Lazarus disagrees with my presentation. His response, though, suggests a transformation of my perspectival ordering somewhat along these lines: to take up his standpoint (more like a dream compared to my initial version of reality) is to occupy a position bizarrely close to the vanishing point. Looking outwards from where Lazarus stands, I am confronted by actors who become monstrously larger the further away they are; their activities have no horizon, but their overwhelming centrality makes inevitable my disappearance.

In Lazarus' account, mental objects familiar enough to me from my childhood education - the Mayflower, the stone of Scone - have taken on radically distinct dimensions, activities and relationships to their place in the kinds of nationalist configurations I am familiar with. Hannibal, the threat to civilisation of my school days, figures for Lazarus as a violent and sexually unruly African who, briefly jumping out of the correct ordering of space-time, is quickly returned to the horizon once more. America, a titanic entity, has come to hasten the end of my fellow indistinguishable others – 'the black'. Social causality is certainly not here the measured rippling outwards of benefits toward the periphery posited by the perspectival politics of diffusion or modernisation: we might picture it instead as a kind of implosion of forces as smaller actors are sucked towards the larger body: an event that marks the end of all causal relationships and all time, the End of All Things.

We are faced, then, with the Arendtian task of trying to understand the common sense of others by getting to grips with our own. A fundamental subjective work I engage in with regard to my available knowledge is surely that of folding cultural discordances back into my common sense by way of the coherent judgements I make about the present (the narratorial centre of which is inevitably myself). This entails being able to map my subjective experiences cosmologically; to gives these elements universal, cosmic validity. There is a constant traversing between my pragmatic subjective engagements with others and a referencing and legitimating of these engagements by reference to a cosmos (whatever examples and exemplars are available to me). That process provokes special difficulties and resulting stratagems in a place like Kingston. Jamaicans including Lazarus recognise themselves as thoroughly modern. Fundamentally, they accept the all-importance of the individual as both a claimer of rights and as a maker of contracts with others. Tradition and habit are, by contrast, contingent and subject to the transformative power of free will (Wardle 2000). But within what cosmological or metaphysical ordering can Lazarus legitimately make these contracts and claim these rights?

His response is both cosmopolitan and cosmopolitical -

if we take the key elements of Beck's and Latour's analyses. In a Beckian sense, he does not ask to be freed from a world that holds the potential of being sharable. In his worldview the process of making meaning is thoroughly subjectivized, thoroughly individualized and this certainly seems the aspect that corresponds most to my way of seeing also. At the same time there is a cosmopolitics here also which transfigures the fundamental spatial and temporal matrix of the 'nature' involved. There is, for instance, no deferring of moral judgement historically in his nature because it is about to come to an end. We both recognize, at least in broad brush, the same actants – Britain, the United States; constitutional symbols, but what we might call their cosmological distribution, size and efficacy is quite distinctly staged. When compared with Lazarus' sharply delineated view, my imagining of these entities becomes a little confused and vague – historical time and a certain kind of perspectival presentiment mediate it, but I am now less able to grasp entirely how. Here we can echo Latour's approving citation of Viveiros de Castro: Lazarus' common sense is already global: it is simply that in his cosmic politics I do not have the place I would have predicted for myself. But we have to employ this rhetoric with a proviso: the refinement of pristine indigenous cosmologies - elaborately articulated symmetric fictions - that provide the foil to a critique of 'Western' society is unsustainable.

Concluding remarks

'Fetishism', remarks Gilsenan (paraphrasing J.S. Khan), 'infects us all, or rather it affects others, because we always seem to escape it' (2000: 603). Beck and Latour combined present the challenge of an anthropology that is simultaneously cosmopolitan and cosmopolitical. Latour's cosmopolitical challenge to Beck involves disavowing cultural code as a neutral medium exchangeable between individual cosmopolitan actors. Cultural code becomes instead an actant in the world of sociologists in the same way as spirits are actants in the world of spiritualists, or Charles Darwin is an actant in the world of socio-biologists. In Latour's view, scientific modernity involves constantly, in Gellner's words, 'invoking the processes of nature to underwrite social arrangements,... allocate responsibilities, and settle disputes' (Gellner 1964:76). The resultant multiplication of natures returns us ever closer to non-modern animism. The anthropologist's task becomes one of demonstrating the moments or nexuses where this underwriting takes place. The Beckian challenge to Latour may consist, by contrast, in recognizing that the 'others', in their generality, will no longer serve as stable points of cosmological reference vis-à-vis 'our' unstable cosmology. 'They' also evidence internalized cosmopolitanism; the rhetorical claim that 'their' cosmological forms evolve in 'their' terms is wearing thin. A comparative anthropology that depends on building ever more rigid geometries around the ideas that certain 'peoples' represent is itself moribund.

If the systems of society and culture have gone then what is left would seem to be divergent histories and a conversation about the present and the future. Here we surely have to agree with Beck that anthropological dialogue can only be pursued on the commonsensical basis that elements of cosmologies can be shared between individual human subjects: human subjects remain the only agents capable of the kind of mutual consideration required. The danger here is the reinvention of what Gellner sarcastically terms the 'Pure Visitor' – an unmediated human ego whose role is to 'quarantine' and arbitrate social truths from a position outside the social (1964:108). At the same time, it is no use reinventing pristine ontologies to serve the same quarantining function. Without resort to either of these implausible guests we are left with an overcrowded universe lacking the geometric simplicities of 'our' versus 'their' cosmologies. If culture is gone, then we need not continue to be spooked by cultural fragmentation: anthropologists will surely still employ diverse heuristics of cosmology and social relationship, but their ethnographies need to be imaginatively open to previously unrecognized, or perhaps politically incorrect, types of agent as well as to new fields and forms of interaction and exchange. Code made the lives of anthropologists easy: 'code presupposes content to be somehow ready-made and presupposes the realization of a choice among various given codes' (Bakhtin 1986:130). Now, by contrast, we find ourselves 'in it together' but with competing definitions of 'we', 'it' and 'together'. How to understand subjectivity comes to the front at this juncture as the crucial object of reflection.

References

Arendt, H. 2003. *Responsibility and Judgement*. New York: Schocken Books.

Bakhtin, M. 1990. *Art and Answerability*. Texas: University of Texas Press.

De Beaumont, L. 1919. *Emanuel Swedenborg*. London: Nelson and Sons.

Beck, U. 2002. 'The Cosmopolitan Society and its Enemies' *Theory, Culture and Society*, 19(1-2):17-44.

Beck, U. 2004 'The Truth of Others: A Cosmopolitan Approach' *Common Knowledge*, 10(3):430-449

Beck, U. 2006. *The Cosmopolitan Vision*. Cambridge: Polity Press.

Engels, F. and K. Marx 1963. *The German Ideology*. New York: International Publishers.

Bohannon, L. 1966. 'Shakespeare in the Bush' *Natural History* 75:28-33.

Cook, J., J. Laidlaw and J. Mair. 2009. 'What if There is No Elephant? Towards a Conception of an Un-sited Field' In *Multi-Sited Ethnography: Theory, Praxis, and Locality in Contemporary Social Research*. (ed.) M-A. Falzon.

London: Ashgate: 47-72.

Derrida, J. 2006. *Spectres of Marx*. Oxford: Routledge.

Fortes, M. 1959. *Oedipus and Job in West African Religion*. Cambridge: Cambridge University Press.

Fortune, R. 1963. *Sorcerers of Dobu*. New York: E.P. Dutton and Co.

Hannerz, U. 1989. 'Notes on the Global Ecumene' *Public Culture* 1(2):66-75.

Hannerz, U. 1997. 'Fluxos, fronteiras, híbridos: palavras-chave da antropologia Transnacional' *Mana* 3(1):7-39.

Hannerz, U. 2006. 'Two Faces of Cosmopolitanism: Culture and Politics' Barcelona: *Documentos CIDOB: Dinamicas Interculturales*, 7.

Kant 1952. *The Critique of Judgement*. Oxford: Clarendon University Press.

Kant 1983. *Perpetual Peace and Other Essays*. Indianapolis: Hackett Publishing Co.

Kant 2006. *Anthropology from a Pragmatic Point of View*. Cambridge: Cambridge University Press.

Latour B. 1996. *Aramis, or the Love of Technology*. Cambridge MA: Harvard University Press.

Latour B. 2004a 'Whose Cosmos, Which Cosmopolitics? Comments on the Peace Terms of Ulrich Beck' *Common Knowledge* 10(3):450-462.

Latour B. 2004b. *The Politics of Nature*. Cambridge MA: Harvard University Press.

Latour B. 2005. *Reassembling the Social: An Introduction to Actor-Network Theory*. Oxford: Oxford University

Press.

Latour B. 2009. 'Perspectivism: "Type" or "Bomb"?' *Anthropology Today* 25(2):1-2.

Mackay 2005. *Stirner: His Life and his work*. South Carolina: Booksurge.

Palmie, S. 2006. 'Creolization and its Discontents' *Annual Review of Anthropology* 35:433-456.

Plato. 1997. *Apology*. Illinois: Bolchazy-Carducci.

Simmel 1955. *The Web of Group-Affiliations*. New York: Free Press.

Simmel 1978. *The Philosophy of Money*. London: Routledge and Kegan Paul.

Stirner 1907. *The Ego and His Own*. New York: Benjamin R. Tucker.

Trouillot 2001. 'The Anthropology of the State in the Age of Globalization' *Current Anthropology* 42(1):125:138.

Veblen 1884. 'Kant's Critique of Judgement' *Journal of Speculative Philosophy* 18(July): 260-274.

Wardle 1995. 'Kingston, Kant and Common Sense' *Cambridge Anthropology* 18(3):40-55.

Wardle 2000. *An Ethnography of Cosmopolitanism in Kingston, Jamaica*. New York: Edwin Mellen.

Wardle 2007. 'A Groundwork for West Indian Cultural Openness' *Journal of the Royal Anthropological Institute* 13(3):567-583.

Weber 1948. *From Max Weber: Essays in Sociology*. London: Routledge and Kegan Paul.

Weber 1978. *Economy and Society: An Outline of Interpretive Sociology*. Berkeley: University of California Press.

Whitehead 1978. *Process and Reality*. New York: The Free Press.

Chapter 3

WHAT DID KANT MEAN BY AND WHY DID HE ADOPT A COSMOPOLITAN POINT OF VIEW IN HISTORY?[1]

Thomas Sturm[2]

Introduction

It is widely held – and not false – that Kant's philosophy of history expresses the Enlightenment hope for a stepwise progress of humankind towards freedom or morality. However, we are nowadays suspicious of models of a stadial development of human history, especially teleological ones. Furthermore, Kant's model of historical development is burdened with problems of its own, concerning its epistemic status, and its position within his philosophy in general. To deal with these issues, scholars have mostly focused on connections between Kant's philosophy of history and his ethics or his views about teleology. They have downplayed or neglected another context, namely, the theories of historiography that he was faced with. I shall show how Kant reacts to debates about a theory and practice of historiography highly influential in his time, especially in his German environment. It was called "pragmatic history".

In part I, I indicate what major versions there existed of this approach. I then outline three crucial problems that emerged with the requirement, set up by many pragmatic historians, of a stage model of humankind's development. Among other things, I shall point to how the debate about the meaning of 'pragmatic history' became connected to the idea of a 'cosmopolitan viewpoint' in history, an issue that was discussed particularly between August Ludwig Schlözer and Johann Gottfried Herder. In part II, I report on Kant's reception of pragmatic history, and what he found lacking in the most important versions of it – namely, an appropriate understanding of human nature, which he himself developed more fully in his lectures on pragmatic anthropology. I shall thereby try to clarify how his own "cosmopolitan" idea of the development of human nature through history is likewise entangled with the notion of pragmatic history, and that his notion of a cosmopolitan idea itself has three different aspects, responding to the three problems outlined. Thus, relating Kant's philosophy of history to contemporary debates can make his views more intelligible than merely analyzing their connection to other parts of his critical philosophy.

I. Pragmatic History and Models of Human Historical Development

1. What Is 'Pragmatic History'?

By the 18th century the study of history is growing quickly not only in terms of institutions and literary output but also in terms of the level of the debates about its theoretical and methodological presuppositions. In the German countries, this debate takes often shape under the heading of a "pragmatic" orientation. To mention but a few examples, eighteenth-century authors before Kant write pragmatic histories of the Jesuits and Protestants, the rulers of Braunschweig, the school reform in Bavaria, of literature, medicine, the souls of humans and animals, and even of sleep. And many historians at the time have a serious intention with this. As the Göttingen professor Johann Christoph Gatterer, the most influential organizer of historical research in the eighteenth century, writes, in "history, *pragmatic* is just what in the proper sciences is called *systematic*".[3]

But which requirements pragmatic historiography need fulfill becomes controversial. In the debate, the following four requirements become introduced stepwise:
  i. Most conceptions of pragmatic historiography take it for granted that the *object* of investigation is *human action*, particularly in more or less widely conceived areas of social life (at certain times and places).
  ii. In methodological terms, a history can be pragmatic if it studies the *causes*, particularly the motives or intentions of human agents.
  iii. A historical study can be called 'pragmatic' if it is tied to a *universal history of mankind* – either by helping to write that history or by presupposing it. Being "universal" does not necessarily mean that it has to cover all historical details, but at least the major factors and/or stages of human history.
  iv. Finally, history can be called 'pragmatic' if *practical consequences* or lessons for human (particularly social) action can be derived from it.

These elements are not mutually exclusive. However, some pragmatic historians require only some of these features, while others demand that all be satisfied; furthermore, some authors claim that a certain requirement is more important than others; and, occasionally, some requirements are developed and discussed more closely and thereby become understood in different ways.

For instance, in the early eighteenth century, Johann David Kö(h)ler claims that a historical study is already pragmatic if it treats of public matters, especially the official and social deeds of rulers, and if it offers practical orientation in civil life, having in mind specifically political action and the design of public affairs.[4] But no later than in the 1750s, such a meaning of "pragmatic history" becomes viewed as overly narrow. This is accompanied by a growing awareness that there might be a pragmatic historiography of the "highest level" or in the "truest understanding" of the term, which has to be distinguished from lesser degrees and incorrect meanings.[5] To begin, a number of authors stresses that pragmatic histories must also inform readers of "impelling forces" (*Triebfedern*)[6], motives, and other causes.[7] Gatterer himself, who voices this point with particular emphasis, does not claim that previous historians had never sought out "causes and effects, means and intentions".[8] Thucydides and Polybius clearly did. Gatterer's main criticism is directed at the genres of mere annals, chronicles, and genealogies, and the accompanying conception that history merely records particular facts of the past. The causes behind historical events seldom coincide with periods or commencements of rule, and outcomes often extend beyond the dates covered by annals.

Gatterer moreover argues that the "*highest level* of what can be considered *pragmatic* history" can only be achieved by developing a universal history, by embedding historical investigation in "the idea of the overall connection of things in the world (*Nexus rerum Universalis*)" – that is, causal explanations in history must be embedded in a system of world history:

> For no occurrence in the world is – as it were – *insular*. Everything is connected, is produced, is induced, and in turn produces and induces. The affairs of the noble and the lowly, individual persons and all of them together, private life and the world at large, indeed, even those of reasonless and lifeless entities and humans; all are intertwined and interconnected.[9]

While these requirements are all repeatedly emphasized by the majority of authors, requirement (iv) remains relatively negligible for Gatterer, unlike for others. He hints at it in one of his earlier writings[10], but later on clearly rejects the view that it would be constitutive of the idea of pragmatic history.[11] He also makes fun of the view, held by several authors, that one could derive practically useful conclusions from mere annals, chronicles or genealogies.[12] One might also think here of Lord Bolingbroke's well-known dictum that "history is philosophy taught by examples".[13] Obviously, Gatterer denies that such views help to raise the rank of history – to approximate it to the *bona fide* sciences.

While Gatterer becomes the most influential German historian of his times, his conception of pragmatic history does not remain undisputed. For instance, the Church historian Johann Matthias Schroeckh (1733-1808) favors a combination of all four requirements: A truly pragmatic history should focus upon human actions, provide causal explanations, develop and use a system of universal human history, and attempt to draw practical lessons on the basis of the first three requirements.[14] Also, other authors raise questions about various requirements. Some already discuss the possibility of giving causal explanations in history, while others are concerned about whether pragmatic histories ultimately have to study humankind as a whole, and whether such histories – if they aim at practical conclusions at all – should instruct particular individuals or groups or humankind as a whole.

2. *The Requirement of a System of Universal History*

Of special relevance here is the call for a system of history as a whole (requirement iii). How should or even could one write "the" complete history of humankind's development? Most authors agree that it will not suffice to collect and order all existing special studies, and then continue them. That had been tried before. Schroeckh emphasizes that causal explanation demands various kinds of *weighting*. It is not easy, he writes, to describe the universal historical "Nexus" in a way that gathers and lists all causes and outcomes. It is not necessary, for instance, to note every historical detail or every slight causal connection. On the contrary, it is the difficult task of the historian to select the facts relevant for an adequate explanation of events. As Gatterer remarks, one has to identify and structure the "revolutions" of human history. Only these will help to identify the really important causes of human actions in history.[15]

His colleague at Göttingen, August Ludwig Schlözer (1735-1809) works out this approach in his *Vorstellung seiner Universal-Historie* (1772-73). He claims that one needs a unifying viewpoint in order to be able to select and order facts and turn them into a system:

> World history can be imagined from a double perspective: Either as an aggregate of specialized histories, a collection of which, if it is complete, constitutes a whole in its own way; or as a system, in which the world and humanity constitute the one entity, for which from among all the parts of the aggregate some are preferably selected and ordered purposefully.[16]

Furthermore, Schlözer demands that for this we need to single out factors that "interest not individual nations or classes of the human race, but that are significant for the cosmopolitan [*Weltbürger*], for man as such".[17] More specifically, he claims that Roman history – from the city's founding, the formation and division of the world empire, to its decline – provides the best focal point:

> [Roman history] is the overall guiding thread [*Leitfaden*] that throughout various concurrent courses of almost innumerous peoples prevents chronological confusion. Rom deserves this honor: For which empire of the world has had greater influence on the fate of the world?[18]

3. Three Problems with the Requirement of Universal History

While the requirement for a structured system of universal history has its attractiveness for authors at the time, it has several problems.

(I) A first problem concerns an assumption about human nature, and it can best be explained by the impact of Hume. He does not, neither in his *History of England* (1754-62) nor elsewhere, use the term 'pragmatic history'. Yet, German reviews praise the *History* as an example of pragmatic work and applaud Hume's skill at "using his knowledge of human nature to enlighten and promote the usefulness of history".[19] Two of Hume's philosophical theses on human nature and history – to be found in the *Treatise* and the first *Enquiry* – are of particular importance here. He claims, first, that the historian may and should presume that human nature is *constant*, or subject to unchangeable causal laws. Second, he advances the methodological claim that by studying history we can discover these laws:

> Mankind are so much the same, in all times and places, that history informs us of nothing new or strange in this particular. Its chief use is only to discover the constant and universal principles of human nature, by showing men in all varieties of circumstances and situations.[20]

Pragmatic historians often follow Hume on these points.[21] But this raises problems for their views. Many of these historians also stress that human history includes "revolutions", necessitating a system of the most important developments. Also, as one reviewer of Hume's *History* points out, impartiality is seen as vital to causal explanation: In order to reveal true causes, it is crucial to assess the past not in terms of maxims of the historian's time, but in terms on those that held in the period and place under investigation[22]. However, these points only make sense given that modes of human conduct change substantially over time. Moreover, if pragmatic history should be used to draw practically relevant conclusions, then such conclusions may repeatedly lead to *new* principles for conduct – which threatens the Humean claim of the constancy of human nature as well.

(II) Second, how ought one to structure human history as a whole? If you take dominant nations as in Gatterer's and Schlözer's proposals: Should universal history first depict their histories and then turn to the subordinate countries? Or should the mutual influence of countries on one another be examined together?[23] Moreover, besides dominant nations, natural, economic, technological and intellectual factors are important too. Schlözer himself stresses that earthquakes, floods and epidemics, or also "the discovery of fire, bread and alcohol, and so on, are facts equally as important as the battles at Arbela, Zama, and Merseburg".[24] Can all the factors be arranged within a single system of human history? In a review of 1772, Johann Gottfried Herder complains that Schlözer merely presents a plan lacking clear execution. In 1774, Herder furthermore suggests that what one reads "in almost all so-called *Pragmatic Histories of the World* is nothing but the disgusting tangled mass of 'the time's prized ideals'".[25] In other words, Schlözer's cosmopolitan orientation may in the best case be useless and in the worst case be the expression of an ideology.

(III) Finally, what is the epistemic role and status of the stage models of human history? The views here are quite divided. The outlines by Gatterer, Schlözer, and others are shaped by tangible tasks of empirical history. Claims about dividing the past into epochs, or questions of chronology are viewed as subject to empirical scrutiny. However, even the very same authors characterize their historical ideas and frameworks as "conjectural" or "philosophical". This indicates that their function and status is not clear.

To sum up: One can see that the shift towards pragmatic history, reasonable as it was when compared with other traditions of history writing, led into serious new predicaments.

II. Kant on Pragmatic History and the Development of Humankind

4. Kant's Reaction to Pragmatic History

Now to Kant. First, a bit about his standpoint towards pragmatic history. From the mid-1770s on, he presents his views especially in his annual lectures on anthropology. Here, he praises Hume's *History* for not confining itself to chronicles of wars and rulers, but relating to humanity in general.[26] Also, Kant is familiar with the *Enquiries*. And in his early statements, one can see Kant as understanding and sharing the idea of pragmatic history along Humean lines: as a study of individual and social intentions causing actions, ideally useful for a practical instruction of agents in the social sphere. At least until 1775-76, he also accepts the ontological thesis that human nature is constant, linking it even to his own conception of anthropology. At the same time Kant becomes also interested in the genre of histories of the stadial development of humankind, including the idea of genuine change in human history.

In the 1780s, he suddenly scathes pragmatic historians for lacking the knowledge of human nature they pretend to have:

> ... since the authors of many history books have little knowledge of human nature, they have no idea of pragmatic history and much less of how to write it.[27]

I will explain in a moment what he means. Before this, I need to briefly comment on a related passage in the *Groundwork*. Here, Kant first distinguishes between pragmatic principles as leading to prudence, and notes that there are two different notions of prudence: *Weltklugheit* and *Privatklugheit*. The first is the competence to use other human beings for one's purpose, the second is the competence to order one's purposes such that one approximates one's own happiness. He also says that *Weltklugheit* should serve *Privatklugheit*, because knowing how to manipulate other persons but not doing so for furthering one's own well-reflected purposes isn't very bright. But all this expresses not his fully considered opinion on what 'pragmatic' means but, rather, a report on widely held views. Just one page later he gives his own viewpoint:

> It seems to me that the proper meaning of the word pragmatic could be determined thus most precisely. Pragmatic are called the sanctions which do not properly follow from the law of states as necessary laws, but from the precaution for general welfare. Pragmatically written is a history if it makes prudent, that is if it instructs the world how to reach its advantage better, or at least as well as its preceding world.[28]

So what he wants pragmatic history to do is not to teach us how to use other human beings simply for our personal purposes. But what would be wrong with that (leaving moral concerns aside here)? And what does he really have in mind with the „general welfare"? His answers stem from the background of his then developing anthropological views about what it means to be a citizen of the world. This then leads him to a specific notion of a cosmopolitan standpoint in history.

5. Kant's Response to the Three Problems of Universal History

Let me explain this by reference to Kant's response to the three problems of the various approaches to universal history described earlier on (section 3 above).

(I) First, Kant comes to reject a naïve view of the constancy of human nature. He does so by means of assumptions concerning basic factors of the dynamics of social interaction developed in his anthropology lectures. Six basic claims are necessary here.[29]

(1) *Human dependency upon society.* Human beings need education, and later on other forms of social cooperation to achieve our goals, to improve action possibilities and to uphold our self-regard.

(2) *Human egoism.* At the same time, unfortunately, human beings are mostly driven by self-interested inclinations. We do not trust each other; we are jealous; we try to manipulate and exploit one another. The conjunction of (1) and (2) Kant famously calls the "unsocial sociability" of humankind.

(3) *The first-person point of view.* That such things are possible is rooted in other, basic human facts. There is an important difference between our having of mental states and our having of physical states. Not only can we note that we are in such-and-such a mental state – say, that we feel a pain or have a desire. Unlike mere animals, we can be happy or sad about that, or we can view these states – and those of other persons as well – with a critical eye, reflect upon and change them. This requires a first-person point of view upon first-order mental states: To know that one is unhappy about a certain pain, and that one wishes that the pain goes away, requires knowing whose pain it is. Also, egoism and self-regard as well would be impossible without such a first-person point of view.

(4) *Prudence and learning to adopt the third-person point of view.* But what can we do about the dilemma of our unsocial sociability? Kant's answer: If I want to act prudently, I have to learn that others have that egoism as well, and that it can be useful to take into account their first-person point of view.

(5) *Invention of new social roles and rules.* Thereby, however, social interaction becomes easily extremely complex. Not only do I perceive others as having egoistic motives and as having abilities for hiding such motives; they perceive me in the same way. Hence, our basic purposes of receiving respect and support must not be exerted too

obviously, and we must be able to find *new* ways by which to pursue our goals prudently. This leads to iterated forms of role-playing in society, to a concealing and dissembling of egoistic intentions before others.

(6) *New roles and rules become "another nature"*. In this interaction, humans therefore develop *new* rules of interaction, or "another nature".[30] But that means that our actions do not simply fall under rules as if they were natural laws; rather, we *follow* certain rules with a greater or lesser amount of rational deliberation. We can thus be producers instead of being mere products of our development.

From all this derives a first sense of cosmopolitanism in Kant's work, which is related to human nature: We are citizens of the world in the sense that our nature is partly plastic, and more specifically that we ourselves produce our rules of action and, thereby, our social world. This is a fact that holds, in principle, for each of us, and which each of us better recognizes in social interaction – instead of expecting to extract more superficial kinds of egoistic prudence from history.

(II) How does this notion of cosmopolitanism relate to the project of universal history? Kant – like Schlözer – claims that the historian needs a guiding "idea", and again characterizes this idea by claiming that it centers on the human being as a "citizen of the world". But, unlike Schlözer, Kant gives this notion a distinctive and not implausible meaning: the knowledge about the plasticity of human nature and its conditions is the knowledge he finds lacking in many pragmatic historians.

In *Idea* Kant then first outlines basic features of human social dynamics and explains afterwards how an adequate universal history would have to look like. It should start with ancient Greek history, for the contingent reason that only here a real source-based historiography could start. But the further steps should not look at dominant people and then wonder how to include other important factors; they should focus upon the development of forms of society that reduced aggression and war (such as the introduction of international commerce), introduced different elements of a republican constitution (the French Revolution becoming later on the outstanding "sign" of such a history), and that may lead to the establishment of a league of nations. This is obviously a second, richer notion of cosmopolitanism, but one presupposing the first. It flows from the former in the sense that such institutions help us to realize more fully the possibilities inherent in our nature, and to cope with our unsocial sociability.

(III) Finally, what about the epistemic role and status of this cosmopolitan idea? The answer is not surprising. No universal history should or even could aim a sum-total of all past events. Instead, by using the idea as guiding thread – another notion already to be found in Schlözer, as cited above, but not clarified by him – helps to find concepts and principles for selecting, linking and organizing historical knowledge in a certain way. The idea thus has a regulative function. Still, history seen from that perspective can be connected to empirically discoverable occurrences and developments.

There might be other perspectives, of course; but these have to be brought to the fore first. Kant emphasizes the sketchy nature of the *Idea* essay, it being "only one of the thoughts that a philosophical mind (that incidentally must be well-versed in history) might also toy with from a different standpoint".[31] Kant does not claim that the propositions he sets forth about the development of human capacities, the mechanism of unsocial sociability, and the resulting sequence of forms of social or political order of humankind are already to be taken as full-blown developmental principles of history. Rather, he explicitly aims to provoke contemporary historians to develop better ideas and frameworks. This is further evidence that his views should be seen as responding to contemporary debates rather than internal problems of his own philosophy only.

Conclusion

It would be a misunderstanding to view my foregoing considerations as a complete defense of Kant's views. I tried to add an important facet to the existing interpretations. What this contextualization cannot explain (and, *a forteriori*, defend) are the strongly teleological claims of his views on human history, or their exact relation to his ethical theory. Even then, critics might either reject the very demand for a grand-scale model of human history, or at least claim that Kant's sketch is useless for, say, current historical research. But note that I have tried to reduce his claims about human social dynamics to their most simple, largely innocent basic points. Given this, and given the epistemological modesty of his claims about human development, perhaps things look better for a kind of reflection about the question of how we could give meaning to the fragmented masses of historical knowledge.

Notes

1. The OAC working paper that appears here was based on chapters in Thomas Sturm's 2009 monograph and a similar version appeared in Sturm, T. 2013. 'What did Kant mean by and why did he adopt a cosmopolitan point of view in history?' In: *Kant und die Philosophie in weltbürgerlicher Absicht: Akten des XI. Kant- Kongresses 2010.* Ed. by S. Bacin, A. Ferrarin, C. LaRocca & M. Ruffing. Berlin: DeGruyter, 853-865.

2. Thomas Sturm is ICREA Research Professor at the Department of Philosophy at the Autonomous University of Barcelona (UAB). He specializes in Kant, theories of rationality, and the history and philosophy of science. Among his publications are two books, including *Kant und die Wissenschaften vom Menschen* (2009) and articles in *Kant-Studien, Kantian Review, Kant Yearbook, Studies in History and Philosophy of Science, Synthese, Erkenntnis,*

Metascience, Philosophical Quarterly, Philosophical Psychology, History of the Human Sciences, Inquiry, and *Journal of the History of the Behavioral Sciences.*

3. Gatterer, Johann Christoph: "Vorrede von der Evidenz in der Geschichtkunde." In: *Die Allgemeine Welthistorie die in England durch eine Gesellschaft von Gelehrten ausgefertiget worden.* Ed. by F. E. Boysen. Halle. 1767, vol. I, 1-38, here 12.

4. Kö(h)ler, Johann David: *Lectorem benevolum programmate de historia pragmatica.* [Altdorf.] 1714.

5. See Anonymous [Abbt, Thomas]: "Hundert und ein und fünfzigster Brief. Anmerkungen über den wahren Begrif einer pragmatischen Geschichte." In: *Briefe, die neueste Literatur betreffend* 9 (No. 151, 1761), 118-125, here 119; Gatterer, Johann Christoph: "Vom historischen Plan und der sich darauf gründenden Zusammenfügung der Erzählungen." In: *Allgemeine historische Bibliothek* 1 (1767), 15-89, here 84; Anonymous: "J. M. Schröckh, *Christliche Kirchengeschichte.*" In: *Königsbergische Gelehrte und Politische Zeitungen* (No. 79, September 30, 1768), 315f.

6. Anonymous: "Hundert und ein und fünfzigster Brief", 118f.

7. See e.g.: Köster, Henrich Martin Georg: *Über die Philosophie der Historie.* Giessen. 1775, 9 and 14.

8. Gatterer, "Plan", 79f.

9. Gatterer, "Plan", 84f.

10. Gatterer, "Plan", 27.

11. Gatterer, Johann Christoph: "*Ueber die Philosophie der Historie,* von H. M. G. Köster." In: *Historisches Journal* 6 (1776), 164-166.

12. Gatterer, "Plan", 77f.

13. Bolingbroke, Henry St. John: "Letters on the Study and Use

of History" (1735). In: *The Works of Lord Bolingbroke*. Ed. by H. G. Bohn. 4 vols. London. 1844, vol. II, 173-334, here 177.

14. Schroeckh, Johann Martin: *Christliche Kirchengeschichte*. Frankfurt a.M. 1768, vol. I, 251-278.

15. Schroeckh, *Kirchengeschichte*, 264-275; Gatterer, "Plan", 86-88.

16. Schlözer, August Ludwig: *Vorstellung seiner Universal-Historie*. 2 vols. Göttingen. 1772-73, vol. I, 14. – Schlözer rejects to characterize his approach to universal history as a pragmatic one, at least in the sense of giving practical lessons to the reader – these, the reader should draw himself (ibid., vol. I, 26).

17. Schlözer, *Vorstellung*, vol. I, 30. Similarly Schroeckh, Johann Martin: *Lehrbuch der allgemeinen Weltgeschichte*. Berlin. 1774, 24f.

18. Schlözer, *Vorstellung*, vol. I, 80f.

19. Anonymous: "D. Hume, *Geschichte von Großbritannien*. Dt. Übers." In: *Neue Zeitungen von gelehrten Sachen* 59 (July 23, 1764), 467f.

20. Hume, David: *Enquiries Concerning Human Understanding and Concerning the Principles of Morals* (1748-51). Ed. by L. A. Selby-Bigge (3rd ed. by P. H. Nidditch). Oxford. 1975, 83f.

21. See, e.g., Gatterer, "Plan", 84f.; Schlözer, *Vorstellung*, vol. I, 15 and 19; Schroeckh, *Kirchengeschichte*, 275-278.

22. Anonymous: "D. Hume, *History of Great Britain, Vol. 1*." In: *Göttingische Anzeigen von gelehrten Sachen* 147 (December 8, 1755), 1350-1354, here 1350f.

23. Köster, *Philosophie der Historie*, 55-62.

24. Schlözer, *Vorstellung*, vol. I, 29f.

25. Herder, Johann Gottfried: "A. L. Schözers *Vorstellung seiner Universal-Historie*." In: Idem: *Sämtliche Werke*. Ed. by B. Suphan. Berlin. 1877ff., vol. V, 436-440. – Idem: *Auch eine Philosophie zur Geschichte zur Bildung der Menschheit* (1774). In: Ibid., vol. V, 555.

26. V-Anth/Fried, AA 25: 472. These references point to the German original in the Academy edition (Kant, Immanuel: *Gesammelte Schriften*. Ed.: Vol. 1-22 Preussische Akademie der Wissenschaften, vol. 23 Deutsche Akademie der Wissenschaften zu Berlin, vol. 24ff. Akademie der Wissenschaften zu Göttingen. Berlin 1900ff.).

27. V-Anth/Mron, AA 25: 1212; see also V-Menschenkunde, AA 25: 857f. – As to how far Kant knew the works of relevant historians, see Sturm, *Kant*, 332-338.

28. GMS, AA 04: 417, footnote.

29. For detailed textual evidence for the following points, see Sturm, *Kant*, 429-446.

30. Anth, AA 07: 121.

31. IaG, AA 08: 30.

Chapter 4

CAN THE THING SPEAK?

Martin Holbraad

It may appear that the last thing that the study of 'things' needs right now is another manifesto, as the echo of Spivak's 1980s subaltern radicalism (1998) in my title may suggest. As archaeologist Severin Fowles has recently observed (2008, 2010), the rise of 'the thing' in social theory at the turn of our century has emancipatory tonalities that echo the emancipation of 'the native' (or the 'subaltern') a generation earlier. If for too long things, under the guise of 'material culture', had 'hibernat[ed] in the basements of museology', as Tim Ingold puts it (2007: 5), their study in recent years has been all about achieving their visibility: making the thing manifest or, in Peter Pels' phrase, allowing it to 'speak back' (Pels 1998: x).

To see why these are more than echoes of expression, consider the analogy of purpose. Notwithstanding their variety, late 20th century arguments tagged as 'post-colonial' and valorised as 'de-colonizing' can also be characterised as emancipatory (*sensu* Argyrou 2002).

This insofar as they typically take the form of what I will call 'widening the circle of the human'. The move turns on a basic diagnosis of the colonial condition as, in one way or other, a deficient attribution of humanity to the colonial subject (the native, the subaltern): a denial of its history, its agency, its subjectivity, its rationality, in short, its human dignity. The response, then, takes the form of a more equitable distribution of these attributes, a move to globalise the sense of justice which they express, in a kind of extension of the global-political dominion of the categorical imperative. The colonised subject is elevated, its subjectivity recognised, its voice heard. The conceptual mould of the agenda, if not its historical precedent, is perhaps the emancipation of slaves, from relative object-commodities to (relative...) subject-persons (cf. Guyer 1993).

An analogous agenda, argues Fowles, is pursued in the more recent literature on the rise of the thing (material culture studies, thing-theory, ANT, speculative realism, post-phenomenology etc.). Here too polemical writing has been motivated in large part by a diagnosis of a deficit of humanity – an obvious one when it comes to things, of course, though all the more powerful for it. And the remedy too has been various species of widening the circle of the human. 'Agency' has been the most vocal term, perhaps due to its relative neutrality, though its corollaries of personhood, history, voice, freedom and responsibility, and other dignities of the kind are never far off in the emancipatory agenda. Indeed, the political tenor of the move is certainly evident in these writings, as is its post-colonial aesthetic. Fowles cites, among others, Bruno Latour, who calls for a 'democracy extended to things' (including a 'parliament' of them); Danny Miller, who renounces the 'tyranny of the subject' and 'the corpse of our imperial majesty: society' in favour of a 'dialectical republic in which persons and things exist in mutual self-construction and respect for their mutual origin and mutual dependency'; and fellow archaeologist Bjørnar Olsen, who calls his colleagues to 'unite in a defence of things, a defence of those subaltern members of the collective that have been silenced and "othered" by the imperialist social and humanist discourses.' (Latour 1993: 12, Miller 2005: 45, 37, Olsen 2003: 100, all cited in Fowles 2008).

Now, the faint sarcasm of calling all this an agenda for 'emancipation' is really more of an irony, since I have subscribed to this agenda myself, along lines that are not dissimilar to the ones Fowles describes – particularly in the volume *Thinking Through Things*, which I co-edited and co-introduced with Ami Salmond (nee Henare) and Sari Wastell (2007), as well as in a couple of single-authored publications related to it (Holbraad 2005 and more explicitly 2009). In the latter part of the present paper I revisit those arguments in some detail, in an effort to clarify what I have since come to see as the somewhat confused way in which they bundle together the two parallel agendas of Fowles's analogy. As I shall argue, however, this is worth doing, not in order to recoil from the agenda of emancipating the thing, but to move it forward. In a nutshell, I want to show that while the approach set out in *Thinking Through Things* (henceforth 'TTT') is offered partly as a way of emancipating things as such, the weight of its argument ends up subsuming this task to that of emancipating the people for whom they are important.[1] If things speak in TTT, they do so mainly by ethnographic association with the voice of 'the native' – a kind of anthropological ventriloquism.

Hence the question: might there nevertheless be a sense in which things could speak for themselves? And what might their voices sound like? Suitably reconsidered and improved, I argue, the approach of TTT is indeed able to articulate answers to these questions, complementing the anthropological concern with native voices with what in the Conclusion I shall call a 'pragmatological' (cf. Witmore forthcoming) engagement with the voices of things – voices which, to anticipate my core suggestion, stem from the contingent material characteristics that make things most obviously thing-like. In order to prepare the ground for this argument, we may begin by fleshing out, with reference to the recent literature on things, the guiding distinction between emancipating things 'by association' with persons as opposed to emancipating them 'as such' – a pretty tricky distinction, as we shall see, and subject to all sorts of caveats.

Emancipation as the entanglement of persons and things

In line with Fowles's analogy with writings in post-colonialism, the past twenty years' or so literature on the rise of the thing could be plotted as a trajectory of increasingly (self-consciously) 'radical' attempts to dislodge or even erase the line that divides things from people. Consider, just as an illustration, the shift from proposing that things acquire 'biographies' and a 'social life' of their own through their complex involvement in the lives of the people who engage with them (Appadurai 1986), to saying that the very distinction between people and things (or humans and non-humans) should be eliminated from the way we think about such engagements (Latour 1993, cf. Pinney 2005). Or the difference between suggesting that people and things emerge out of each other dialectically (Miller 1987, 2005) and claiming that in certain contexts they are best conceived as being identical (Strathern 1988, 1990). Such differences may be said to correspond to two broad stages on the axis of radicalism, which, following Haraway (1991, cf. Webmoor & Witmore 2009), I shall tag as 'humanist' and 'posthumanist' respectively. The distinction turns on contrasting stances to the ontological division between humans and things. Humanist, then, would be approaches that seek to emancipate the thing in terms of this division, while posthumanist would be ones that do so by going beyond it. The move from one towards the other, I argue, can also be understood as a move from emancipating things by association, i.e. by letting some of the light of what it is to be human shine on them too, to emancipating them as such, i.e. showing that they can radiate light for themselves – though in a way that, as we shall see, is not altogether satisfactory. Let us explore this with reference to some of the most influential contributions to the literature.

Danny Miller's introduction to his edited volume *Materiality* (2005, cf. Miller 1987) presents a transparent example of what I'm calling a humanist approach, as well as of the emancipation of things 'by association', with reference to the role in the lives of humans, that such approaches tend to imply. Miller is fully cognizant of the importance to anthropological discussions of materiality of 'philosophical resolution[s] to the problematic dualism between people and things' (Miller 2005: 41), and includes as an example his own preference for theorizing the relationship between people and things in terms of the forms that emerge out of a Hegelian dialectical processes of objectification, rather than through the 'mutual constitution of prior forms, such as subjects and objects' (2005: 9). The job of the anthropologist, he argues however, cannot be simply (or complexly) to reinvent such philosophical wheels, not least because the people he or she studies ethnographically so often have a much more 'commonsense' understanding of things, including all sorts of ways of distinguishing them from people, spirits and so on. Ultimately, Miller is saying, the role of an anthropology that is seriously committed to reflecting ethnographically on the world in which we live, and to theorising what it is to be human, must recognise and 'respect' (2005: 38) material objects and the implicit as well as explicit ways in which they give form to people's lives. Its aim, through strategic combinations of dualism-busting philosophical models and ethnographic sensitivity and empathy, must be to show the myriad ways in which 'the things people make, make people' (ibid).[2]

It is perhaps not entirely clear how Miller squares the circle (not to say wheel) of the contrasting demands of a philosophical impulse to overcome dualism and an anthropological one to dwell on the myriad forms in which it may play itself out ethnographically.[3] Still, what he makes abundantly clear is that his heart lies with the messiness of the ethnography, and the 'vulgar' study of 'the way the specific character of people emerges from their interaction with the material world through practice' (Miller 2007: 26), as he and his students at UCL have been doing for some time. If he is interested in emancipating the thing from the 'tyranny of the subject', that is because doing so gives us a more profound understanding of what it is to be human. Material culture studies may displace an anthropology obsessed with the imperium of the social, but only to replace it with a better anthropology humble enough to recognise the ways in which things also so pervasively contribute to our humanity. Which is exactly the kind of stance I have in mind when talking of humanism and its emancipation of things by association.

Alfred Gell's argument in *Art and Agency* (1998) provides another example of this approach, though a less straightforward one. Certainly, the idea for which Gell's landmark book most often gets cited, namely that things can be understood as possessing agency in the same sense as humans do, may well appear as an attempt to emancipate things 'as such'. In contrast to, say, Miller, the flag of emancipation (if such it is) is here pinned not on things' role in making human beings what they are (although this is a central concern for Gell too), but rather on the extent to which things may themselves be more like humans than we might assume. Insofar as things (e.g. cars, bombs, effigies) can be construed as indices of a prior intention, as they so often are (e.g. an intention to make us late for work, Pol Pot's desire to kill, the blessing of a benign deity), they themselves become something akin to humans, and thus could be said to be emancipated as such rather than by association.

Nevertheless, as a number of discussions of Gell's argument have tended to show, there is some ambiguity as to how far agency really attaches to things themselves in his scheme. Indeed, in reading the book, one is never quite sure how seriously Gell wants us to take the, after all, rather scandalous notion that things can be ascribed with intentions. Part of the problem is that in his analysis Gell tends to treat as equivalent ascriptions of agency that, ethnographically speaking, vary rather vastly in the degree to which they are taken seriously by those who engage in them. Broadly put, if swearing at one's car for failing to start is meant to be a phenomenon of the same order as praying to an effigy, then one wants to know whether the latter ascription of agency is supposed to be taken as lightly as the former surely should be (which makes Gell look rather dismissive of devotees who take their prayers and effigies very seriously indeed), or whether the agency of the car should be imagined as being as weighty as that of the effigy (in which case Gell would look like a bit of a New Age mystic). Indeed, when it comes down to it, it does seem that Gell's scheme is slanted towards the former option. As James Leach has argued, a close reading of Gell reveals that agency for him is only ever an indirect attribute of things, its origins lying ultimately with a *human* agent, whose intention the thing in question only indexes – hence, for example, the significant distinction Gell makes between the 'secondary' agency of indices and the 'primary' agency of the intentions they are abductively surmised to index (Leach 2007, cf. Gell 1998: 17-21). Things, for Gell, cannot *really* be agents, if by that we mean anything more than the kind of attribution of agency involved in swearing at a car for making us late. As Miller puts it in his own critique, 'Gell's is a theory of natural anthropomorphism, where our primary reference point is to people and their intentionality behind the world of artefacts' (Miller 2005: 13). Indeed, Gell's emancipation of things by conferring them with agency turns out to be more similar to Miller's than may at first appear. Where Miller raises the profile of things by making them operative in the making of human beings, Gell does so by making them operative in acts of human agency.

So, in sum: humanist approaches, which leave the ontological distinction between things and people unmodified, cannot but emancipate things by association. The whole point about the common sense distinction between people and things is that the former are endowed with all the marks of dignity, while the latter are not. So if you want to emancipate the thing while leaving the ontology untouched, then all you can do is find ways to associate it more intimately with the person.

Post-human approaches, by contrast, can be seen as taking up just that challenge: they propose a different ontology of people and things and thus precipitate a re-definition of their properties (i.e. rather than merely a re-distribution of them across the person/thing divide). This tack does indeed raise the hope of an emancipation of the thing 'as such', although one immediately has to add the proviso that 'the thing', following its ontological re-constitution, is no longer the thing as we ordinarily know it.

Think, for example, of Latour's denial of human/ non-human purification in favour of the flat ontology of the Actor Network. All the 'entities' that modernist purification takes as 'people' and 'things' are refashioned analytically 'hybrid' knots of mutually transformative relations. Each element of which these relations are composed (itself a relation – hence the network's fractal structure, à la Strathern 2004 [1991]) is an 'actant' inasmuch as it has a transformative effect on the assemblage (i.e. the contingent and analytically localised aspect or moment of the Network.)

So agency for Latour is not the effectuation of a human intention (e.g. as it is for Gell). It is a property of networks of relationships (hybrid ones, involving all the elements that a modernist ontology would want to distinguish from one another) that emerges as and when the elements they involve make a difference to each other. The classic and much cited example being Latour's discussion of the gun debate in the USA (e.g. see 1999: 180). The responsible agents are neither the guns themselves (as the anti-gun campaigners argue) nor the people who use them (as the gun-lobby would have it – 'guns don't kill, people do'). It is the hybrid assemblage, or 'collective', which gun users and guns form together: the 'person-with-gun'.

There can be no doubt that, thus ontologically revised or redefined, things are indeed emancipated 'as such'. The new kind of analytical entity that Latour proposes, the hybrid assemblage of humans and non-humans in mutual transformation, is an agent in as serious a sense one might wish to take that term: its very constitution is defined by its ability to act as such. Indeed, the bold political philosophy that Latour has been building on the back of his move to networks of things-and-people in recent years is testimony to this: 'political representation of nonhumans seems not only plausible now but necessary, when the notion would have seemed ludicrous or indecent not long ago', he writes, and raises the prospect of a 'parliament of things' (Latour 1999: 198).

Yet, in terms of the framework of the present argument, there is also a significant irony involved in Latour's tack of emancipation. In order for him to avoid emancipating things 'by association' to humans, as per Miller or Gell, Latour ends up defining them, in a revisionist move, *as* associations (assemblages, collectives, networks), thus binding them to humans by ontological fiat. This, however, begs a question: to what extent and, if at all, how does the dignity conferred on the actants of a Latourian network rub off on the things a pre-Latourian metaphysic would call 'things'? Does the Latourian revision of the constituents of the world get us any closer to answering our question of whether *the thing* can speak? Of course, from a Latourian point of view, these questions are either meaningless or foolish. There is no 'thing', other than in the modernist chimera. To raise the very question – Can the thing speak? – is to engage in an act of purification. One should rather bite oneself and ask, Can the thing – I mean the actor network! – speak? (Answer: yes.)

Yet, I want to suggest that something important is lost in this act of analytical (because ontological) censorship. Far be it from me to propose any kind of return to modernist ontology – not even for the sake of an anthropological commitment to vulgar common sense à la Miller. Indeed, I am not even sure at this stage of thinking about the matter whether the sense of dissatisfaction I express here points to a principled flaw in Latour's analytic or an accidental feature of the way

Latourian analyses tend to get done. Still, so often when reading such analyses one gets the impression that all the qualities that seem peculiar to 'things' as one ordinarily conceives of them – I mean the aspects of things we would ordinarily tag is their 'material' qualities, such as those studied by material scientists – somehow get muted, lost in the Latourian translation. I am not saying they don't get a mention, or that they do not play a significant role in Latour's often highly sophisticated empirical analyses, as well as those of his followers. For example, Latour's refutation of the technological determinism of saying that guns kill people does not stop him from emphasising the particular forms of agency that a gun's technological characteristics – the mechanics of detonation, velocity, accuracy and so on – contribute to the man-with-a-gun assemblage. What I am saying is that the net effect of Latour's ontological amalgamation of such characteristics with the people they act to transform renders them (or at least tends to render them) corollaries of projects and concerns that a lay non-Latourian account would interpret as irreducibly human: what is important about Boyle's air-pump is its contribution to modernity (1993a), the significant thing about sleeping policemen is that their concrete curvature participates in the patrolling of traffic (Latour 1993b), what the elements that make for a gun's firing power do is they engender the potential to kill (1999).

All this may indeed be a contingent function of the particular questions on which Latourian analyses have been put to work.[4] Nevertheless, one can make the principled point that Latour's prime ontological revision, namely the 'symmetry' of treating the entities that a modernist metaphysics purifies as persons 'or' things as hybrid relations of persons 'and' things (see also Viveiros de Castro 2002), renders any interest in those aspects of things one would ordinarily view as distinctively thing-like considerably harder to pursue. Qualities one would call 'material' are, as such, always in deep ontological entanglement with the (also) human projects that they help constitute, so one wonders whether in practice, let alone in principle, a Latourian take on things could at all let one disentangle them and allow them to be explored as such. One suspects that with the metaphysical bathwater of 'materiality' (as opposed, that is, to 'humanity') goes also the baby of 'materials' as a legitimate analytical concern.

This way of putting it shows how close this worry comes to one expressed recently by Tim Ingold (2007). Fed up with what he sees as perversely abstract and intractably abstruse debates about 'materiality' in recent years, Ingold urges anthropologists to 'take a step back, from the materiality of objects to the properties of materials [... -] a tangled web of meandrine complexity, in which – among myriad other things – oaken wasp galls get caught up with old iron, acacia sap, goose feathers and calf-skins, and the residue from heated limestone mixes with emissions from pigs, cattle, hens and bears' (Ingold 2007: 9). Ingold, we may note, makes no secret of the fact that his manifesto for a renewed focus on materials is itself metaphysically motivated, and bound up with a particular way of viewing the relationship between humans and things. Inspired by Gibson as well as phenomenology, Ingold sees humans and things as submerged on an equal ontological footing in 'an ocean of materials' (2007: 7). He writes:

> Once we acknowledge our immersion, what this ocean reveals to us is [...] a flux in which materials of the most diverse kinds – through processes of admixture and distillation, of coagulation and dispersal, and of evaporation and precipitation – undergo continual generation and transformation. The forms of things, far from having been imposed from without upon an inert substrate, arise and are borne along – as indeed we are too – within this current of materials. (ibid.)

One might say that Ingold's tactic for emancipating the thing involves a kind of inverse humanism (for this is not materialism as we know it), in which, rather than raising things to the power of the human, humans and things alike are factorised down to their primordial material denominator: Life on Earth (ibid). Nevertheless, my point here is that Ingold's plea for materials can be taken independently of the theoretical agenda from which it may flow, and heeded as a powerful reminder of a whole terrain of investigation that any attempt to take things seriously – even to emancipate them in the terms developed here – cannot afford to ignore.

Indeed, it is with Ingold's plea for materials that I want to cut to the chase of what asking for things that speak could mean. The problem is one of, if you like, wanting to have one's cake and eat it. Eating the cake, in this case, is taking fully on board the post-human (e.g. Latourian) point that a proper emancipation of the thing must eschew any principled distinction between it and humans as a starting-point. Having the cake is finding a way nevertheless to credit the Ingoldian intuition that a full-hog emancipation of the thing must place those characteristics that are most think-like or 'thingy' (the designation is purely heuristic, with no metaphysical prejudice!) at the top of its agenda. Asking whether the thing can speak, then, is to ask for it to speak on its own terms – in its own language, if you like. Any interesting answer to this question, I suggest, would have to start form the rather blatant observation that it would be a shame if such a language – call it 'thingese'? – turned out to have no sonorities of what we take to be the most obvious distinguishing feature of so-called things, namely their material characteristics. It is in answer to this question that a critique of the argument of TTT may be useful.

Rethinking through things

Plotted onto the trajectory of increasingly radical attempts to erase the human/thing divide, TTT should probably be placed at the far posthumanist extreme. Indeed, were one permitted to compound this already horrible term, the argument of TTT is post-posthumanist, in that it takes on board the Latourian suggestion that the distinction between people and things is ontologically arbitrary, but adds (contra Latour among others) that, this being so, the solution for emancipating the thing must not be to bind it to an alternative ontological order (e.g. that of the Actor Network), but rather to free it from any ontological determination whatsoever. TTT, in other words, operates within the economy of the literature announcing and articulating the rise of the thing, and its self-conscious polemic purports to offer a corrective even to the most extreme proponents of this (otherwise) common emancipatory goal. Let me indicate briefly how our attempt to emancipate the thing was supposed to work

As put forward in the Introduction of TTT, the argument involved two key claims – one critical and one positive. The critical move, which took off directly from Strathern (see above), went as follows. If in any given ethnographic instance things may be considered, somehow, also as non-things (e.g. an artefact that, ethnographically speaking, is a human being, as per Melanesian gifts, or a river that is a spirit), then the notion of a 'thing', anthropologically speaking, can only have a heuristic, rather than an analytical, role. So attempts to analyse the things we call objects, artefacts, substances, or materials in terms of their objectivity, substantiality or, as has become most popular, their 'materiality', are locked in a kind of ethnographic prejudice – they are, to use the dirty word, ethnocentric. And this goes also for attempts theoretically to emancipate things by attributing them with all sorts of qualities earlier shacklers would take to belong only to humans, such as sociality, spirituality, and again, most popularly, agency. In other words, if what a thing may be is itself an ethnographic variable, then the initial analytical task must not be to 'add' to that term's theoretical purchase by proposing new ways to think of it – e.g. as a site of human beings' objectification (Miller), an index of agency (Gell), an on-going event of assemblage (Latour), or what have you. Rather it must be effectively to de-theorise the thing, by emptying it out of its many analytical connotations, rendering it a purely ethnographic 'form' ready to be filled out contingently according only to its own ethnographic exigencies. Treating the thing as a heuristic (i.e. just as a tag for identifying it as an object of study) was indeed, then, a way for us to allow it to speak in its own terms – which in ethnographic principle may be as varied as there are things to listen to – from behind the clamour of social theoretical attempts to theorise such a thing as the thing as such. Things do speak, ran the thought, but the problem is how to hear them past all the things we say about them.

If half of the way towards addressing this problem is to empty out the notion of 'thing' of its contingently a priori metaphysical contents – thing-as-heuristic –, the other half is to formulate a way of allowing it to be filled by (potentially) alternative ones in each ethnographic instance. This can be seen as the second and positive emancipatory move of the TTT argument, which is captured by a complementary methodological injunction: 'concepts = things'. The move is complementary in that it follows directly from the issue that motivates the heuristic approach in the first place, namely the possibility – and in so many instances the fact – that the things we call 'things' might not ethnographically speaking be things at all, or not in the way we might initially assume them to be. For note that the things-as-concepts injunction is determinedly *not* proposed as some new theory of the thing. The idea is emphatically not to propose some kind of revisionary metaphysic, to the effect that, where people have so often assumed things and concepts to belong to opposite ontological camps, we should all from now on recognise them as belonging to the same one (viz. the kind of approach Latour and Ingold advance in different ways, as we have seen). To the contrary, the 'things = concepts' formula is offered as a further methodological clause for side-stepping just such theoretical prescriptions. In particular, it is supposed to foreclose a very real danger when it comes to thinking anthropologically about the different ways in which things may feature ethnographically, namely that of parsing them as different ways in which people may think about (represent, imagine, socially construct) them. This is to parse ethnographic alternatives to our metaphysic of things in terms of it – in fact, in terms of what nigh all-thing emancipators consider its crassest version, namely the idea of inert and mute things invested with varied meanings only by human fiats of representation. It is, in effect, to raise the erasure of things to the power of a necessity for thinking of them.

So the 'concepts = things' clause is meant to placate just this danger. Put very simply: instead of treating all the things that your informants say of and do to or with things as modes of representing the things in question, treat them as modes of *defining* them. The immediate advantage of this way of parsing the issue is that it renders wide open precisely the kinds of questions that lie at the heart of the emancipatory agenda, namely questions about what kinds of things 'things' might be. Instead of merely offering sundry ways of confirming the base metaphysic of mute things invested with varied meanings by humans, the things-as-concepts tack holds up that very ethnographic variety as a promise of so many ways of arriving at alternative metaphysical positions – *whatever* they might be. If every instance anthropologists would deem a different representation of a thing is conceived as a potentially different way of defining what such a thing might be, then all the metaphysical questions about its character qua 'thing', what materiality might be, objectification, agency – all that is now up for grabs, as a matter of ethnographic contingency and the analytical work it forces upon us.

As we did in the Introduction to TTT itself, let me illustrate the approach with reference to my own chapter in the book, in which I elaborate an analysis of *aché*. *Aché* is a *mana*-type term that Afro-Cuban diviners use to talk both about their power to make deities appear during divination, and about a particular kind of consecrated powder that they consider as a necessary ingredient for achieving this. The terminological coincidence, I argued, corresponds to an ontological one: a diviner's power is also his powder and the powder (*qua* consecrated) is also his power. Now, this is obviously a counter-intuitive suggestion, of the order of 'twins are birds' (Evans-Pritchard 1956, cf. Holbraad 2010). If we know what powder is at all, we know that it is not also power in any meaningful sense (it's just powder!), and much less can we accept that power (a concept with proportions as grand as Nietzsche or Foucault) might also be just powder (of all things!). Hence the classical anthropological type of question: why might Cuban diviners 'believe' such a crazy idea? For as long as our analysis of *aché* remains within the terms of an axiomatic distinction between things and concepts, we cannot but ask the question in these terms. We know that powder is just that dusty thing there on the diviner's tray (see below). So the question is why Cubans might 'think' that it is also a form of power. How do we explain it? How do we interpret it?

Alternatively, we could treat the distinction between concepts and things merely as a heuristic device, as per TTT's first move. This would allow us to ask questions about that powder that we would intuitively identify as a 'thing', without prejudicing the question of what it might be, including questions of what it being a 'thing' might even mean. Answers to such questions, then, would be culled from the ethnography of all the data we would ordinarily be tempted to call people's 'beliefs' about this powder, including the notion that it is also power. As per the second move of the TTT method (concept = thing), we would treat such data as elements of a conceptual definition of the thing in question. So: Cuban diviners do not 'believe' that powder is power, but rather *define* it as power. Note, crucially, how this way of setting up the problem raises the metaphysical stakes. Since our own default assumption is that powder is *not* to be defined as power (it's just a dusty thing, we assume), the challenge now must be to *reconceptualise* those very notions and their many ethnographic and analytical corollaries (powder, power, deity etc. but also thing, concept, divinity etc.) in a way that would render the ethnographically-given definition of powder as power reasonable, rather than absurd. It is just this kind of analytical work I attempted to carry out in my chapter in TTT (I shall cover more of that ground later).

At the time we presented this mode of analysis in TTT, I for one imagined it as having cracked the problem of the thing's emancipation as I have been outlining it here. Taken together, I thought, our argument's two key moves effectively opened up the space for things themselves, as one encounters them heuristically in any given ethnographic instance, to dictate their own metaphysics – to dictate, if you like, the terms of their own analytical engagement. Just what I have in mind when asking for an approach that allows things to speak for themselves, in their *own* language! Yet, to see why I may have been wrong, one needs only to contemplate how the prospect of things speaking in the 'own' language in this TTT-sense measures up to the Ingoldian caveat, namely that a proper emancipation of things 'as such', whatever that may mean or involve, should place their material characteristics centre stage – that things should speak in thingese, and that thingese should somehow be an expression of things' peculiarly material qualities. In the sometimes flamboyantly programmatic pronouncements of the TTT Introduction, nothing is in fact made of such qualities, and certainly their role in 'thinking through things' is left largely unspecified.

In fact, it is indicative that this first dawned on me (at any rate) when faced with a searching question by an archaeologist in a conference at which my co-editors and I presented our argument (see also Holbraad 2009). Being himself consigned to working with things without the benefit of rich ethnographic information about them, he admitted, he found himself at a loss as to how archaeologists might deploy our approach to any effect. Notwithstanding our claim to have found a way to let things speak for themselves, our argument seemed at most a method for allowing the *ethnography* of things to speak on their behalf – to set, indeed, the terms of their analytical engagement. If what motivates the whole approach is, as explained above, the fact that in varied instances people speak of or act with things in ways that contradict our assumptions about what a thing might be; and if, furthermore, it is just those ways of speaking and acting around things that are supposed to provide the 'content' of their potentially alternative metaphysics; then how might archaeologists, for whom, *what* people might have said or done around the things archaeologists call 'finds' is so often *the primary question*? If anyone ever needed a way of letting things speak for themselves that is the archaeologist, for whom things are so often all he has to go on. Our unproblematised reliance on, and unabashed love for, ethnography in our way of 'thinking through things' is of no huge help. The clue is in the book's subtitle: 'theorising artefacts ethnographically'.

These misgivings go to the heart of the problem I wish to tackle here, and are tellingly connected to another worry that as a social anthropologist I have had myself (privately!) about the TTT argument, namely the fact that the analytical experimentations it seeks to promote seem in one way or other to be wound around ethnographic phenomena one might broadly call 'magical' or even 'animist' in one sense or other. Cigarettes that make Port Morsby inmates' thoughts fly out of prison, Maori and Swazi legal paraphernalia that have metaphysical efficacy, shamanic costumes that transport Mongols to legions of skies, and family chests and photographs that contain their life force, divinatory powder that is the power to reveal deities: these are the things contributors to our volume thought through, along with the people who 'informed' them ethnographically about them. In line with the archaeologist's comment, I suspect that this 'magical realist' tenor of the chapters is not accidental. The leverage for thinking out of the metaphysical box that so entranced us as editors was owed, at least to a large extent and at the first instance, to the chapters' ethnographic magic, to coin a phrase, rather than the specifically 'thing-like' character of their subject-matter.

It emerges, then, that TTT's claim to offer an emancipation of the thing along the lines I have been discussing is open to a critique that is analogous to the one advanced earlier in relation to Latour. Latour, we saw, emancipates the thing by entangling it ontologically with persons – subsuming both under the terms of his revisionary ontology of networks comprising people-and-things. TTT does something similar, though now at the level of analytical methodology. It emancipates the thing by entangling it heuristically with all that the people concerned with it say and do around it, subsuming things and their ethnographic accounts under the terms of our revisionary methodology. Indeed, just as a Latourian might object that to demand an emancipation of the thing 'as such' is flatly to deny the significance of Latour's ontology of networks, so we might want to contend that that same demand merely contradicts our methodological injunction of concept = thing. As far as TTT is concerned, things as such just *are* what our ethnographic descriptions of them define them to be. Still, if this is emancipation by ethnographic 'association', the Ingoldian bugbear remains: what of materials and their properties?

Yet, I want to argue that the force of this line of critique pertains more to the rhetoric of the TTT argument than to its substance. Suitably reconsidered, the methodological approach of TTT is indeed able to give 'voice' to material characteristics, making analytical virtue of them as such. The fact that this prospect remained mute in the way we pitched the argument when we wrote it relates directly to the guiding homology with which I began this paper, between the postcolonial agenda of emancipating the native and the thing-theoretical one of emancipating the thing. With particular reference to Viveiros de Castro's ongoing project of de-colonizing anthropological thinking by using ethnography to subvert its most domineering (because ontological) presuppositions (see Henare et al 2007: 8-9, cf. Viveiros de Castro 1998, 2002), ours was pitched above all as an attempt to put the ethnography of things at the centre of such an endeavour. If for Viveiros de Castro the emancipation of the native in anthropology is a matter of opening up space for her 'conceptual self-determination' (2002) within it, then the TTT argument amounted mainly to the addendum that the ethnography of (people's engagement with) things is a prime site for pursuing this goal. In other words, whatever emancipation TTT might offer to things was rhetorically subsumed under the older (but surely no less pressing) political agenda of emancipating the native. Indeed, TTT's two-step methodology reflected this directly. The 'thing-as-heuristic' move opened up 'things' as a locus of ontological self-determination, while the 'concept = thing' clause allowed the ethnography of what natives do and say around them to provide it with ontologically variable contents.

What, then, of the substance of this argument? Might it, albeit inadvertently, provide a way for things to speak, not as proxies for ethnographic natives, but for themselves? In a longer, fully written up version of this paper I plan to use three examples of anthropological and archaeological analyses of things in order to explore the question concretely.[5] Here I limit myself to making the argument from first principles, and illustrating it briefly with reference to my Cuban powder-is-power case.

It all depends, of course, on what one takes 'things that may speak' to mean – what counts as a thing that speaks for itself? It is on this point that I think the homology with Spivak's question about the subaltern is most instructive. We have already seen that attempts to transpose the humanist agenda of postcolonial emancipation onto things by including them in 'the circle of the human' provide only half-hogged emancipations, 'by association'. But we have seen also that there is an alternative to humanism in the struggle to de-colonise anthropology – not least in the rhetoric of TTT itself, as well as in the work of Viveiros de Castro. Captured by Viveiros's slogan of 'conceptual self-determination', this is the project of constructing an anthropology that opens spaces for natives to set the terms of our anthropological engagements with them, positing them as producers of concepts rather than, say, consumers of ours. Rather than worrying about how far natives might (or should) be considered as humans, agents, subjects and so on, we should be asking *what concepts* of humanity, agency, subjectivity and more our anthropological engagement with them might yield, and be fully prepared to be surprised by what we find (*sensu* Strathern 2005). It is this notion of emancipation, then, that I propose to transpose onto things: things can speak insofar as they can set the terms of their anthropological engagement by acting as the originators (rather than the objects) of our anthropological conceptualisations. Things can speak if they can yield their own concepts.

This way of putting the matter already gets us much closer to seeing why TTT might after all be suited to stage such a move. Bracketing for this purpose the underlying postcolonialist concerns to which it was put to use, the 'concept = thing' formula speaks directly to the problem at hand. All one needs to do is read the formula backwards (in school we called this 'symmetry of equality'): 'thing = concept'. Indeed, the thought is in a pertinent sense the reverse (though not the opposite) of the one advocated explicitly in TTT. If there the formula 'concept = thing' designated the possibility of treating what people say and do around things as manners of defining what those things are, here its symmetrical rendition 'thing = concept' raises the prospect of treating the thing as a manner of defining what we (analysts now, rather than natives) are able to say and do around it. At issue, to coin another phrase, are a thing's conceptual affordances.

Indeed, thinking of the present argument as a symmetrical reversal of the one made in TTT also allows us to flesh the thought out in Ingold's direction, towards the question of materials and their properties. As I noted when outlining the TTT position, the promise of conceptual experimentation that it holds up is grounded in ethnographic contingency. Having emptied the notion of 'the thing' of any conceptual presuppositions of what may count as one, we fill it back up with alternative conceptualisations drawn from the contingent ethnographic data we find around it. One way of describing the procedure, it strikes me, would be as a form of 'empirical ontology', where 'empirical' denotes its ethnographic grounding. So we may ask: what is the equivalently empirical grounding of the reverse procedure that I seek to articulate here for things? Following through on the symmetry of our reversal-strategy, the answer can be found only in the material characteristics of the thing itself. What was empirical about (ethnographically driven) concepts that defined things must now be so about (let's say, 'pragmatographically' driven) things that now define concepts. With what other 'stuff' can things feed their conceptualizations than the very stuff that makes them what they are, as heuristically marked 'things'? The data that make a (conceptual) difference, in this case, are no longer what we hear and see people say and do around things, but rather what we hear, see, smell, taste and touch of the thing as we find it (heuristically) as such.

The difference from Ingold, however, is that, in line with his phenomenologically inclined vitalism, he is content to revel at this material and sensuous level of things, to explore their mutual 'enmeshment' with people and other organisms, as well as their 'affordances' for them in the broader ecology of living. By contrast, in raising the question of the *conceptual* affordances of materials and their properties, my interest is not in the ecology of their material alterations but rather in the economy of their conceptual transformations: how their material characteristics can dictate particular forms for their conceptualization. At issue, if you like, is not the horizontal traffic of materials' enmeshment in forms of life, but rather what one might imagine as a vertical axis of materials' transformation into forms of thought – mainly for fun, I'd call this the 'intensional vertizon' of things (to mark its orthogonal relationship to phenomenological notions of things' 'intentional horizon' in, say, Husserl). Simply put, this vertizonal movement would be what 'abstraction' would look like were it to be divorced from the ontological distinction between concrete (things) and abstract (concepts). Indeed, this is just what the 'thing = concept' clause of our analytical method would suggest. Where the ontology of things versus concepts would posit abstraction as the ability of a given concept to comprehend a particular thing, external to itself, in its extension, the heuristic continuity of 'thing = concept' casts this as a movement internal to 'the thing itself' (to echo Husserl again): the thing differentiates *itself*, no longer as an instantiation 'of' a concept, but a self-transformation *as* a concept.

I am of course aware that this way of thinking takes us into deep philosophical waters which I am incompetent to chart (although one may note with pleasure that this is exactly as it should be: one would hardly hope for the scandalous idea of things that speak to have tamer philosophical implications). Indeed, in my amateur understanding, there is a line in Western philosophy, which runs from Heraclitus through Leibniz and up to Deleuze, that deals with many of the relevant problems. Still, adopting a distinctively anthropological slant with reference to Marilyn Strathern's notion of 'partial connections' (1991), Morten Pedersen and I have elsewhere tried to articulate in some detail the analytical implications of things' capacity for vertizonal transformation – we called this form of self-motion 'abstension', to indicate the intensive (as opposed to extensive) character that abstractions acquire when they are thought as self-differentiating transformations of things-into-concepts (see Holbraad & Pedersen 2009). Rather than cover this ground again for present purposes, however, I close by showing what this kind of analytical movement looks like with reference to the example of *aché* which I began to discuss earlier. (Indeed, in retrospect, it seems remarkable that this line of argument was pasted over, not only in the Introduction to TTT, where the notion of a powder that is power is used as an illustration as we saw, but even in my own chapter in the book, where the actual analysis of this material is carried out.)

If, as I have argued, the problem with TTT is that it emancipates the thing only by associating it in ethnography with an ontologically emancipated native, then my analysis of *aché* in my TTT chapter is certainly an instance of this. We have already seen, for example, that the very problem that article was devoted to solving – what might a powder that is also power be? – was ethnographically driven: it was not powder that told me it is power, it was my diviner informants. And certainly, a host of ethnographic data serve to frame and develop the problem itself, as well as parts of its analytical solution. Crucially, for example, since what powder might be in this instance depends on the notion of power, part of my attempt to articulate the question involves developing its various dimensions ethnographically. In a nutshell, I provide an account of Afro-Cuban divinatory cosmology based on informants' responses, to show that for diviners power consists in the ability to render otherwise absent divinities present during the divinatory ceremony, and that this power manifested in divination as the 'signs' the diviners mark with their fingers on the powder that is spread in the surface of their divining board, which are called 'oddu', and said to 'be' divinities in their own right. On the basis of this ethnographic information, I go on to show that the notion of a powder that 'is' power emerges as a solution to an age-old theological conundrum, familiar in the anthropology of religion (e.g. Keane 2007): apparently transcendent deities are rendered immanent on the surface of the divining board, allowing those present in the divination to relate to them directly. Conceptualising powder as power, then, requires us to understand analytically how Afro-Cuban divination effectively *solves* this 'problem of presence', to recall Matthew Engelke's book on a related conundrum (2007). And it is to this question that powder, finally, speaks:

> Powder gives us the answer [...]. As we saw, spread on the surface of the divining board, powder provides the backdrop upon which the *oddu*, thought of as deity-signs, 'come out'. In this most crucial of senses, then, powder is the catalyst of divinatory power, ie the capacity to make [deities] 'come out' and 'speak' [...]. Considered prosaically, powder is able to do this due to its pervious character, as a collection of unstructured particles – its pure multiplicity, so to speak. In marking the

oddu on the board, the *babalawo*'s fingers are able to draw the configuration just to the extent that the 'intensive' capacity of powder to be moved (to be displaced like Archimedean bathwater) allows them to do so. The extensive movement of the *oddu* as it appears on the board, then, presupposes the intensive mobility of powder as the medium upon which it is registered. [In this way] powder renders the motile premise of the *oddu*'s revelation *explicit*, there for all to see by means of a simple figure-ground reversal: *oddu* figures are revealed *as* a temporary displacement of their ground, the powder. [...] This suggests a logical reversal that goes to the heart of the problem of transcendence. If we take seriously *babalawos*' contention that the *oddu* just *are* the marks they make on *aché*-powder [...], then the constitution of deities as displacements of powder tells us something pretty important about the premises of Ifá cosmology: that these deities are to be thought of [not as] entities, but rather as *motions*. [...] If the *oddu* [...] just are motions [...], then the apparent antinomy of giving logical priority to transcendence over relation or vice versa is resolved. In a logical universe where motion is primitive, what looks like transcendence becomes distance and what looks like relation becomes proximity. [So, *qua* motions, the deities have inherent within themselves the capacity to relate to humans, through the potential of *directed movement* that] *aché*-powder guarantees, as a solution to the genuine problem of the distance deities must traverse in order to be rendered present in divination. (Holbraad 2007: 208-9)

It in not an accident that the content of this analysis (i.e. the relationship between transcendence and immanence) is recursively related to its form (i.e. the relationship between analytical concepts and ethnographic things) – in the article itself I made much of this. Here, however, I want only to focus on the latter question, to draw attention to the work powder does for the analysis, by virtue specifically of its material characteristics. If ethnography carries the weight of the analytical problem, in this argument, it is the material quality of powder that provides the most crucial elements for its solution. If deities are conceptualised as motions to solve the problem of presence, after all, that is only because their material manifestations are just that, *motions*. And those motions, in turn, only emerge as analytically significant because of the material constitution of the powder upon which they are physically marked: its pervious quality as a pure multiplicity of unstructured particles, amenable to intensive movement, like the displacement of water, in reaction to the extensive pressure of the diviner's fingers, and so on. Each of this series of material qualities inheres in powder itself, and it is by virtue of this material inherence that they can engender vertizonal effects, setting the conceptual parameters for the anthropological analysis that they 'afford' the argument. As an irreducible element of the analysis of *aché*, it is *powder* that brings the pivotal concepts of perviousness, multiplicity, motion, direction, potential and so on into the fray of analysis, as conceptual transformations *of itself*, as per the 'thing = concept' clause. In that sense, I submit, it speaks for itself – louder, in fact, than any other element of the analysis presented.

Conclusion: anthropology and/or pragmatology

By way of conclusion, it may be worth clarifying a little how I see the dividends, as it were, of the kind of amplification of things' voices in anthropological analysis that I have sought to articulate. In particular, it is important at this point to be rather precise about the degree and manner in which this way of sourcing anthropological conceptualizations in things counts as a way of emancipating them 'as such'. Indeed: one might be tempted to object that, whatever the merits of the case I have sought to make for things speaking 'as such' in our analyses, their emancipation in this way nevertheless remains unavoidably circumscribed by the human-oriented agendas to which these analyses – anthropological after all – are directed. Sure (the objection would go): powder may be operative in the analysis of my Cuban example, providing the material source for my conceptual abstensions, as I called them, of such analytical ingredients as perviousness, multiplicity, intensive motion, and so on. Still, these ingredients are part of a longer recipe, so to speak, which includes not only things like powder, but also divinities, diviners, their clients and so on. And what this analytical recipe is meant to cook is an argument about Cuban practitioners of divination – that is people, my informants – and how we may best conceive of their notion that powder, in a divinatory context, is a form of divine power. While part of our answers to such questions, in other words, might be driven by things 'as such' in the manner I have indicated, their anthropological significance is nevertheless a function of their association, in the economy of anthropological analysis, with people and the ethnographic conundrums they pose to us. So the aforementioned archaeologist's bemused complaint, it seems, remains after all: could things really speak without their association to human (in this case ethnographically talkative) subjects?

The correct response, I would suggest, is to bite the bullet. Anthropological examples such as the one on Afro-Cuban powder indeed *do not* demonstrate that things can speak of their own accord, and seem bound to continue to render them subservient to the analysis of the human projects into which they enter. Arguably, however, this line of scepticism is contingent squarely on the anthropological – by which I mean also human-centric – character of the example. Indeed, while admittedly staying within the economy of undeniably anthropological analyses, what I have ventured to argue is that such analyses may involve an irreducibly thing-driven component or phase – one we might call 'pragmatological', borrowing somewhat subversively a term coined, tellingly, by the archaeologist Christopher Witmore (forthcoming). Indeed, while the analytical difference things can make pragmatologically might in this instance be gauged with reference to the anthropological mileage they give, the very notion that things might make such a difference of their own accord, 'as such', does, it seems to me, ultimately raise the prospect of pragmatology as a sui generis field of inquiry.

Allow me, then, to indulge in a final and absurdly programmatic speculation. Might one imagine a thing-centric discipline called pragmatology in which things' material properties would form the basis of conceptual experimentations that would be unmediated by, and run unchecked from, any human projects whatsoever? I have to admit that my own conception of what such a discipline might look like is hazy to say the least... Certainly, notwithstanding my earlier comments, I don't think archaeology would be enough to provide a model, if only because archaeology shares the anthropo-centric slant of social anthropology, its problem being mainly that its otherwise thing-oriented methodology suffers from a deficit of human conformation. Theoretical physics may come considerably closer, since so much of it apparently takes the form, precisely, of radical conceptual experimentations in the service of understanding the material forms of the universe. Still, this also has problems, partly due to physicists' still encompassing demand for causal explanation (a demand that is certainly distinct, and possibly incompatible, with our pragmatological concern with conceptualization). At any rate, there is no reason to limit our putative pragmatology to physicists' takes on matter, to the exclusion of those of, say, chemists, biologists, engineers, or, indeed, artists, sculptors or musicians. In fact, I suspect the closest one might get to the kind of inquiry pragmatology could involve would be an inverse form of conceptual art – construed, of course, very broadly indeed. If the labour of the conceptual artist is supposed to issue in an object that congeals in concrete form a set of conceptual possibilities, the work of the pragmatologist would be one that issues concepts that abstend in abstract form a set of concrete realities. Pragmatology, then, as art backwards.

Notes

Acknowledgements. Versions of this paper has been presented at departmental seminars in Aberdeen, SOAS and UCL, as well as at the *Things and Spirits* conference in Lisbon (September 2010) and the *TAG 2010* conference at Bristol. I thank James Leach, Ed Simpson, Victor Buchli, Ricardo Roque and Joao Vasconcelos and Dan Hicks for their respective invitations, and to the participants in each of them for their valuable comments. I am also grateful to Lise Philipsen for illuminating conversations during writing.

1. While my comments here speak to the argument as presented by all three of its authors, I do not claim that Salmond and Wastell would agree with the retrospective critique I develop here (although they may well do so, at least in part).

2. Chris Tilley (whose own dualism-busting efforts draw mainly on phenomenology), puts it most simply, in defence of the notion of 'materiality': 'The concept of materiality is required because it tries to consider and embrace subject-object relations going beyond the brute materiality of [things] and considering why certain [things] and their properties become important to people.' (Tilley 2007: 17)

3. On this point Miller, for one, resorts to a rather elaborate metaphor about philosophical wheels and the anthropological vehicles they help along which does not, to my mind, express very clearly the relationship between the two analytical demands (see Miller 2005: 43-46).

4. There may exist out there a Latourian analysis of an assemblage of actants consisting only of the things we'd call things, though the prospect seems more speculative at present – see Harman 2009.

5. My favourite candidates are Pedersen's forthcoming analysis of shamanic costumes in Mongolia (Pedersen 2011), in which he claims that these artefacts 'provide an analysis of

themselves', Strathern's commentary on Battaglia's analysis of Sabarl pick-axes (Strathern 1991), in which she argues that these artefacts 'contain their own contexts', and the archaeological debate about skeuomorphism, where, I want to argue, materials analyse each other through translating prior forms into novel contents (material analysis as concretions of abstractions).

References

Appadurai, Arjun, 1986. 'Introduction: commodities and the politics of value'. In: *The Social Life of Things: Commodities in Cultural Perspective*, A. Appadurai (ed.). Cambridge University Press, Cambridge, 3-63

Argyrou, Vassos, 2002. *Anthropology and the Will to Meaning: a Postcolonial critique*. London: Pluto Press

Engelke, Matthew, 2007. *A Problem of Presence: Beyond Scripture in an African Church*. Berkeley: University of California Press

E.E Evans-Pritchard, 1956. *Nuer Religion*. New York & Oxford: Oxford University Press

Fowles, Severin, 2008. 'The perfect subject: Postcolonial object studies'. Paper at Annual Conference of *Theoretical Archaeology Group*, May 24, Columbia University, New York.

Fowles, Severin, 2010. 'People without things'. In: *An Anthropology of Absence: Materializations of Transcendence and Loss*, M. Bille *et al* (eds.). New York: Springer, 23-41

Gell, Alfred, 1998. *Art and Agency: An Anthropological Theory*. Oxford: Clarendon Press

Guyer, Jane, 1993. 'Wealth in people and self-realisation in equatorial Africa'. *Man* N.S. 28(2): 243-265

Haraway, Donna. (1991) *Simians, Cyborgs and Women: The Reinvention of Nature*, Free Association Books: London.

Harman, Graham, 2009. *Prince of Networks: Bruno Latour and Metaphysics*. Re.press

Henare, A., M. Holbraad & S. Wastell, 2007. 'Introduction'. In *Thinking Through Things: Theorising artefacts ethnographically*, Wenare *et al* (eds.). London: Routledge, 1-31.

Holbraad, Martin, 2005. Expending multiplicity: money in Cuban Ifá cults. *Journal of the Royal Anthropological Institute* (N.S.) 11(2): 231-54

Holbraad, Martin, 2007. The power of powder: multiplicity and motion in the divinatory cosmology of Cuban Ifá (or *mana* again). In A. Henare *et al* (eds.) *Thinking Through Things: Theorising Artefacts Ethnographically*, London: Routledge, 189-225

Holbraad, Martin, 2009. 'Ontology, ethnography, archaeology: an afterword on the ontography of things'. *Cambridge Archaeological Journal* 19(3): 431-441

Holbraad, Martin, 2010. Ontology is just another word for culture: against the motion. Debate & Discussion (from GDAT 2008, S. Venkatesan (ed.)). *Critique of Anthropology* 30(2): 179-185

Holbraad, Martin & Morten A. Pedersen, 2009. 'Planet M: the intense abstraction of Marilyn Strathern'. *Anthropological Theory* 9(4): 371-94

Ingold, Tim, 2007. 'Materials against materiality'.

Archaeological Dialogues 14(1): 1-16

Keane, Webb, 2007. *Christian Moderns: Freedom and Fetish in the Mission Encounter*. Berkeley: University of California Press

Latour, Bruno, 1993. *We Have Never Been Modern*. Translated by C. Porter. London: Prentice Hall.

Latour, Bruno, 1993b. 'On technical mediation: philosophy, sociology, genealogy'. *Common Knowledge* 2: 29–64

Latour, Bruno, 1999. *Pandora's hope: Essays on the reality of science studies*. Cambridge, MA: Harvard University Press

Leach, James, 2007. 'Differentiation and encompassment: a critique of Alfred Gell's theory of the abduction of creativity'. In: *Thinking Through Things: Theorising artefacts ethnographically*, Wenare *et al* (eds.). London: Routledge

Miller, Daniel, 1987. *Material Culture and Mass Consumption*. Oxford: Basil Blackwell

Miller, Daniel, 2005. 'Materiality: an introduction'. In *Materiality*, D. Miller (ed.). Durham & London: Duke University Press, 1-50

Miller, Daniel, 2007. 'Stone age or plastic age?'. *Archaeological Dialogues* 14(1): 23-7

Olsen, B. 2003. 'Material culture after text: re-membering things'. *Norwegian Archaeological Review* 36(3):87–104

Pedersen, Morten A., 2011. *Not Quite Shamans: Spirit Worlds and Political Lives in Northern Mongolia*. Ithaca:

Cornell University Press

Pels, Peter,1998. 'The spirit of matter: On fetish, rarity, fact and fancy'. In *Border Fetishisms: Material Objects in Unstable Places*, Patricia Spyer (ed.), New York: Routledge, 91-121.

Pinney, Chris, 2005. 'Things happen: or, from which moment does that object come?'. In: *Materiality*, D. Miller (ed.). Durham & London: Duke University Press, 256-72

Spivak, Gayatri Chakravorty. 1998. "Can the Subaltern Speak?" in *Marxism and the Interpretation of Culture.* Eds. Cary Nelson and Lawrence Grossberg. Urbana, IL: University of Illinois Press, 1988: 271-313

Strathern, Marilyn, 1990. 'Artefacts of history: events and the interpretation of images'. In *Culture and History in the Pacific*, J. Siikala (ed.). Helsinki: Transactions of the Finish Anthropological Society, 25-44

Strathern, Marilyn, 2004 [first published 1991]. *Partial Connections (Updated edition)*. Walnut Creek: Altamira Press

Strathern, Marilyn, 2005. *Kinship, Law and the Unexpected: Relatives Are Always a Surprise*, Cambridge: CUP

Tilley, Christopher, 2007. 'Materiality in materials'. *Archaeological Dialogues* 14(1): 16-20

Viveiros de Castro, Eduardo, 1998. *Cosmological Perspectivism in Amazonia and Elsewhere*. Lecture series delivered at Dept. of Social Anthropology, University of Cambridg, *17 February – 10 March*

Viveiros de Castro, Eduardo, 2002. *And*. Manchester:

Manchester Papers in Social Anthropology.

Webmoor, Tim & Christopher Witmore, 2008. 'Things are us! A commentary on human/things relations under the banner of a 'social' archaeology'. *Norwegian Archaeology Review*, 41(1), 53-70

Witmore, Christopher, Forthcoming 2011. "The realities of the past: Archaeology, object-orientations, pragmatology." In B.R. Fortenberry and L. McAtackney (eds) *Modern Materials: Proceedings from the Contemporary and Historical Archaeology in Theory Conference 2009*. Oxford: Archaeopress.

Chapter 5

DEVOURING OBJECTS OF STUDY:
FOOD AND FIELDWORK

Sidney Mintz

Back in 1978,[1] when thinking about food seriously was becoming a crotchet among scholars, Joseph Epstein wrote a column for *The American Scholar* about the subject:

> Judging from the space given to it in the media, the great number of cookbooks and restaurant guides published annually, the conversations of friends – it is very nearly topic number one. Restaurants today are talked about with the kind of excitement that ten years ago was expended on movies. Kitchen technology-blenders, grinders, vegetable steamers, microwave ovens, and the rest-arouses something akin to the interest once reserved for cars.... The time may be exactly right to hit the best-seller lists with a killer who disposes of his victims in a Cuisinart (Aristides 1978:157-8).

If Professor Epstein was so in awe more than thirty years ago, he must now ponder with added bewilderment – as should we all – what has happened since. One keeps expecting the fascination with food to fade away but it has not – anyway, not *yet*. The anthropological study of food-related behavior has also changed and expanded radically during the last three decades, though no one is ready to explain its momentum. Some years back, Christine Du Bois and the author (Mintz and Du Bois 2003) sought to document briefly in text, and with bibliographical underpinning, some of the major problem areas this interest has entailed, to enable us to highlight a few changes. One such problem area has to do with studies of single plants or animals, food substances, or ingredients – buckwheat or quinoa, shrimp or muskrats, collagen or lecithin, vinegars or oils. It is with that problem area in particular, in relation to anthropology, that the following remarks are concerned.

Redcliffe N. Salaman's remarkable *History and Social Influence of the Potato* appeared in 1949, yet the number of kindred studies that followed it during the subsequent three decades or so was small. I wrote a book on sugar (sucrose), published now twenty-five years ago (Mintz 1985). Since then, similar works have multiplied. We have seen books on maize (Warman 2003), saffron (Willard 1999), rhubarb (Foust 1992). potatoes (Zuckerman 2000), pasta (Sirventi and Sabban 2000), bananas (Jenkins 2000), eels (Schweid 2002), codfish (Kurlansky 1997), wedding cakes (Charsley 1992), Coca Cola (Pendergrast 1993, Foster 2008), two on guinea pigs (Morales 1995, Archetti 1997), at least two on salt (Kurlansky 2002. Laszlo 2001 [1993]), at least three on rice (Ohnuki-Tierney 1993, Hess 1992, Carney 2001), at least two on milk (Wiley 2010, Valenze 2011 [forthcoming]), at least three more on capsicums (Long-Solis 1986, Naj 1992, Schweid 1999 [1987]), and even a quintet, by a prolific popular food writer, on peanuts, popcorn, ketchup, and two on tomatoes in America (Smith 1994, 1996, 1999, 2000, 2002). The supplementary list of volumes since 2003 and now forthcoming or in progress is, if anything, even more intimidating. Only some of these works are by anthropologists (I have starred them above). But anthropological books on food now float amid a veritable sea of food studies. The anthropological interest in food came about by a distinctive route. If we go back to two of the founding food-centered studies by American anthropologists – Frank Cushing's essay on Zuñi breadstuffs (1920) and Franz Boas's work on salmon among the Kwakiutl (1921) – we can see why. Though each focused on a single food, one plant and one animal, their aim was to describe that food in cultural context. Otherwise said, each dealt with a subsistence mainstay that was food for all, inside what was conceived of as a small, specific, geographically distinct society; and both works were based on fieldwork. Most important, production, distribution and consumption are treated in each as integral – as coherent within a single social and economic system. Trade was certainly known to the Zuñi and was important to the Kwakiutl, yet food-linked economic activity appeared to be mostly endogenous.

Of course social and economic boundaries between them and their neighbors were crossed. But such boundary crossing was noteworthy. Food-related activity took place almost entirely within the society itself; and it was, and was considered, absolutely critical to survival. In both societies the issue of adequate food figured, ceremonially and ideologically, in the lives of the people. For anthropologists at that time, at least, the reasons for studying food systems were crystal clear: how could you know how the society worked, if you did not know how it got and used its food? If one looks, for example, at Clark Wissler's *The American Indian* (1917), in its time a bible for beginning students of the indigenous peoples of North America, one discovers that Wissler's culture areas are above all *food* areas, built on Otis T. Mason's earlier work on "ethnic environments" (Mason 1895).

How better to begin to sort out the complexity of indigenous hemispheric life than to look at which people ate salmon, which acorns, and which maize? While some groups, such as those of the Northwest Pacific, lived rather high on the hog (so to speak), most had it much harder; none, especially to judge by their folklore, had it easy. For all New World peoples food was, both literally and figuratively, part of the central challenge of life. Turning back to works on the aboriginal peoples whose cultures most interested the anthropologists of a century ago, we remember that those societies produced most of what they consumed, and consumed most of what they produced. Yet such societies were not isolates. Alexander Lesser (1961) pointed this out in a brilliant paper, as had others before him. Still, most of the economic activities remained within definable borders. When anthropology moved away from societies that were largely self-sufficient (or that the ethnographers *took to be* largely self-sufficient), our task changed. Our ability to treat production, distribution and consumption as a coherent system ended, once that real (or in some cases spurious) self-sufficiency disappeared. One simply couldn't write a monograph about Muncie, Indiana that made it look like Malinowski's *Coral Gardens and Their Magic*, or Firth's *A Primitive Polynesian Economy*, no matter what sorts of blinders the ethnographer wore.

The enlargement of anthropological focus beyond the so-called "primitive" came slowly, even painfully; and a full recognition that the job requirements for anthropologists had become different arrived yet more uncertainly. I ask your forbearance, in commenting briefly on that shift, by referring to my own experience. More than half a century ago, when such fieldwork by anthropologists was still rare, I worked in a rural proletarian community on the south coast of Puerto Rico. Nearly everyone there worked in the sugarcane. Indeed, one could argue defensibly that *the community was defined* by the activities of a foreign sugar corporation, which employed nearly every inhabitant. To have tried to picture that community as some sort of isolate, self-contained, definable in terms of itself, would have been as convincing as imagining it to be on the moon.

But understanding what had happened does not end there. I discovered that much of the social fabric of that community would remind me more of what I had been reading about in Malinowski and Firth than of Muncie, Indiana, in spite of the industrial ambience. I would come to conclude that this seeming contradictoriness was real. Learning about sugarcane and sugar production was essential to making sense of people's lives there. Understanding something about the Boston corporation that managed its production and sale clarified other things about Puerto Rican life. Yet I knew I was making a community study, even while realizing that the local economy was utterly dependent upon forces external to it. Its people were not tribespersons or peasants; they were rural proletarians (Mintz 1951). They had no means of production beyond their labor; they were nearly as stripped of such means as any dishwasher in a New York City restaurant. They sold their labor power to a North American corporation. They produced hardly anything that they ate, ate nothing they produced. That is an exaggeration, but only a slight one. Economically speaking, their lives would have been empty without sugar.

Yet their lives as a community were real enough. Indeed, in the tenor of daily life, they seemed to me in my short life much more like a living community than anywhere else I had lived up to that time. I saw sugar as an element in the shaping of their lives, not as the subject of my research. It was not until thirty-five years later, when I decided to write a book on the history of sugar, that I first began to think of myself as a serious student of a single substance. It was lecturing on that book that made me a student of food. In the question period following a lecture on sugar history, I might be asked what I had to say about salt – about which I knew nothing; or about honey, of which I knew too little; or about Equal, or HFCS, or maple syrup – or why people everywhere seemed to like sweet foods, anyway. It was in response to my listeners' questions that I became serious about the study of food. I recount this only to indicate to the reader how accidentally one can – or anyway, I did – wander into something like the anthropology of food.

The truth is, of course, that *Sweetness and Power* is not really *about* food – it is about the rise of capitalism. Sugar (sucrose) was simply an illustrative instance of that process, a long thread in the social and economic fabric of Western history – and the histories of peoples then buried by western historiography.

While I think that sugar is interesting in its own right, in *Sweetness and Power* my interest in sugar was only incidental. I was trying to uncover how holders of power in the West were establishing themselves at an early time in the world outside Europe on the one hand, and relating themselves in new ways to their own laboring classes on the other. I realized that one of the ways they were discovering how to do so was by manipulating the material universe. The one concrete substance that I knew about personally was sugar.

As the governing classes learned to take the measure of their own people and of subjected peoples elsewhere, we are able to see how the fates of different lands and their inhabitants as producers and as consumers became linked in various ways to the fates of particular substances. In effect, the ruling classes of the societies of the West, who had long seen themselves as entitled to enjoy both substances and experiences not available to others, must have been beginning to think more consciously about what ordinary people might want – and then, more importantly, under what conditions it might benefit *them*, the rulers, to see that ordinary people *got* some of what they wanted. This is a highly original line of thought if it turns up in societies where inequalities were inherited – to control others and to benefit from their existence, not by beating them with a stick, but by offering them some carrots. In practice this doesn't work so well with donkeys, about whom it is commonly said; but some persons thought maybe it would work with humans. It did; and it does. Gradually a social and economic system was born, within which people could fashion their identities as much from what they consumed as from what they could learn, work at, or create.

Of course such a line of thought is highly speculative, even though it may sound persuasive. But what we knew about how capitalism as a system of consumption had taken shape, from writers such as Marx, Sombart and Veblen; and what I knew already about the history of sugar, made it seem worth my while to look harder. Even without the *inner* story of sugar, some uncovering of its nature in relation to human desires – and of the human capacity to braid together desire and habit – the larger, *outer* story of power might be narrated. But if I did only that, we would not have an example of what I intended to uncover. I hoped to show how, by looking at one revealing niche of activity, an ever-larger economic system could be discerned, operating pretty smoothly, though not entirely visible.

To achieve my aim, there had to be – at least for me – a definable and concrete object of study. Of course there were and are alternative ways to study sugar or any other such product. Perhaps it would have been more useful to do a discursive analysis of books on power and the tropics; or to study the history of capitalism on a larger canvas, such as the general nature of human food, the ubiquitous power of capitalism, the generalized hegemony of its leaders. I even wondered about writing about the works of whoever wrote about sugar. I had been studying those, and a lot of people, some of them interesting, had indeed written about it.

But I would not have been able to do that work well. Being of my generation, with a strong liking for the concrete, I went ahead with my own plan. That involved – though I did not anticipate it as such at the time – putting my ideas and what I learned within a framework of the sort sometimes now referred to, not very respectfully, as a "master narrative." I suppose the truth is that I am a sucker for master narratives. Back when I was living on the edge of a sugar plantation in Puerto Rico in 1948, it surely seemed to me that sugar fitted within a larger chronicle of the rise of capitalism, of the use of forced labor outside the capitalist heartland, of *fin de siècle* U.S.

imperialism, and of the long-term success of linking a safe site of production and a guaranteed market for consumption: at home and in the colonies, and preferably without others quite noticing it.

This looked to me like a lengthy chronicle, going back as it did for nearly five centuries, involving Europe, Africa and the tropical New World, using forced labor in many guises, and perfecting a characteristic form of industrial organization, one that blended field and factory into one efficient, productive and vicious enterprise. I did not see any of those features in sugar's history as inevitable. Indeed, I came to take positions on the relationship of slavery to capitalism, and on the geographical locus of the first centers of industrial production, that put me in positions that no orthodox Marxist or economic determinist would want to find herself. And I surely did not believe that my version was by any means the only such narrative of the past. In fact, in a much earlier book, I had put together unawares much of the same story, taken from the mouth of a single narrator (Mintz 1960).

In chronicling sugar, I wanted to be as objective as I could. At times I wondered whether there might be some way to get enough distance from my subject to attain the objectivity that apparently comes with successfully situating oneself outside of, or above, the capitalistic system. I admit that some anthropological scholars had apparently succeeded at doing that, and at first I wanted to do it, too. But when I thought about where my university salary came from; who pays for the fellowships that my school supplies its graduate students; the light that proper attention to politics still sheds upon plantation owners in the right places, even today; and other such truths (not opinions) in today's world – I could not elude my feeling that I, at least, was living within capitalism, not floating invulnerably above it. I decided to write my study of sugar in an old fashioned way: as if I lived in a capitalist society myself, and so I did.

As Redcliffe Salaman's remarkable study of the potato

eloquently demonstrated, the idea of studying a single plant, animal, food, or food ingredient is by no means new; and work such as Boas's and Cushing's in an earlier era makes plain that anthropologists had thought of it long ago. But it is worth noting afresh, because when we look at Malinowski's work with the Trobrianders, or Firth's with the Tikopia, we see much of the same, because they could define social groups that produced what they consumed, and consumed what they produced. In such analytical works production and consumption were not amputated from each other; the near-obsession with consumption that we have seen in food studies in recent years was absent. Put simply, in those societies the relation between supply and demand was much less influenced by market forces than is true for most of the modern world. Missing from those monographs is concern with the economic relationships among producers, and their influence over consumers. In those societies producers did not aim at enlarging, changing, or cornering a part of the market. They were not competing for buyers, nor were the consumers searching for alternate sellers. Each economic act in those societies was also a social act. A diminishing supply did not automatically result in price rises. When such indicators, having to do with the nature of capital, of the market, and of the market value of factors of production such as labor, are not present, their absence signals that a fully developed capitalism is still wanting. But I believe that it is near impossible to study food production or consumption almost anywhere in the world today without taking such forces into account.

In the modern world, the extent to which economic factors become deeply interwoven with the role of government in the economy makes the picture additionally complex. For example, where does profit stop and the FDA begin? Should ephedra be taken off the market, rather than being sold with warnings to the consumers? Should we regulate the so-called nutraceuticals at all? To what extent should General Foods lobbyists or sugar lobbyists – or for that matter, congressmen underwritten by lobbyists – determine how the food triangle is depicted graphically, and what pictures and words go in it?

Now the interpenetration of government and the private sector poses almost daily challenges to our conceptions of individual freedom and the definition of general welfare. If one contemplates the facts about food-borne diseases and what consumers can do to protect our children from the "modern" system of food production, we have a wordless but eloquent demonstration of our near total helplessness.

But these are questions with which our anthropological ancestors did not have to deal when they studied food. They concentrated on other food-related matters, such as coral gardens and their magic, or salmon recipes on the Northwest coast. In very large measure, the doing of the anthropology of that earlier era is gone, even if – one hopes – not forgotten. But we can still study the way human beings behave, and the rules and patterns of their behavior, as did our forbears; we can still learn about different value systems, and their internal logics. We can, in short, still profitably do fieldwork, which is what we are supposed to be good at.

I was reminded of our distinctive methodological gift a few years back, when I asked two colleagues if I might read their unpublished manuscript. Professors Frederick Errington and Deborah Gewertz had based what became their book (2002) on the New Guinea fieldwork they had carried out over two decades and on their recent Morgan Lectures. I asked to read the manuscript because it is about sugar. In it they describe events leading up to the creation of a plantation and the construction of a modern sugar mill in Papua New Guinea. Since the history of the industrial production of sugar goes back at least to the 17th century in the Caribbean region, I tend to associate it with slavery and the destruction of cultural origins, both Native American and African. But in Papua New Guinea, making a sugar industry was intimately associated with creating a nation – not so much with destroying local cultures, as with aiming at the conception of a national culture.

The early planning discussions there, Errington and Gewertz report, had to do with whether the Papua New Guinea sugar industry would supply only the national population, or undertake to export sugar besides. Much discussion concerned the quality of sugar to be produced, as well as the quantity. People wanted PNG to have a modern industry, so the country would look modern to the outside world. So both quality – in this case, to produce fully-refined white, or the less "modern" brown – and quantity were argued over. Once decided, the next issue became that of location and employment. On grounds of fair play, and to avoid localism, the labor force for the new industry was to be drawn from peoples across the nation – a deliberate attempt was made to avoid provincialism or "wantokism" ("one-language-ism"); and by aiming to treat individuals as equals, the hope was to contribute to the building of a national identity. With the work force recruited from every part of the country, both to prevent kin, village or language-group cliques from forming, and to impose equality of treatment on all, the sugar industry became a bulwark for fostering national feelings, as against local loyalties. To at least some extent, the plan succeeded (or at least at that time the authors thought it had.). Errington and Gewertz had to learn about the sugar industry, as have many other anthropological field workers before them in other places; but what they learned shows the way that the world is changing, and the power of anthropological fieldwork to document in detail the changes taking shape. When one reads what was done with the labor force for the PNG sugar complex – organized by the Booker-Tate Corporation, one of the great capitalistic enterprises that lay behind the development of Caribbean sugar – one is stunned to see to what extent the efforts made to create a genuine landless wage-earning proletariat in Papua New Guinea paralleled those that marked the coming of U.S. power to the Puerto Rican south coast, a century before.

Even more remarkable, those efforts also reveal

provocative similarities to what happened sociologically with the enslaved Africans brought in to work on Caribbean plantations centuries earlier. What I mean here is that a nation was being deliberately constructed; in Caribbean history, pre-existing cultural patterns were being deliberately broken down.

What I read about in Errington and Gewertz's book was the imposition of a time-conscious industrial process upon people in a newly-emergent nation – people whose vision had been, and in large measure still is, conditioned by kin group, village and linguistic group that provide the circles of meaning by which the people identified themselves, as individuals and as group members. The sugar industry there reveals that they are now being circumscribed by a still larger circle – one we social scientists have variously labeled with terms such as secularization, industrialization, urbanization, acculturation or some other, but which also end up meaning at some point "modernity" within global capitalism.

I do not mean to suggest by this description that there is some single interpretive or explanatory high road to the study of food – any food – or toward our richest understanding of human behavior and its past. If we look at the work of other "sugar scholars," after this brief glance at Errington and Gewertz, we see how rich and varied are the approaches that serious scholars have taken. Monographs by historians and anthropologists about sugar, no two of them alike – Ortiz in *Cuban Counterpoint*, Moreno Fraginals in *El Ingenio*, Attwood in *Raising Cane*, Scheper-Hughes in *Death Without Weeping*, Mazumdar in *Sugar and Society in China*, and many others – have advanced our understanding of the relationship among substance, society and behavior; and though sugar figures importantly in all of their work, it would be mistaken to claim that they wrote "books about sugar." My intention in this paper was to keep the notion of concrete objects of study – in this instance, foods and food substances, and one in particular – front and center. Yet none of these books is only about sugar, even though each of them is very much about sugar. Their authors' eyes were firmly fixed on the substance through which their protagonists, and the social forces of which they were part, interacted. Of this list of monographs, all of them excellent, two – *Death Without Weeping* and *Raising Cane* – were written by anthropologists, and both display handsomely how the study of the material world and the methods of anthropology can meet fruitfully in fieldwork. The purpose of these remarks was to reflect upon fieldwork and the study of foods or food-related substances. But permit me to conclude by making a final point.

My aim was to suggest that there are still many different ways to do anthropology, and within the subfield of food studies that is still true. We food anthropologists need to do careful fieldwork and lots of it. But we want it to help us to understand, *if possible*, something larger than itself. That is not always possible; and the fieldwork can still be well worth doing. But if we aim to reach a larger readership than our colleagues; and if we want what we have found out and think to serve some useful purpose beyond self-education, we should aim at exploring the larger messages our data offer us.

Notes

1. This paper was first delivered as the David Skomp Distinguished Lecture on April 30, 2003, for the Department of Anthropology, Indiana University. It was then published separately, the same year and with the same title, by the Department. I have made a few small changes in the text for this online edition. It is posted here by permission of the Department of Anthropology, Indiana University. Requests for copies of the original lecture may be addressed to the Department of Anthropology, Indiana University, 701 E. Kirkwood Avenue, SB 130, Bloomington IN 47405.

References

Archetti, Eduardo. 1997. *Guinea-Pigs*. Oxford: Berg.

Aristides [Epstein, J.J.] 1978. Foodstuff and nonsense. *American Scholar* 47 (2): 157-63.

Attwood, Donald. 1992. *Raising Cane*. Boulder: Westview Press.

Boas, Franz. 1921. *Ethnology of the Kwakiutl*. 35th Annual Report of the Bureau of American Ethnology. Washington: Government Printing Office.

Carney, Judith. 2001. *Black Rice*. Cambridge: Harvard University Press.

Charsley, Simon. 1992. *Wedding Cakes and Cultural History*. New York: Routledge.

Cushing, Frank. 1920. Zuñi Breadstuffs. *Indian Notes and Monographs* 8. New York: Museum of the American Indian. The Heye Foundation.

Errington, Frederick, and Deborah Gewertz. 2004. *Yali's Question: Sugar, Culture, History*. Chicago: University of Chicago.

Firth, Raymond. 1939. *A Primitive Polynesian Economy*. London: G. Routledge and Sons.

Firth, Raymond. 1951. *Elements of Social Organization*. London: Watts.

Foust, Clifford. 1992. *Rhubarb*. Princeton: Princeton University Press.

Gillin, John. 1947. *Moche. A Peruvian Coastal Community*. Smithsonian Institution Institute of Social Anthropology, No.3. Washington: Government Printing

Office.

Hess, Karen. 1992. *The Carolina Rice Kitchen. The African Connection*. Columbia SC: The University of South Carolina Press.

Jenkins, Virginia. 2000. *Bananas*. Washington: Smithsonian Institution Press.

Kurlansky, Mark. 1997. *Cod*. New York: Penguin.

Kurlansky, Mark.. 2002. *Salt*. New York: Walker & Co.

Laszlo, Pierre. 1998. *Salt: Grain of Life*. New York: Columbia.

Lesser, Alexander. 1961. Social fields and the evolution of society. *Southwestern Journal of Anthropology* 17: 40-48.

Long-Solis, Janet. 1986. *Capsicum y cultura*. Mexico City: Fondo de Cultura Econ6mica.

Malinowski, Bronislaw. 1935. *Coral Gardens and Their Magic*. 2 vols. London: Allen & Unwin.

Mason, Otis. 1895. Influence of environment upon human industries or arts. *Smithsonian Institution Annual Report*: 639-65.

Mazumdar, Sucheta. 1998. *Sugar and Society in China*. Cambridge: Harvard University Press.

McPhee, John. 2002. *The Founding Fish*. New York: Farrar, Straus and Giroux.

Mintz, Sidney W. 1951. *Caiiamelar: The Culture of a Rural Puerto Rican Proletariat*. Ph.D. thesis, Columbia University.

Mintz, Sidney W. 1960. *Worker in the Cane: A Puerto*

Rican Life History. New Haven: Yale University Press.

Mintz, Sidney W. 1985. *Sweetness and Power.* New York: Viking-Penguin.

Mintz, Sidney W. and Christine Du Bois. 2002. The anthropology of food and eating. *Annual Review of Anthropology* 31: 99-119.

Morales, Edmundo. 1995. *The Guinea Pig.* Tucson: University of Arizona Press.

Moreno Fraginals, Manuel. 1977. *El ingenio.* 3 vols. Havana.

Naj, Amal. 1992. *Peppers.* New York: Knopf.

Nestle, Marion. 2002. *Food Politics.* Berkeley: University of California Press.

Ohnuki Tierney, Emiko. 1993. *Rice as Self.* Princeton: Princeton University Press.

Ortiz, Fernando. 1947. *Cuban Counterpoint.* New York: Knopf.

Pendergrast, Mark. 1993. *For God, Country and Coca Cola.* New York: Charles Scribner's Sons.

Salaman, Redcliffe. 1949. *History and Social Influence of the Potato.* Cambridge: Cambridge University Press.

Scheper-Hughes, Nancy. 1992. *Death Without Weeping.* Berkeley: University of California Press.

Schweid, Richard. 1987. *Hot Peppers.* Chapel Hill: University of North Carolina.

Schweid, Richard. 2002. *Consider the Eel.* Chapel Hill: University of North Carolina Press.

Sirventi, Silvano, and Françoise Sabban. 2000. *Pasta*. New York: Columbia University Press.

Smith, Anthony. 1994. *The Tomato in America*. Columbia: University of South Carolina Press.

Smith, Anthony. 1996. *Pure Ketchup*. Columbia SC: The University of South Carolina Press.

Smith, Anthony. 1999. *Popped Culture*. Columbia SC: The University of South Carolina Press.

Smith, Anthony. 2000. *Souper Tomatoes*. New Brunswick NJ: Rutgers University Press.

Smith, Anthony. 2002. *Peanuts*. Urbana: University of Illinois Press.

Warman, Arturo. 2003. *Corn and Capitalism*. Chapel Hill: Uniiversity of North Carolina Press.

Warner, William. 1976. *Beautiful Swimmers*. Boston: Little Brown & Co.

Willard, Pat. 2002. *Secrets of Saffron*. Boston: Beacon Press.

Wissler, Clark. 1917. *The American Indian*. New York: Oxford University Press.

Zuckerman, Larry. 1998. *The Potato*. Boston: Faber & Faber.

Chapter 6

COSMETIC COSMOLOGIES IN JAPAN: NOTES TOWARDS A SUPERFICIAL INVESTIGATION

Philip Swift

Tiger and Bond stood in the shade of the avenue of giant cryptomerias and observed the pilgrims, slung with cameras, who were visiting the famous Outer Shrine of Ise, the greatest temple to the creed of Shintoism. Tiger said, 'All right. You have observed these people and their actions. They have been saying prayers to the sun goddess. Go and say a prayer without drawing attention to yourself.'

Bond walked over the raked path and through the great wooden archway and joined the throng in front of the shrine. Two priests, bizarre in their red kimonos and black helmets, were watching. Bond bowed towards the shrine, tossed a coin on to the wire-netting designed to catch the offerings, clapped his hands loudly, bent his head in an attitude of prayer, clapped his hands again, bowed and walked out.

'You did well,' said Tiger. 'One of the priests barely glanced at you. The public paid no attention. You should perhaps have clapped your hands more loudly. It is to draw the attention of the goddess and your ancestors to your presence at the shrine. Then they will pay more attention to your prayer. What prayer did you in fact make?'

'I'm afraid I didn't make any, Tiger. I was concentrating on remembering the right sequence of motions.'

'The goddess will have noticed that, Bondo-san. She will help you to concentrate still more in the future. Now we will go back to the car and proceed to witness another interesting ceremony in which you will take part.'

—Ian Fleming, You Only Live Twice (1965) p.90-91

A superficial citation, to be sure, but deployed with a more significant (I do not say deeper) end in mind: to pay attention, in this essay, to the significance of superficiality in Japan. By this, I mean the well-documented tendency of Japanese sociality to invest a serious amount of energy in the creation of surfaces.[1] For the moment, though, let us stick with this trivial epigraph, for it is instructive. In *You Only Live Twice*, James Bond – on a mission in Japan – is instructed in becoming Japanese by Tiger Tanaka, head of the Japanese Secret Service. As described by Fleming, James Bond's Japan is a kind of technicolor theatre state, parcelled up in ritual. A country of pure exteriority that Fleming invents by papering it with clichés (so often italicised): *samurai, sake*, Suntory whisky, *ninja* and nightingale floorboards. How then to go undercover in a world of surfaces? Not so difficult, when identity too is just a façade. In a doubly dubious moment of mimesis,

Double-O Seven play-acts at being Japanese by the easy expedient of cosmetics: black hair dye and skin-tanning lotion. Later on, Bond gives up his Japanese disguise in favour of something even more implausible. He pretends to be an anthropologist! (Fleming 1965: 121)

Ironies aside, however, consider the scenario quoted above; the prayer exercise at Ise Shrine. Suppose, for a moment, that an anthropologist were present at the scene, loitering perhaps behind a giant cryptomeria; spying on the spy. Observing Bond perform a sequence of actions and overhearing the subsequent bit of dialogue – *You did well...What prayer did you in fact make? – I'm afraid I didn't make any* – our eavesdropping anthropologist might well be led to ask herself the following question: Did James Bond pray or not? After all, he got the actions right, but then he says that actually he didn't pray; yet Tanaka, his mentor, seems to think that he did. Which is it then? Our anthropologist is fazed, both shaken *and* stirred. For while she is able to accept that, on the surface, Bond seems to pray, what she most wants to know is what's *really* happening deep down. Perhaps she remembers reading Geertz and his Rylean doctrine of thick description. The job of ethnography, she recalls, is to codify occurrences according to their particular significations, to sort out 'real winks from mimicked ones' (Geertz 1993: 16). Well then, how to tell the difference between someone making a prayer and someone faking one?

If I indulge in these fictional speculations, it is in order to create a conceptual space for the staging of analysis. Fleming's account is a fabrication – obviously – but it is, I suggest, effective nonetheless in terms of delimiting certain aspects of the ethnographic problem of prayer in Japan. In fact, more than that – to deploy this ersatz example as a means of enacting my general thesis: it is effective to the extent that it is fabricated.

To see how this passage of Fleming might turn out to be ethnographically useful – in spite of its evident exoticism, its double-O orientalism – consider the following description offered by Thomas Kasulis (2004: 27-8). He reports on the sort of typical exchange he would have with the businessmen he would often see praying at a certain shrine in Tokyo.

'"Why did you stop at the shrine?"' asks Kasulis.

Says the businessman: '"I almost always stop on the way to work."'

Kasulis presses him further. '"Yes, but why? Was it to give thanks, to ask a favor [sic], to repent, to pay homage, to avoid something bad from happening? What was your purpose?"

"I don't really know. It was nothing in particular."

"Well then, when you stood in front of the shrine with your palms together, what did you say, either aloud or silently to yourself?"

"I didn't say anything."

"Did you call on the name of the *kami* [divinity] to whom the shrine is dedicated?'

"I'm not really sure which *kami* it is."

So there you have it. Everything happens as if the invocation is simulated, seemingly going no further than the curve and contact of surfaces – clapping, bowing, and the pressing of palms together.[2] Roland Barthes possibly gestures at this image of prayer as pure exteriority at the end of his famous meditation on the 'system' he calls Japan. 'Empire of Signs?' asks Barthes. 'Yes, if it is understood that these signs are empty and that the ritual is without a god' (Barthes 1983: 108; 2005: 149). Certainly, the model 'Japan' that Barthes engineers is too heavily invested with the elements of an idealized Zen, with the result that his system puts too much stress on emptiness. At the same time, however, the merit of his analysis is its disavowal of depth; instead, it traces planes and sticks to surfaces. Consider, by contrast, a mode of inquiry that moves very differently; one for which surfaces are encountered as obstructions, when what it really wants is not more walls to run up against, but windows to look through. Just such a model of method is employed by a Cambridge Professor of Anthropology, Alan Macfarlane, with stumbling-block consequences. Writing of the goings-on at the Ise Shrine (where James Bond 'didn't' pray) and other such places, Macfarlane registers confusion:

> There is no God or gods and there is no other separate supernatural world. With what can ritual communicate? When thousands visit the Ise shrine or go to Buddhist or Shinto shrines and wash their hands, clap, make little monetary offerings, write up their wishes and hang them on trees, what are they doing?

> There is a widespread attempt to communicate with something spiritual...But it is difficult to find out what exactly is happening. (2007: 186)

This moment of incomprehension reminds me of nothing so much as the opening lines of the song, 'For What It's Worth', by Buffalo Springfield: *There's something happening here/What it is ain't exactly clear*. Here, from the point of view of a method fixated with the location of foundations, there is, as Barthes disconcertingly observed, 'nothing to *grab hold of* ('*rien à saisir*'; 2005: 150). In other words, the problem would seem to be that there are too many surfaces and no evident way of accessing that subterranean zone of motivations that would make them intelligible. This issue of 'access' is one which, for example, scholars of religious conversion – keener than believers in their need to finally, really see just what is actually going on – have rather quaintly called the 'problem of observability' (see Cowan and Bromley 2008: 218).[3] In short, the problem of what we might call the credibility gap between the envelope of action (clapping, bowing) and the interior intention.

The problem surfaces once more in Nelson's ethnography of the daily life of a Shinto shrine in Kyoto, when he remarks of the various activities that shrine-goers engage in that 'the observer cannot know for certain what degree of belief accompanies such acts' (Nelson 1996: 141; cf. 136). Now this is a perfectly unobjectionable statement, quite in keeping with Nelson's sensible emphasis on the importance of allowing for a wide range of motivations (where these can be ascertained) of those who visit the shrine. But it is precisely this statement's seeming reasonableness that makes me hesitate. That is to say, I am bothered by the elementary epistemology it presupposes; for why, in this particular case, should the observer suppose *any degree of* association between such acts and certain inner states (such as beliefs) that might authorise them? Certainly, nothing in Nelson's own data suggests that 'belief', whether present or absent, has anything to do with the activities that take place at Shinto shrines. If this is so, then perhaps we have been using the wrong language, for, as currently articulated, our analytical expressions concerning these Japanese practices seem to be marked by that 'constitutive unhappiness' that, as Latour (2004: 212) says, forever hangs over the language of epistemology; the sense of regret that, although our descriptions can never get beyond the surface of practice, this is what they *ought* to be doing if they aim to reach that real, interior space of explanation. To be sure, as with other analysts of Japanese religiosity, Nelson makes it clear that 'praxical' (rather than 'creedal') concerns count (1996: 121; cf. Reader 1991: 1-22), but he reaches nevertheless for a readymade language of analysis in which a familiar space is maintained for the possibility of the presence of belief. As a consequence, the same doubts and concerns about surfaces remain, because they are lodged in the language itself; hence the sense of uncertainty, vis-à-vis belief, is a problem of our own making, for, rather like a frustrated dermatologist, who really wishes he had taken up neurology instead, we are left with a feeling that the skin is all there is; and even if it isn't, we would never know anyway.

But what if the problem of 'what exactly is happening' (as articulated by Macfarlane, for example) was a problem best left at the level of the surface itself? In other words, if the Japanese practices we have been considering here appear to be much less cosmic than cosmetic – if, that is, they strike us as superficial – then, I suggest, that is because the cosmological in Japan is so often constituted at the cosmetic level. This, anyway, is the argument I intend to trace out in the rest of this paper. *Paper* – the very thinness of which we take to be proverbial in our everyday definitions of the superficial. But in Japan – and this is my point – surfaces might be conceptualised very differently. Paper, that is to say, might not always be indicative of the trivial. Indeed, the zigzagging strips of paper (*shide*) often to be found in Shinto shrines index the presence of divinities.

Cosmology and difference deferred – the anthropology of Japan

If my anthropological argument is inclined towards the cosmological, then it does no more than follow a certain recent trend within the discipline (e.g., Taylor 1999; Viveiros de Castro 2001; and especially Handelman 2008). Of course, anthropological interest in cosmology is by no means new – it goes back at least as far as Boas (1996) who, in famously advocating the science he called 'cosmography', was himself taking a cue from Humboldt's Cosmos, that massive atmospheric project that sought to relate the farthest star systems to the thinnest skins of lichen 'over the surface of our rocks' (Humboldt 1860: 68). But if there has been a renewed interest in the cosmological (a move not without its critics, as I consider below), then this would not yet seem to have had much impact on the anthropology of Japan, that distant, disciplinary star at the outer arm of the anthropological galaxy. While there are, assuredly, some outstanding exceptions (including Clammer 2001; Ohnuki-Tierney 1987; Yamaguchi 1977; 1991a; 1998),[4] it seems to me that indifference towards cosmology as a possible resource for thought might be related to a more general disciplinary suspicion towards the invocation of difference. To simplify considerably, the emergence of these doubts about difference was in part the result of the powerful attacks launched against orientalism (spearheaded, of course, by Edward Said). But the inclination to tone down difference was also a reaction against certain indigenous discourses (the so-called *nihonjinron* literature – or 'theories of the Japanese') in which Japan is presented as so utterly other that only the Japanese are capable of understanding it (Dale 1995). Caught between orientalisms – 'ours' and 'theirs' – the easiest exit strategy has been to downplay difference altogether. But this is merely a methodological dodge that creates its own contradictions, for, as Clammer puts it, the result has been that a discipline dedicated 'to the study of a particular Other, paradoxically fears the very differences out of which its object is constituted' (2001: 94).

Maybe, therefore, we require new strategies, new-fashioned languages of analysis; in other words, we need *other words* (though this paper is no manifesto; I am just trying to feel my way around). Hence, what I am in search of is a style of thought that would – as the philosopher François Jullien says of his own thinking on Chinese thinking – succumb neither to a 'lazy humanism' that would efface all differences, nor to a 'lazy relativism' that would make differences absolute and inscrutable (Jullien 2003: 17). Or, put differently – if you'll pardon my revision of an old trope – we would need to avoid the Godzilla of orientalism, on the one hand, and the Charybdis of universalism, on the other.[5]

It is therefore with an eye to the careful figuration of difference that I aim to understand Japanese practices of prayer, glossed as cosmological. But since, as Clammer observes, 'The question of difference will not just go away' (2001: 3), how can we address it? And what might a cosmological angle add to the endeavour? One possible way of clarifying these difficult issues would be to consider some recent, programmatic remarks made by Jennifer Robertson, which are enlightening for the very reason that they are not concerned with the cosmological at all.

In an introduction to a handbook on the anthropology of Japan, Robertson draws attention to the persistence (in Euro-American accounts of Japan) of a particular figurative device used to evoke Japanese difference: the metaphor of the mirror (Robertson 2005: 6-7; cf. Robertson 2002).[6] The device that Robertson has in mind is the age-old trope of symbolic inversion; that is, the perception and construction of other societies as being exactly contrary to our own, of which a classic and ancient instance is Herodotus' description of the Egyptians who (in opposition to the Greeks) do everything back to front – the women urinate standing up; the men urinate sitting down, etc.[7] It is the enantiomorphic effect of mirrors – their exact reversal of the image in reflection – that makes them so obviously attractive for the figuring of other societies (Fernandez 1986). And Japan came to be figured in the same way. Indeed, inversion as a means of conceptualising Japanese otherness became such a commonplace in Western descriptions that Chamberlain was able to dedicate an entry to 'Topsy-turvydom' in his quirky, turn-of-the-century dictionary of Japanese culture (2007: 512-514). To slightly different effect, Ruth Benedict (1967) took up the mirror and deployed it for partly satirical purposes, angling it at Japan and America in such a way as to make one wonder which culture it was that was topsy-turvy. While sympathetic to Benedict's efforts, Robertson is critical of ethnographies such as hers which resort to this mirror-imaging technique, and she stresses the connection between this Japan-as-mirror literature and the popular conception of anthropology as a 'mirror' of and for 'culture' (as it was for Kluckhohn, for example). As she observes, mirrors are quite capable of other tricks as well; so seemingly deep, they may act as solipsistic traps, specular deceptions (Robertson 2005: 6; 2002:

786; cf. Fernandez 1986).[8]

In addition, according to Robertson, it is also the ubiquity of this particular tropological technique that accounts for the large number of books on Japan that feature the word 'mirror' in the title (2005: 6-7). Robertson only cites one example, but something of the range can most easily be grasped in the most superficial way possible, by simply tallying up the book titles: *Mirror, Sword and Jewel*; *A Japanese Mirror*; *The Empty Mirror*; *The Monkey as Mirror*, and so on and so forth.[9] To be sure, it is hard to see otherwise why these titular mirrors keep reappearing, unless (the whims of uninspired editors notwithstanding) we were to put it down to some strange phenomenon of specular proliferation. The latest addition to this mirror literature is Alan Macfarlane's *Japan Through the Looking Glass* (2007), a curious kind of magical mystery tour of the country; and, certainly, some of the criticisms that Robertson levels at the Japan-as-mirror literature could be applied even more forcefully here. For instance (and with acknowledgement to Lewis Carroll), Macfarlane's Japan is seemingly a place where the people are able to 'believe six impossible things before breakfast' (2007: 153).[10] It is an exceptional, paradoxical and therefore almost unintelligible culture, which Macfarlane signals many times over by saying that the Japanese 'mirror' is difficult to see into (2007: 204, 212, 213, 215, 229, etc.) As for the Japanese environment, it is:

> a magical landscape of the kind which I had only previously encountered in fairy stories and the poetry of Wordsworth, Keats and Yeats. This is the last great fairy-land on earth, but it did not take Disney to create it. (2007: 47-8)

It is perhaps no great surprise why Macfarlane's mirror is difficult to look into, if it keeps getting steamed up by sentimentality of this sort. In the end, however, for all his talk about the incommensurability of Japan – which, whatever one makes of it, at least has the merit of stressing *difference* – he ends up saying that Japan can only be made intelligible if it is 'put into a *universal* frame which would bring it back into our comprehension' (2007: 213; italics mine). But then, whither difference? Like the Cheshire Cat, it vanishes.

Returning to Robertson, her criticisms assuredly hit the mark with regard to books like this. Her own concern is, I take it, with finding a way of figuring difference differently, without recourse to mirror-imaging which, she writes, 'can deflect recognition of the need to learn more about Japan on terms relevant to the dynamic and intertwined histories of localities and subjective cultural formations and practices within that country' (2005: 6). I take her point. In addition, I freely admit that my effort here, to try to imagine how a cosmology might inform certain practices at shrines, necessarily abridges and compresses all manner of local formations and histories. And yet, Robertson's critique is too all-encompassing, linking, as it does, mirrors as tricky instruments for the imaging of Japanese culture to the titular mirrors of so much literature on Japan. Because, as she recognises elsewhere (2002: 791), it is not only anthropologists who do things with mirrors and, equally, their epistemological capacity as imaging devices may be only one of their functions (see Viveiros de Castro 2007: 165). For indeed – the trope of mirror-imaging aside – Robertson overlooks an alternative possibility that would account for the prevalence of the mirror in writings on Japan, which is that it might in fact be conceptually indebted to Japanese thought itself. Thus, one such source of the mirror metaphor is, I suggest, the historical Japanese practice of naming descriptive or historical accounts as 'mirrors' (*kagami*) because they purport to 'reflect' some place or series of events.[11] But the image of the mirror has alternative sources as well, because in Shinto shrines it is very often the case that divinities reside *within mirrors*. This is exactly what I would regard as the crucial cosmological angle that Robertson's account passes over.

But before exploring what the consequences of this might be for a cosmological understanding of Japanese practices of prayer, I want to weigh up a specific criticism of cosmology as a resource for anthropological thinking. In the first paper published in this series for the OAC, Huon Wardle (2009) takes up the topic of cosmopolitics, by way of an evaluation of a debate between Ulrich Beck and Bruno Latour that was enacted in the journal, *Common Knowledge*. Wardle's argument is acute and powerfully stated, and – if I understand it correctly – aims, by means of Kant's notion of common sense, to create a space for an ethical and reflexive subjectivity, as part of a more cosmopolitan conception of anthropology.[12] But the part of his argument that concerns me here is his rebuke of the use of explicit cosmological contrasts – 'us' and 'them' stagings – of the kind made by Viveiros de Castro (whose work is often championed by Latour). Says Wardle: 'the refinement of pristine indigenous cosmologies – elaborately articulated symmetric fictions – that provide the foil to a critique of "Western" society is unsustainable' (2009: 22). I must confess that finding an adequate response to this doesn't come easily, except to say, lamely no doubt, that I do not wholly agree. I remain of the view that difference, deployed tactically in something like this fashion, is still a viable device for arriving at anthropological insights (see Robbins 2002). Nevertheless, my intent here is much less ambitious and I have no designs on scaling up a cosmology and ascribing it to something massive called 'Japan'. My aims are considerably more local and superficial. But it is also partly for these same reasons that I am not sure that Kantian insights would be of much help to my argument either. Though I cannot claim to know much about Kant's thesis of common sense (beyond Wardle's excellent exposition), his writings on religion make me hesitate. His universalizing pretensions and strong moral sense of what should constitute reasonable religion lead him to treat all manner of diverse practices as the same in so far as they are equally ineffective. For, as Kant has it, 'Differences of external form [*den Unterschied in der äußern Form*]...count equally for nothing' (1998: 168) in so far as belief in the sensuous and transgressively technical nature of ritual or adherence to inflexible dogma erases all differences, as he says, between the Tungus shaman, the Bishop and the Connecticut Puritan (Kant 1998: 171).

But Kant's anti-ritualism and thorough distrust of surfaces allow me to foreground, by means of cosmological contrast, the Japanese practices of praying at shrines with which my inquiry is concerned. For here, it is, in part, precisely the sensuous and technical aspects – the surfaces – of ritual form that make it efficacious. And this is where cosmology comes into the picture. Of course, in our everyday talk, we might be liable to assume that cosmology must refer to something of gigantic size and infinite depth (*deep space*) or to stories of absolute origin (*Big Bangs*) (Tresch 2005: 352), but the cosmology I aim to model here is arranged along its surfaces and is open to the efficacy of simulation. In characterising it as 'cosmetic', I do not mean to refer to make-up per se – though how curious that we give the name of *foundation* to that thinnest skin of emulsion, sponged across a face! Rather, what I intend is to exploit this obvious etymological relation between cosmetics and cosmos, in order to imagine how a cosmology might be constituted in facades and fabricating practices.[13] Practices of prayer in Japan seem difficult to fathom because, *at depth*, there appears to be little there. In fact, such practices, we might feel, almost smack of the theatrical (what Kant would denounce as 'pious play-acting and nothing-doing'; 1998: 168). But such feelings, I would hazard, are arguably the kinds of anxieties triggered when a 'depth ontology', as Daniel Miller christens it, comes up against a counterforce of thought that takes surfaces seriously. As Miller goes on to observe, the devaluation of outsides, of the ephemeral, as somehow lacking content 'becomes highly problematic... when we encounter a cosmology which may not share these assumptions, and rests upon a very different sense of ontology' (Miller 1994: 71).

Belief or efficacy?

Japanese practices that centre on shrines are thoroughly pragmatic engagements. I recall once, almost ten years ago, paying a visit to the Hitomaru Shrine in Akashi (western Japan). With me came Maeda-san (the owner of a prominent local business selling soy sauce), in his early seventies though very much *genki* (fit and cheerful), with a puckish sense of humour. Having made some perfunctory prayers – tossing a coin into the offering box, clapping and bowing – I decided to buy an *ema*, a votive plaque. With the felt-tip in my hand, still thinking about what I ought to write, Maeda-san shouted at me across the precinct, 'The god won't understand English!' (*kami-san wa eigo wakarahen de*); both a joke and a dismissal. Notice here that there is no talk of believing, just a half-serious concern with getting the language right. It strikes me now that what Maeda-san was getting at was the question of efficacy – the issue of whether or not the message would work. And, in its way, this crucial sense of efficacy, to my mind, recalls the lesson of Niels Bohr's horseshoe. The story goes that someone once asked Bohr whether he believed that the horseshoes hanging over his door would bring him luck. 'No,' he replied, 'but I am told that they bring luck even to those who do not believe in them' (Elster 1983: 5). Not belief then, but efficacy. As Pirotte points out, the famous physicist was, at that moment, articulating animist principles (2010: 203).[14]

I guess that, were we to take this story seriously – to take it in and nail it above all our doors, as it were – our accounts of Japanese shrine-going might gain a little more felicity (to advert to a term of J.L. Austin's; Austin 1962). This is so because, although much is made of the sheer performativity and pragmatism of everyday Japanese religious practice, scholars who write on these matters often end up, *anyway*, in the position of assuming some inner space populated by beliefs or some similar 'backstage artiste' (another Austinian expression; 1962: 10). To give an instance: in an excellent and thoroughgoing ethnography of quotidian religion in Japan, Reader and Tanabe confront the well-documented ethnographic problem 'that people sincerely purchase amulets but do not really believe in them' (1998: 129). From this they deduce that such activities do not involve what they call 'cognitive belief' and they caution against 'the common error on the part of investigators' to suppose that an inner domain of well-formed representations must be motivating the surface of practice (1998:130-31). Nevertheless, rather than draw (what I would regard as) the obvious animist consequences from this observation, they go on to suggest that the system of practice is founded on what they designate as 'affective beliefs', by which they mean intimate and emotional attachments to such things as amulets (1998: 129-31). Yes – but why persist in calling these 'beliefs'? Something of the confusion of their position is, I think, evident when they try to explain that there are, of course, multiple means of apprehending a world, hence, 'cognition and intellectual thought are not the only ways by which the world can be affirmed and *believed in*' (1998: 129; my emphasis). But to say that there are many ways, beyond the cognitive, in which a world can be believed in is still to suppose that the foundational relation is one of belief. This is exactly the problem with the notion of 'affective belief'; it merely consecrates the concept of belief and establishes it at an even more fundamental level.

In an argument that lacks even the nuance of Reader and Tanabe's discussion, Martinez, writing of a fishing community in Western Japan, engages in an inconsequential excursus on Japanese religion in general in which she seems to say, on the one hand, that the Japanese don't believe, and then, on the other, that after all, they do (2004: 70-72). In a mild rebuke of Reader and Tanabe's position, Martinez claims that Japanese popular religiosity should not simply be understood as praxical and pragmatic because, 'the belief in spirits and ancestor worship still holds a powerful place in the lives of many Japanese', and anyhow, she says straight away, to overly focus on the pragmatic is to overlook 'issues of power and politics' (2004: 72). The reader is then dutifully referred to Asad's (1994) seminal deconstruction of Geertz's thesis on religion. All well and good, perhaps, but I find it strange that someone who is able to cite Asad's argument can so casually and uncritically speak of

Japanese 'belief in spirits'. In discussions such as these, everything happens as if forty years of sustained and critical anthropological attention paid towards the concept of belief never took place.

Of course, none of this is to suggest that Japanese practices do not involve the ideational, the conceptual, etc. Rather, to chime in with the findings of Inge Daniels (2003; 2010), relations with divinities in Japan are neither established by means of belief nor are they conceptualised in these terms.

The efficacy of the artificial

And so, at last, on to matters cosmological. In an influential article (Yamaguchi 1991b), the implications of which have not, I think, been fully appreciated, the anthropologist Masao Yamaguchi draws attention to a Japanese presentational technique known as *mitate* (lit. 'seeing-standing'). This is a kind of imaging technique for the conceptualisation of something presented in terms of something else distant or absent. In the process, a kind of conceptual contiguity is established that directs attention to the invisible or virtual dimensions of the thing so presented. To illustrate this, Yamaguchi cites an example from the famous tenth century *Pillow Book* (*Makura no sôshi*):

> 'In this episode a princess asks her ladies-in-waiting what name they would give a scene of a snow-covered mound in a garden. One of them immediately replies, "The snow on Mount Koro in China" (Koro is the mountain well known in the classics for the beauty of its scenery after a snowfall). The image of the snow-covered mound was given a mythological dimension by associating it with a well-known image from the Chinese classics' (1991b: 58).

Here, a relation of reference is established between a present object (a snow-covered mound in the garden) and an absent one (a Chinese mountain). The former playfully 'quotes' the latter. It is for this reason that Yamaguchi refers to *mitate* as an 'art of citation'. But as Yamaguchi makes clear (1991b: 64), the technique of *mitate* is not limited to rarefied contexts such as this; it is extensively deployed in the presentation of offerings to divinities (*kami*). Thus, in her ethnography of ascetic practices on Akakura Mountain in Aomori Prefecture, Schattschneider (herself drawing on Yamaguchi) describes how worshippers actualize this technique of *mitate* in their presentation of offerings to the mountain divinities (2003: 55-56). The offerings themselves are constructed and arranged as microcosmic 'citations' of the mountain itself; thus, glutinous rice cakes (*mochi*) 'are carefully piled in the shapes of miniature mountains. Mounds of raw rice are shaped into perfect cones. Offered metal bells are sculpted into vertical, mountain-like towers'. In such ways, these offered objects are so many simulations of the mountain itself (2003: 56; cf. Nobuo 1994: 38).

Note that this bringing into relation that *mitate* achieves cannot easily be reduced to a process of metaphor. According to Yukio Hattori, *mitate* is rather 'a powerful procedure for the realization of novel creations' (Hattori 1975: 192; my translation). In a similar regard, Yamaguchi himself likens the notion of *mitate* to Baudrillard's concept of the simulacrum; in the sense, I suppose, that the objects mobilized by *mitate* are not merely copies, but things that are capable of establishing their own realities (1991b: 66).[15] In any case, what the concept of *mitate* articulates is a notion of the efficacy of artificial, material creation. Artificiality is effective, *because* it is artificial – to say this is merely to repeat the insight of Chikamatsu, that great 17th century innovator of the *bunraku* puppet theatre (see Bolton 2002: 739, 744). Or, to put it another way, we find in this idea the recognition that the deliberate mobilisation and manipulation of forms, on a cosmetic level, can have cosmological consequences.

All of this is especially pertinent to the Japanese practices of prayer with which I began my inquiry, because, as Yamaguchi remarks (borrowing his argument from Masakatsu Gunji's study of the aesthetics of festival practices; Gunji 1987), 'Japanese gods do not appreciate true things; they do not accept things that are not fabricated by means of a device' (1991b: 64).[16] To recall the Geertzian injunction that troubled our fictional anthropologist, on the need to sort out real prayers from mimicked ones, it is as if, in this case, the mimicked prayer is the real one – so long as it is well fabricated.

Conclusion

In conclusion, we turn to mirrors again. Mirrors are often the supports or containers (*go-shintai*) within which the *kami* (gods) reside – *kami* being almost always aniconically evoked. The *go-shintai* (lit. 'body of divinity') may actually be any number of things – a painting, a mountain, a sword, a waterfall, etc. But mirrors are said to be the most common containers; not that anyone would know however. The *go-shintai* is generally concealed at the back of the shrine, inaccessible to the public. But there are mirrors that are regularly displayed in shrines, as evocations of brightness and purity. These visible mirrors are associated with the most important object among the 'three imperial regalia' (*sanshu no jingi*), this object being itself a mirror that permanently remains, concealed in multiple boxes, at the Grand Shrine of Ise, in Mie Prefecture. Ise enshrines the imperial divinity of the sun, Amaterasu Ômikami – the deity, incidentally, to whom James Bond did his simulated praying. But it is with a myth of this mirror that I want to end; a myth first recorded in the early eighth century, and systemically simulated ever since.[17]

According to this myth (called *Iwato-biraki*, or 'opening of the rock door'), the *kami* of the sun, Amaterasu, shuts herself up in a cave and so the whole world goes dark. The other divinities devise a scheme to lure her out again. Assembling before the cave door, they suspend a mirror from the branches of a tree while one of them, the divinity Ame-no-Uzume begins to dance in a frenzy of possession. All the *kami* laugh and, hearing their laughter, Amaterasu opens the cave door in curiosity. On seeing herself reflected in the mirror, she believes she is looking at another, superior divinity; while frozen in this moment of bewilderment, the other *kami* block the cave mouth. Light is restored to the world.

Now, a lot could be said about this; but I feel I have already said more than enough. The mirror, as a device, is efficacious *because* it simulates. Commenting on the myth, Schattschneider suggests that

> 'Life itself is thus founded on an initially illusory act of representation, a potent confounding of presence and absence, merging the imitative image with the represented thing itself' (2004: 145).

If this myth contained a credo – which it doesn't; it's not *deep* enough for that – we could well refer to it as the Doctrine of Original Sim, the myth of the genuinely artificial.

As Arata Isozaki (2006: 154) observes, in a discussion of the Ise Shrine and the efficacy of fabrication: 'the gods always reveal themselves at the invitation of mimicry'.

Notes

Acknowledgements. This paper was originally presented at the Cosmology Workshop, Department of Anthropology, University College London. Hence, once again, thanks are owed to Martin Holbraad, Ioannis Kyriakakis, and Fabio Gygi.

1. For example, Buruma (1995); Hendry (1993); Köpping (2005); McVeigh (1997; 2000); Yamaguchi (1977). In arriving at the ideas presented here, I have also drawn inspiration from both Hay's and Zito's studies of the work of surfaces in Chinese cosmologies (see Hay 1994; Zito 1994).

2. I should make it clear that this inference, that the

businessman's prayer is *merely* superficial, in so far as it is in want of something else, is emphatically not one made by Kasulis. Indeed, he is intent on challenging any such notion; his argument being that practice of this sort is an attempt to establish existential connections with divinities in Japan (See Kasulis 2004: 28-37). The problematic of prayer is a useful entry point into issues of Japanese religious practice. Reader (1991: 1-2), for instance, begins his own overview on Japanese religion with a similar vignette.

3. For a critique of these sociological assumptions by means of Japanese ethnographic materials, see Swift (forthcoming).

4. It is worth recalling that Sahlins (1999: 407-9) too made a case for taking Japanese cosmology seriously, by way of a critique of an argument (one of the contributions in Vlastos 1998) that much of the form of sumo wrestling can be explained by the fact that it is a modern invention. Indeed, the Japanese anthropologist Yamaguchi Masao (1998) has explored the cosmological dimensions of sumo and its relations to kabuki theatre and the emperor system. For Yamaguchi, sumo is clearly a dynamic historical formation, in which the cosmological and the commercial are mutually implicated. I therefore fail to understand how the editor of the collection to which Yamaguchi is a contributor can state that Yamaguchi 'implies that this very Japanese "tradition" might well fall into the category of a modern invented tradition' (Martinez 1998: 13). Yamaguchi's exposition is certainly subtle, as the editor points out, and it is precisely because it is that it contains no such simplistic implications.

5. The anthropologist John Clammer has argued this point (with regard to the understanding of Japan) with singularity clarity (Clammer 2001). But see also the collection of papers edited by Gerstle and Milner (1994), a project by various Asian Studies scholars to recover 'otherness' in the light of Said's critique.

6. These remarks that Robertson includes in her introduction were, as she makes clear, in fact first published in 1998 (Robertson 2005: 4).

7. Hdt. 2.35 (Herodotus 1988: 145). For the classic study of such mirror operations in Herodotus, see Hartog (1988).

8. As Yamada (2009) has recently documented of what he calls the 'magic mirror effect' of two-way traffic in representations of Zen – when those others we thought we were representing pick up our depictions in order to represent themselves, then the mirrors multiply to such an extent that all that would seem to be left is the dazzling spectacle of representations rebounding endlessly. Similarly, writing of the problems that foreign anthropologists face in attempting to represent Japan, Caillet (2006: 11) comments that it can seem as if 'our positions disintegrate into a game of mirrors without end' ('*un jeu de miroirs sans fin*').

   Be that as it may, Robertson's critique of mirror-imaging is valuable, but it is hardly new. Horton and Finnegan (1973) already raised a number of these points almost forty years ago (see also Nagashima's essay in the same volume).

9. The references are, respectively: Singer (1997); Buruma (1995); Wetering (1987); Ohnuki-Tierney (1987); and Vlastos (1998). And fanciful no doubt, but is Ian Fleming's title, *You Only Live Twice*, not also suggestive of a certain mirror-like doubling?

10. Accordingly, Macfarlane deliberately identifies himself with Alice (2007: 4), but he might just as well be Dorothy in *The Wizard of Oz*, for, in its supersaturated strangeness, Japan is the Emerald City and to be in Kansai is to be told, like Toto, that we're not in Kansas anymore.

11. Among numerous examples, one could cite the *Great Mirror* (*Ôkagami*), a history of the Fujiwara aristocratic lineage, or the *Great Mirror of Love Suicide* (*Shinjû ôkagami*) that documented a series of scandalous double suicides – a source of much popular fascination during the early 1700s. Or the *Complete Mirror of Yoshiwara* (*Yoshiwara marukagami*), a sort of guidebook (from 1720) to the Yoshiwara pleasure quarters in Edo (i.e., Tokyo).

12. I haven't the space to do justice to Wardle's exposition, except to say here that his observation (2009: 3; cf. 19) that Latour's 'comparative anthropology' may well be too 'insufficiently comparative' is, I think, especially well made.

13. I say that this etymological relation is obvious – it is, at least, to classicists. But I have found little work in anthropology that has explored its implications. An exception is Lamp's (1985) fine study of Temne ritual masking in Sierra Leone. A further exception, recently discovered, is, as I ought to have expected, Lévi-Strauss, who puts it to use in his analysis of Caduveo body painting (Wiseman 2007: chap. 6, esp. 146).

14. I cite Elster's version of the anecdote. Needless to say, I do not agree with his interpretation of it.

15. Joy Hendry (2000: 180) has attempted to utilize Yamaguchi's argument in her ethnography on Japanese theme parks, but her ensuing analysis make abundantly clear that she hasn't understood it. Attacking a vague post-modernist position that she attributes to no one, she attempts to counter it by employing Yamaguchi's discussion of *mitate* as simulation which, she says, is 'close to the original meaning of Baudrillard's "simulacrum", a term too easily translated as "fake"'. Apart from wondering to whom this final caution is supposed to apply (who, after all, is all too easily making such equations?), one can only imagine Baudrillard laughing (somewhere in hyper-reality) about this straight-faced appeal to his *original* meaning! Hendry then goes on (in the same paragraph) to associate *mitate* as simulation with Platonic Forms, seemingly unaware that Plato was the arch-enemy of simulacra.

16. For Gunji's original discussion see Gunji (1987: 88-89).

17. The myth and its subsequent history have very recently been treated by Mark Teeuwen (Teeuwen and Breen 2010: chap. 4).

References

Asad, Talal. 1993. *Genealogies of Religion: Discipline and Power in Christianity and Islam*. Johns Hopkins University Press.

Austin, J.L. 1962. *How to do things with Words* (ed.) J.O. Urmson. Oxford University Press.

Barthes, Roland. 1983. *Empire of Signs* (trans. R. Howard). London: Jonathan Cape.

Barthes, Roland. 2005. *L'Empire des signes*. Paris: Éditions du Seuil.

Benedict, Ruth. 1967. *The Chrysanthemum and the Sword: Patterns of Japanese Culture*. London: Routledge & Kegan Paul.

Boas, Franz. 1996. The Study of Geography. Reprinted in *Volksgeist as Method and Ethic* (ed.) G.W. Stocking, 9-16. University of Wisconsin Press.

Bolton, Christopher A. 2002. From Wooden Cyborgs to Celluloid Souls: mechanical Bodies in Anime and Japanese Puppet Theatre. *Positions* 10 (3): 729-71.

Buruma, Ian. 1995. *A Japanese Mirror: Heroes and Villains of Japanese Culture*. London: Vintage.

Caillet, Laurence. 2006. Introduction. *Ateliers du LESC* 30: 9-34. <http://ateliers.revues.org/71> (Retrieved on: 30/03/06)

Chamberlain, Basil Hall. 2007. *Things Japanese: Being Notes on Various Subjects Connected with Japan*. Tokyo: IBC Publishing.

Clammer, John. 2001. *Japan and Its Others: Globalization, Difference and the Critique of Modernity*.

Melbourne: Trans Pacific Press.

Cowan, Douglas E., & David G. Bromley. 2008. *Cults and New Religions: A Brief History*. Oxford: Blackwell.

Dale, Peter. 1995. *The Myth of Japanese Uniqueness*. London: Routledge.

Daniels, Inge Maria. 2003. Scooping, Raking, Beckoning Luck: Luck, Agency and the Interdependence between People and Things in Japan. *Journal of the Royal Anthropological Institute* 9 (4): 619-38.

Daniels, Inge Maria. 2010. 'Dolls are scary': the locus of the spiritual in contemporary Japanese homes. In *Religion and Material Culture: The Matter of Belief* (ed.) D. Morgan, 153-70. London: Routledge.

Elster, Jon. 1983. *Sour Grapes: Studies in the subversion of rationality*. Cambridge University Press.

Fernandez, James W. 1986. Some Reflections on Looking into Mirrors. In *Persuasions and Performances: The Play of Tropes in Culture*, J.W. Fernandez, 157-171. Indiana University Press.

Fleming, Ian. 1965. *You Only Live Twice*. London: Pan Books

Geertz, Clifford. 1993. *The Interpretation of Cultures: Selected Essays*. London: Fontana Press.

Gerstle, Andrew & Anthony Milner. 1994. *Recovering the Orient: Artists, Scholars,Appropriations*. Chur, Switzerland: Harwood Academic Publishers.

Gunji, Masakatsu. 1987. *Furyû no zuzôshi* [The Iconography of Elegant Custom]. Tokyo: Sanseido.

Handelman, Don. 2008. Afterword: Returning to

Cosmology – Thoughts on the Positioning of Belief. *Social Analysis* 52 (1): 181-95.

Hattori, Yukio. 1975. *Henkaron: kabuki no seishinshi* [The theory of changes: a spiritual history of Kabuki]. Tokyo: Heibonsha.

Hartog, François. 1988. *The Mirror of Herodotus: The Representation of the Other in the Writing of History* (trans. J. Lloyd). University of California Press.

Hay, John. 1994. Boundaries and Surfaces of Self and Desire in Yuan Painting. In *Boundaries in China* (ed.) John Hay, 124-70. London: Reaktion Books.

Hendry, Joy. 1993. *Wrapping Culture: Politeness, presentation, and power in Japan and other societies.* Oxford University Press.

Hendry, Joy. 2000. *The Orient Strikes Back: A Global View of Cultural Display.* Oxford: Berg.

Herodotus. 1988. *The History* (trans. D. Grene). Chicago University Press.

Humboldt, Alexander von. 1860. *Cosmos: A Sketch of a Physical Description of the Universe*, Vol. 1 (trans. E.C. Otté). New York: Harper & Brothers.

Horton, Robin & Ruth Finnegan. 1973. Introduction. In *Modes of Thought: Essays on Thinking in Western and Non-Western Societies* (eds.) R. Horton & R. Finnegan, 13-62. London: Faber & Faber.

Isozaki, Arata. 2006. *Japan-ness in Architecture* (trans. S. Kohso). MIT Press.

Jullien, François. 2003. 'China as Philosophical Tool': François Jullien in conversation with Thierry Zarcone.

Diogenes 50 (4): 15-21.

Kant, Immanuel. 1998. *Religion with the Boundaries of Mere Reason and Other Writings* (trans. A. Wood & G. di Giovanni). (Eds) A. Wood & G. di Giovanni. Cambridge University Press.

Kasulis, Thomas P. 2004. *Shinto: The Way Home*. University of Hawai'i Press.

Köpping, Klaus-Peter. 2005. Masking as Ludic Practice of Selfhood in Japan. *Culture and Psychology* 11 (1): 29-46.

Lamp, Frederick. 1985. Cosmos, Cosmetics, and the Spirit of Bondo. *African Arts* 18 (3): 28-43, 98-99.

Latour, Bruno. 2004. How to Talk About the Body? The Normative Dimension of Science Studies. *Body & Society* 10 (2-3): 205-229.

Macfarlane, Alan. 2007. *Japan Through the Looking Glass*. London: Profile Books.

Martinez, D.P. 1998. Gender, Shifting Boundaries and Global Cultures. In *The Worlds of Japanese Popular Culture: Gender, Shifting Boundaries and Global Cultures* (ed.) D.P. Martinez, 1-18. Cambridge University Press.

Martinez, D.P. 2004. *Identity and Ritual in a Japanese Diving Village: The Making and Becoming of Person and Place*. University of Hawai'i Press.

McVeigh, Brian J. 1997. *Life in a Japanese Women's College: Learning to be ladylike*. London: Routledge.

McVeigh, Brian J. 2000. *Wearing Ideology: State, Schooling and Self-Presentation in Japan*. Oxford: Berg.

Miller, Daniel [inexplicably credited as 'David' (sic!)]. 1994. Style and Ontology. In *Consumption and Identity* (ed.) J. Friedman, 71-96. Chur, Switzerland: Harwood Academic Publishers.

Nelson, John K. 1996. Freedom of Expression: The Very Modern Practice of Visiting a Shinto Shrine. *Japanese Journal of Religious Studies* 23:1-2:117-153.

Nobuo, Tsuji. 1994. Ornament (Kazari) – An Approach to Japanese Culture. *Archives of Asian Art* XLVII: 35-45.

Ohnuki-Tierney, Emiko. 1987. *The Monkey as Mirror: Symbolic Transformations in Japanese History and Ritual.* Princeton University Press.

Pirotte, Philippe. 2010. Absentminded Wandering through an Indeterminate Maze of Intentionality. In *Animism* Vol. 1 (ed.) A. Franke, 203-14. Berlin: Sternberg Press.

Reader, Ian. 1991. *Religion in Contemporary Japan.* Basingstoke: Macmillan Press.

Reader, Ian & George J. Tanabe. 1998. *Practically Religious: Worldly Benefits and the Common Religion of Japan.* University of Hawai'i Press.

Robbins, Joel. 2002. On the Critical Uses of Difference: The Uninvited Guest and *The Invention of Culture. Social Analysis* 46 (1): 4-11.

Robertson, Jennifer. 2002. Reflexivity Redux: A Pithy Polemic on 'Positionality'. *Anthropological Quarterly* 75:4: 785-92.

Robertson, Jennifer. 2005. Introduction: Putting and Keeping Japan in Anthropology. In *A Companion to the Anthropology of Japan* (ed.) J. Robertson, 3-16. Oxford: Blackwell.

Sahlins, Marshall. 1999. Two or three things that I know about culture. *Journal of the Royal Anthropological Institute* 5: 399-421.

Schattschneider, Ellen. 2003. *Immortal Wishes: Labor and Transcendence on a Japanese Sacred Mountain.* Duke University Press.

Schattschneider, Ellen. 2004. Family Resemblances: Memorial Images and the Face of Kinship. *Japanese Journal of Religious Studies*, 31 (1): 141-62.

Singer, Kurt. 1997. *Mirror, Sword and Jewel: A Study of Japanese Characteristics.* Richmond: Curzon Press.

Swift, Philip. Forthcoming. Touching Conversion: Tangible Transformations in a Japanese New Religion.

Taylor, Christopher C.1999. *Sacrifice as Terror: The Rwandan Genocide of 1994.* Oxford: Berg.

Tresch, John. 2005. ¡Viva la República Cósmica! Or The Children of Humboldt and Coca-Cola. In *Making Things Public: Atmospheres of Democracy* (eds) B. Latour & P. Weibel, 352-6. MIT Press.

Tueewen, Mark & John Breen. 2010. *A New History of Shinto.* Oxford: Wiley-Blackwell.

Viveiros de Castro, Eduardo. 2001. GUT Feelings about Amazonia: Potential Affinity and the Construction of Sociality. In *Beyond the Visible and the Material: The Amerindianization of Society in the Work of Peter Rivière* (eds) L.M. Rival & N.L. Whitehead, 19-43. Oxford University Press.

Viveiros de Castro, Eduardo. 2007. The Crystal Forest: Notes on the Ontology of Amazonian Spirits. *Inner Asia* 9: 153-72.

Vlastos, Stephen. 1998. *Mirror of Modernity: Invented Traditions of Modern Japan*. University of California Press.

Wardle, Huon. 2009. Cosmopolitics and Common Sense. *OAC Working Papers Series 1*. Open Anthropology Cooperative Press.

Wetering, Janwillem van de. 1987. *The Empty Mirror: Experiences in a Japanese Zen Monastery*. London: Arkana.

Wiseman, Boris. 2007. *Lévi-Strauss, Anthropology and Aesthetics*. Cambridge University Press.

Yamada, Shoji. 2009. *Shots in the Dark: Japan, Zen and the West* (trans. E. Hartman). Chicago University Press.

Yamaguchi, Masao. 1977. Kingship, Theatricality, and Marginal Reality in Japan. In *Text and Context: The Social Anthropology of Tradition* (ed.) R.K. Jain, 151-79. Philadelphia: ISHI.

Yamaguchi, Masao. 1991a. Cosmological Dimension of the Japanese Theater. In *The Empire of Signs: Semiotic Essays on Japanese Culture* (ed.) Yoshihiko Ikegami, 219-40. Amsterdam: John Benjamins Publishing Company.

Yamaguchi, Masao. 1991b. The Poetics of Exhibition in Japanese Culture. In *Exhibiting Cultures: The Poetics and Politics of Museum Display* (eds.) I. Karp & S.D. Levine, 57-67. Smithsonian Institution Press.

Yamaguchi, Masao. 1998. Sumo in the Popular Culture of Contemporary Japan. In *The Worlds of Japanese Popular Culture: Gender, Shifting Boundaries and Global Cultures* (ed.) D.P. Martinez, 19-29. Cambridge University Press.

Zito, Angela. 1994. Silk and Skin: Significant Boundaries.

In *Body, Subject and Power in China* (eds) A. Zito & T.E. Barlow, 103-30. Chicago University Press.

Chapter 7

WHY DO THE GODS LOOK LIKE THAT? MATERIAL EMBODIMENTS OF SHIFTING MEANINGS

John McCreery

Prologue

I invite you to imagine a tourist visiting Japan. She has seen a number of Buddhist temples and Shinto shrines. Friends take her to Yokohama's Chinatown for dinner. On the way to the restaurant they stop for a look at a Chinese temple, the Guandi Miao. The vivid colors and baroque decoration of the Chinese temple contrasts sharply with the subdued simplicity of Japanese Buddhist temples and shrines (Figures 1, and 2). The red face and piercing eyes of the Chinese deity on this altar (Figure 3) differ dramatically from the lowered eye-lids and meditative serenity of the Japanese Buddhas (Figure 4) she has seen. In Japanese Shinto shrines, the gods are not visible at all (Figure 5). The question she asks is simple but profound: "Why do Chinese gods look like that?"

When, however, we turn to the anthropological literature on Chinese religion, we discover, as Wei-Ping Lin points out, that anthropologists have paid little attention to the material forms that gods take in their statues on Chinese altars (2008:454-455). Instead of looking closely at god statues to discover what they might tell us about the gods in question, we have tended to look *through* god statues in search of something else. The statues themselves are treated as arbitrary signs, as, in effect, texts, whose material form is of no intrinsic interest.

If we adopt, instead, an art historical or connoisseur's perspective, we encounter a different approach. Here the primary focus of interest is iconographic details that that identify the god or the style in which the statue is carved, with the style then further specified geographically and historically. Once again, however, the existence of the statue is taken for granted.

In the Japanese context in which our tourist asks, "Why do Chinese gods look like that?" her question points to larger issues. We have noted that the demeanour of Japanese Buddhas is noticeably different from that of Chinese gods. The contrast sharpens when we turn to Shinto shrines, in which there are no god statues at all; Shinto deities remain invisible. If we go a step further in enlarging our context, we encounter Protestant Christianity, Judaism and Islam, religions that taboo any attempt to represent deity in anthroporphic images.

> Lin tells us that in Wan-nian, the village in Taiwan where she did her fieldwork, she was told that,

> Gods are formless. When you call them, they come! (2008: 459)

> They are three feet above your head (*Gia-thau sann-chioh u sin-bing; Jutou sanche you shenming*)! (2008:460)

They have no shadows and leave no trace (*Lai bo-iann, khi bo-cong; Lai wuying, qu wuzong*).

Why, then, are there statues of gods on Chinese altars? Lin asks a spirit medium,

Why do people need god statues, and what is the relationship between gods with and without form? (2008:460)

The medium responds,

Everyone respects and prays to gods, but they 'have no shadows and leave no trace,' so people carve statues to make the gods settle down where they want them. That means to contain them inside the statues. People should worship the statues, so that a special bond grows between gods and worshippers. If the bond is strong, the spirit won't leave. (208:460)

As Lin points out, the medium's interpretation has several implications: people need images in order to believe. Images are places for gods to reside. They also facilitate a particular kind of relationship.

God statues make the formless omnipresent gods settle down and build a stable connection with the villagers, who worship them in return for protection; this creates a strong reciprocal bond between the villagers and the gods. (208:460)

The remainder of Lin's paper provides a wealth of evidence for this interpretation and focuses, in particular, on steps taken to localize the god's attachment to a particular community. We may note, however, that while this paper explains in detail how god statues are made, consecrated, and localized, it contains no answer to the question why Chinese god statues depict Chinese gods in the way that they do. We are neither shown or told what these particular statues look like. And one nagging, but fundamental, issue remains. Lin's informants tell us that Chinese worshippers require images to reinforce their belief and, further, that god statues contribue to creation of strong reciprocal bonds. But why should this be, when worshippers in other traditions do not require images — in fact, their traditions forbid them?

We are still, then, at the point described by Alfred Gell in "The Technology of Enchantment," when he says of Bourdieu's sociological approach and Panofsky's iconographic approach that the former, " never actually looks at the art object iteself," while the latter, "treats art as a species of writing" and thus fails to consider the object itself, instead of the symbolic meanings attributed to it (2009: 10). My purpose here is to consider what we might learn by going a step further and considering the object itself.

Adding the Material, Thickening the Description

In this case the object itself is a god statue, the statue of Guandi that sits on the altar of the Guandi Miao in Yokohama's Chinatown. To learn more about it, I compare it with other representations of Chinese gods, including, in particular, other images of Guandi himself. I want to emphasize, however, that the approach taken here is to add investigation of the material forms in which Guandi is represented to advance a deeper understanding that also includes the other approaches to Chinese religion sketched above. It does not propose to replace them.

The approach I employ is inspired by Claude Levi-Strauss' injunction in the "Overture" to *The Raw and the Cooked* to search for the logic in tangible qualities (1970:1) and by Clifford Geertz' call for thick descriptions in *The Interpretation of Cultures* (1973). The model I attempt to follow, however, is that provided by Victor Turner in *The Ritual Process* (1969), enriched by recent discussions of the importance of material cultures and objects to cultural understanding (Miller, 1998;

Candlin and Guins, 2009). It is, in other words, informed by Turner's approach to ethnography but also a contribution to what Daniel Miller calls the second stage in the development of material culture studies, in which the goal is to demonstrate, "what is to be gained by focusing upon the diversity of material worlds which become each other's contexts rather than reducing them either to models of the social world or to specific subdisciplinary concerns" (1998: 3).

Context is, however, a particularly tricky issue. When Levi-Strauss looks at tangible qualities, he is searching for universal structures that shape cultures everywhere and pointing to binary contrasts, e.g., the raw and the cooked, that appear fundamental in human thinking everywhere. His context is all of humanity. Geertz directs our attention, instead, to the richness of layered meanings that interpreters of culture must seek to unpack in particular situations. He leaves unanswered, however, a fundamental question: where does the relevant context begin or end?

Is it found in that place and moment where the observation is made or the informant's comment collected? Our tourist is looking at a statue of Guandi in a temple in a Chinatown located in Yokohama, Japan. Is the significance of what she sees confined to this particular temple in this particular location? Or to what someone she meets at the temple may tell her? Or, this being the twenty-first century, should we take as authoritative the account provided on the temple's Website? If not, how far should we search for connections, in Chinese culture and history? In specific Chinese or religious traditions? Across the length and breadth of Asia? There is, I suggest, no a priori answer. Depending on the observation, any and all of these contexts may be relevant.

When working in a conventional social science framework, the limits-of-context problem is easy to overlook. We pre-select the scope of our research, develop an hypothesis within it, then search for evidence that confirms or contradicts the hypothesis we are testing. The same is true when doing qualitative research, if we start with a well-defined topic. The topic's definition defines the limits of relevance.

Invert the problem, however, and start with the observation, the tangible thing itself, a case of something, but we don't yet know of what. As ethnographers we are not supposed to make assumptions. But, as noted in *The SAGE Handbook of Case-based Methods*,

> From a trans-disciplinary perspective, what unites different kinds of cases, regardless of the discipline, is that all cases are complex and multi-dimensional objects of study. Furthermore, all cases are situated in time and space, as are the disciplines within which they might be situated. Arguably, therefore all cases, as objects of study, need to be described in an ever-increasing and changing variety of ways, and each of these ways may in fact be representing something 'real' about the object of study as well. (2009: 141-142)

Thus, for example, when I wrote "Why don't we see some real money here?" (1990) I began by observing the difference between spirit money and offerings of food in Chinese rituals. I wanted to know why the money was mock money, while the food was real food. Combining ideas from Levi-Strauss and James Fernandez and looking at the ritual process, I developed the hypothesis that the food asserts a relationship; the money restores social distance. In "Negotiating with demons" (1995) I began with the text of a Taoist exorcism and three approaches to analyzing magical language, as performative act, metaphor, and formalized, restricted code. Each did, in fact, show something real about the case in hand, and together the three approaches produced a richer thick description than any one approach by itself.

In this case, I will focus on why some representations of gods are fully rounded figures, seated or standing, some in dynamic poses, while others are literally flat tablets on which a title is written. I will argue, in a Levi-Straussian mode, that this contrast embodies the difference between abstract, and thus absolute, claims to authority and concrete, more personal relationships, rooted in reciprocity that opens the way for exchanges of gifts and favors. I will situate this argument in a Geertzian thick description that builds on existing scholarly analyses of Chinese gods that relate the ways in which gods are envisioned to structure and change in Chinese society. I will speculate on possible extensions of this analysis to comparisons between Chinese popular religion and other religious traditions.

First, however, we need some empirical grounding. Here my model is Victor Turner, who taught us that anthropologists always work with three kinds of data: What we observe, what the people whose lives we study tell us about what we see, and information from other places, ideas and other data that inform interpretation. All are parts of the puzzle from which the anthropologist attempts to construct a convincing picture of the whole of what he is writing about. The place to begin, however, is the way in which the people we study explain their own symbols. I begin, then, with the contents of the Yokohama Guandi Miao website (http://www.yokohama-kanteibyo.com/).

A Twenty-First Century Chinese Temple in Japan

The Yokohama Guandi Miao website (http://www.yokohama-kanteibyo.com/) is in Japanese. Its intended audience appears to be Japanese tourists who flock to Yokohama's Chinatown to enjoy a local but exotic experience. The top page displays a link to Yokohama Chinatown's own official website (http://www.chinatown.or.jp/). Three additional buttons are indicated on the photograph of the temple's main gate that is the single largest visual element on the page. Button No. 1 opens a description of the gate, which towers 12 meters above street level. Its elaborate wood carvings are covered with gold leaf, and two dragons sit (one on each side) on the top of its roof. Button No. 2 opens a description of the stone slabs with images of dragons cavorting in the clouds that frame the stairs leading up to the gate. Imported from Beijing, the slabs are single pieces of stone, each weighing four and a half tons. A third, cloud-shaped blue button reads, "Go inside."

The camera has now moved through the gate, and the temple proper fills the frame. Now there are five buttons that point to information on visually interesting details. Button No. 3 describes the colorful tiles on the roof. Like the stone slabs to which Button No. 2 pointed, these, too, were specially ordered from Beijing. They are attached with special hooks to enhance rain and wind resistance. Dragons and other beasts made of glass complete the rooftop decorations. Button No. 4 describes four elaborately carved stone columns, two with dragons, two with images of Guandi in action. These were imported from Taiwan. Button No. 5 describes the main incense burner and notes that it is one of five incense burners. Those who wish to worship are directed to purchase five sticks of incense, one for each of the burners. Button No. 6 shows the reception building where incense and spirit money can be purchased. Button No. 7 describes the stone lions that guard the temple, noting that they were imported from Taiwan and survived the fire that in 1986 destroyed the previous version of the temple. Another blue cloud invites the visitor to enter the temple.

Now the image contains five pictures, each with a button of its own. The largest, which fills three quarters of the frame, shows the main altar, where a seated Guandi, stroking his long beard, looks straight toward the visitor. Button No. 8 reveals the following brief description.

> The divine form of Guanyu, a Chinese general who lived around 160 a.d. His loyalty and fidelity have made him a god of commerce worshipped around

the world. On his left stands his adopted son, Goan Ping, on his right his faithful follower Zhou Zang. Both also receive worship.

Beneath this description are four phrases highlighted in blue, indicating prayers for which Guandi is especially efficacious: traffic safety, business success, entrance exams, and study.

Buttons No. 9, 10, and 11 point to descriptions of other deities worshipped at the temple: Earth Mother, the Bodhisattva Kwannon, and Tu-di Gong. These also include areas in which these deities are particularly efficacious. Earth Mother, for example, is especially good for those who pray to be safe from disasters and to enjoy good health.

To the left of screen is a menu offering additional information. Here we can discover that this temple is is the fourth in a series, the first of which was built in 1873, shortly after the opening of the port of Yokohama in 1859. The site was enlarged in 1886 and a larger temple built in 1893. That temple was destroyed in the Great Kanto Earthquake of 1923. The second-generation temple that replaced it was destroyed by Allied bombing in 1945. Its replacement, the third-generation temple, was destroyed by fire in 1986, though miraculously its god statues remained unharmed. Construction of the current temple was completed in 1990. We can also learn that as Chinese began to emigrate overseas in large numbers during the 19th century, temples dedicated to Guandi were built in Chinatowns the world over.

With these facts in mind, we turn now to anthropological and historical discussions of Chinese gods.

Celestial Bureaucracy, The Limits of Metaphor

When our tourist asks, "Why do the gods look like this?" the first answer that comes to mind is that Chinese conceive of their gods as celestial bureaucrats. They wear official robes, and their temples resemble the yamen from which imperial officials governed the Chinese empire. Their ranks correspond to the scale of the territories for which they are responsible. On closer inspection, however, all of these propositions turn out to be dubious.

The idea that Chinese conceive of their gods as celestial bureaucrats was forcefully articulated by Arthur Wolf in the "Introduction" to Religion and Ritual in Chinese Society (1974), a collection of papers that marked a pivotal moment in the anthropological study of Chinese religion and framed subsequent debates. Should Chinese religion be treated as an integrated whole tightly linked to Chinese social structure or a motley bricolage of traditions that, as Donald Deglopper put it (Personal communication; see also 1974: 43-69), stood in relation to Chinese society as the colors refracted by the oil on the surface of a puddle stand to the water in the puddle, a far looser and more liquid relationship?

When this collection appeared, the dominant theories in the anthropology of Chinese society were the structural-functionalism of Maurice Freedman's studies of lineage organization and the standard marketing regions of G. William Skinner. Synthesized by Stephen Feuchtwang, they provided a plausible grounding for the notion that Chinese spirits fall into three broad categories, gods, ghosts and ancestors. Ancestors were kin whose descendants looked after their worship and afterlife. Ghosts were prototypically hungry ghosts without descendants, angry at their fate. The gods were the spiritual counterparts of government officials, the celestial bureaucrats in charge of dispensing both favors and punishments to those whose lives they ruled. Like their earthly counterparts, they formed a spatial hierarchy, with officials at different levels in charge of smaller or larger geographical areas.

Subsequent research, however, would enormously complicate this picture. Shahar and Weller's *Unruly Gods*

(1996) provides numerous examples of deities who slip betwixt-and-between Wolf's categories. Gods, it turned out, frequently started their careers as demons. The Wang-yeh, whose demonic role is to spread plagues, are one example (Katz, 1995). Powerful females like Guan-yin and Mazu had no obvious place in what should have been, in principle, an all-male officialdom. The local gods of the soil, Tu-di Kong, were frequently said to have been virtuous individuals raised to divine status after death; but the territories they governed were at a level far below that to which imperial China's bureaucracies extended. There is also the awkward fact that the last of the Chinese empires on which the celestial bureaucracy is supposed to be modeled had, by the time that the anthropologists cited here began their research in the 1960s and '70s, long since ceased to exist. The Republic of China had been founded in 1911, and the Peoples Republic of China had followed in 1949.

A case might be made for similarity between the powers and habits of modern Chinese bureaucrats and their imperial predecessors. That argument could then be extended to the proposition that Chinese worshipers approach Chinese deities in a way analogous to that in which they approach mortal officials. But as Steve Sangren asks, "If gods are modeled on peasants' images of officials, why officials so different from any in most peasants' experience?" (1987: 130). Adam Chau, writing about his observations in Shaanbei, notes that in northern China, too, people liken deities to bureaucrats. He then goes on to note, however, that,

> The relationship between local state agents and ordinary peasants in Shaanbei is strained, to put it mildly. Indeed, the image of local bureaucrats in the minds of Shaanbei peasants is most negative: they take things away from you but rarely give anything back (2006:73).

Expectations of bureaucrats and expectations of gods appear to be strikingly different. In *Way and Byway*

(2002), historian Robert Hymes proposes that Chinese deities are conceived in terms of two analytically separate models, one bureaucratic, the other personal. On the one side are officials. Described abstractly, in terms of name, rank, and title, these gods are temporary appointees who represent a multilevel authority imposed from the outside. On the other are individuals with rich biographies; stories about their miracles are legion. Instead of appointed officials, these are extraordinary persons, with inherent powers enhanced through self-cultivation. They enter into direct, dyadic relations with persons and places and are see as permanent fixtures in the localities where they are worshipped. In these respects, they resemble the gods worshipped in Wannian, the community studied by Lin Wei-ping, who like the Daoist immortals studied by Hymes, traveled to a particular place where they settled, where their statues are not only consecrated to bring them to life but also localized through rites that attach them to this particular place.

From this perspective, however, the Guandi who sites on the altar in the Guandi Miao in Yokohama's China is problematic. He is, on the one hand, an intensely individual god. He has a rich biography, elaborated with stories of numerous miracles. He epitomizes abstract virtues, loyalty and righteousness; but is also said to be particularly efficacious in dealing with problems related to traffic safety and achieving business and academic success. His virtues and powers are his own; but the god who occupies his statue may, in fact, be only a delegate, like those said to be worshipped in his place in thousands of temples throughout China and around the world. Neither his virtues nor his stories attach him to one particular place. He is, on the contrary, a favorite deity of overseas Chinese, who have taken him with them as traveled to new places in search of new opportunities. From from being a deity with strong local ties, Guandi is, arguably, the most cosmopolitan of Chinese gods.

Not surprisingly, how Guandi is perceived and the stories told about him vary from place to place and speaker to speaker. How he is seen and represented has been subject for centuries to a process that Prasenjit Duara calls "superscription," elaboration and editing to suit a variety of purposes (1988:778). In this respect he resembles Lü Dongbin, the Daoist immortal of whom Paul Katz writes that, "*more than one* Lü Dongin existed in the minds of the late imperial Chinese" (1996: 97). One way of summarizing the argument of this essay would be to say that, like the murals of the Yongle Gong studied by Katz, god statues that represent Guandi are works of art that "have not been adequately used as sources for the study of Chinese hagiography" (1996:72); with the additional caveat that, like the historical documents analyzed by Duara, Chinese god statues are also subject to superscription. They, too, can be elaborated and edited to fit various purposes. These depend, in at least one important respect, to how the relationship between worshipper and god is conceived.

The Importance of Being *Ling*

One point on which anthropologists of China and their informants appear to agree is that gods are supposed to be *ling*, i.e., efficacious. How *ling* should be interpreted is the focus of several attempts to explain the relationship between Chinese deities and the mundane realities of Chinese society.

To Sangren, *ling* embodies a logic that pervades the whole of Chinese culture and, "can be fully understood only as a product of the reproduction of social institutions and as a manifestation of a native historical consciousness" (1987: 2). *Ling* refers to situations in which Yang, the principle of order, encompasses and overcomes Yin, the principle of disorder. Deities are *ling* because they operate at the margin where Yang confronts Yin.

Chau offers a more mundane interpretation that turns on a familiar saying, *ren ping shen, shen ping ren* (people depend on gods and gods depend on people). A god, he says, is *ling*, efficacious, when the god responds effectively to his worshippers' prayers, which leads to the *hong huo* (red heat) of ritual celebration, which enhances the god's reputation and makes the god appear more *ling* (2006:9).

In his review of *Miraculous Response*, Feuchtwang agrees that Chau is onto something by focusing on the Durkheimian social effervescence that reflects and sustains a god's reputation for being *ling*. What is left unaccounted for, he observes, is the "disavowal of human agency" involved in attributing efficacy to the god (2006:978).

Like Sangren, Feuchtwang bases his own analysis on the notion of collective representations that precede and define the attribution of ling to deities. Feuchtwang, however, is not content with a cultural logic that, while pervasive in Chinese rites and religion, is so pervasive that it ceases to account for the different local and historical contexts in which ling appears. He agrees that ling appears at the margins that define the spaces and times in which Chinese individuals find themselves but argues that the frames of reference are multiple — household, community, region, and, only ultimately, China as a whole (Feuchtwang, 2000).

These brief summaries hardly do justice to the complex and subtle arguments of which they are, at best, caricatures. The gods may be Yang overcoming Yin, mark boundaries on several levels of territorial hierarchy, or have won reputations for efficacy reinforced by lavishly decorated temples and noisy celebrations. But, why do they look like that? Why do they display the particular tangible qualities that motivate our tourist's question? What if, in fact, some representations replace ling, efficaciousness in addressing specific requests, with uncompromising authority? This is an issue to which we will soon return. First, however, we consider iconography, the details by which art historians and collectors identify particular deities and styles of representation.

The Collector's Eye

Keith Stevens is a collector. According to his *Chinese Gods: The Unseen World of Spirits and Demons* (1997) he became interested in the iconography of Chinese deities in 1948 and, by the time he wrote this book, had visited more than 3,500 Chinese temples in China, Taiwan, Hong Kong, Macao, and across Southeast Asia. His personal collection included over 1,000 god statues and 30,000 photographs of temples and images. He had documented the legend and folklore surrounding approximately 2,500 deities.

Stevens candidly describes his book as, "An introduction to the imagery of Chinese deities and demons and their legends and beliefs in relation to the common people, as observed from a Western point of view" (1997:11). His description of Chinese popular religion is consistent with what anthropologists have written. There are, he notes, two orders of deities: a higher order of gods associated with Daoist and Buddhist pantheons and a lower order of humans deified for exceptional accomplishments while alive or miraculous powers after death. The deities on Buddhist altars generally appear in conventional sets; those on Daoist altars or in the temples of popular religion tend to be a more mixed lot. Broadly speaking, he says, there are three standard forms of images.

1) In Buddhist images, the faces are calm and characterless, lacking distinctive features. The deities are dressed in simple priestly robes and cross-legged.
2) Daoist images may lean, stand or be seated. Characteristic features include black beards, tiny Daoist crowns, and hands holding either a gourd or fly switch.
3) The standard deity of popular religion is a seated scholar-official with a full black or red beard, holding a tablet with both hands in front of his chest. Alternatively his hands may rest on arm rests or his knees, or one hand may clutch his

official girdle. Alternative elements include the cap, crown or helmet.

These standard forms are only prototypes with numerous variations. Buddhas may be depicted standing, and the deities who serve as their guardians may be demonic in appearance. Daoist images include figures on mythical beasts, like Zhang Dao-ling on his tiger. As previously noted, the deities of popular religion include females and demonic figures whose scowls and gestures are inconsistent with official restraint.

Of particular interest, however, is the way in which Stevens describes his research. Deities can, he notes, be identified in several ways, including titles on placards associated with them or the names of their temples. The groupings in which they appear may also be indicative. Some are easily identified by distinctive iconographic features. But for others there is no recourse but what informants say, and this may be problematic. Here it is, I believe, worth quoting Stevens at length.

> A major problem has involved the contradictory stories and legends, with the temple staff giving different versions during successive visits. These contradictions would appear to be due to sheer lack of interest on the part of the temple custodian or to an unwillingness to admit to a foreigner ignorance of the identity of the deities in their temple. Suggestions are usually offered in a confident voice, suggesting unequivocal accuracy. It is only later, on revisiting and perhaps talking to others, that the positive identification becomes less certain. It has been somewhat surprising to me how little many temple watchmen, devotees and even god-carvers know of the myths, legends and histories behind the deities in their own temples and shops (1997:11).

Our second collector, Liu Senhower (劉 文 三), the author of *The God Statues of Taiwan*, brings an insider's perspective to Chinese popular religion. Born in 1939,

Liu was a child during World War II. He has vivid memories of his mother, a true believer in popular religion, who made sure that everyone in his family knew how to light incense, bow and worship properly. These memories were reinforced when his father was drafted by the Japanese army and sent to Hainan and his mother prayed day and night for his safety. Then came the Allied bombings and hearing his mother repeating the names of the gods as the family huddled together in their air raid shelter. A story circulated among their neighbors about a bomb that fell into a fishpond instead of the village, diverted by divine intervention. As an artist, author and collector, Liu knows intellectually that god statues are simply blocks of wood, brought to life as works of art by the god-carver's craft. When he's tired or troubled, however, they seem to be something more. Liu has a Chinese intellectual's mixed feelings about the gods, with nuances added by his personal history. He has, however, no trouble identifying the thirty gods whose statues, background and iconography he presents in his book. These are all among the most popular and best documented gods.

With these two collectors to guide us, let us return now to our tourist in Yokohama, looking at the statue on the altar of the Yokohama Guandi Miao (Figure 6).

Describing Guandi

What our tourist sees is an image consistent with the classic description of Guanyu, the hero who would later be deified as Guandi, in *The Romance of the Three Kingdoms*.

> Xuande [Liu Bei] took a look at the man, who stood at a height of nine chi, and had a two chi long beard; his face was the color of a dark jujube, with lips that were red and plump; his eyes were like that of a crimson phoenix, and his eyebrows resembled reclining silkworms. He had a dignified air, and looked quite majestic.

(http://en.wikisource.org/wiki/Romance_of_the_Thre
e_Kingdoms/Chapter_1#11)

The first of our collectors, Keith Stevens, notes that the legends surrounding Guangong have become the subject for prints, story tellers, operas and plays. He recounts two examples with a more earthy tone than the stories that appear on the Yokohama temple's website. According to the first, Guanyu was a simple bean curd hawker who rescued a girl from an evil magistrate, whom he killed. He then fled and joined the army. Near Beijing he encountered a butcher who challenged passersby to lift a 400-lb stone off the well in which he stored his meat. Guanyu lifted the stone, took the meat, and was pursued by the butcher, who turned out to be Zhang Fei. The two were fighting when Liu Bei intervened. According to the second, when Guanyu was captured by Cao Cao, he and the wives of Liu Bei were given a single room to share. Guanyu stood by the door all night holding a candle, to avoid any hint of impropriety.

Liu Senhower provides two additional tales. According to one, collected in the countryside in Taiwan, the Jade Emperor, the supreme god in the popular pantheon, had come down to earth to investigate conditions there. Appalled by the human misbehavior he discovered, he was about to punish humanity with devastating disasters and plagues. Hearing of these plans, Guangong prostrated himself before the Jade Emperor and tearfully begged the Jade Emperor to show mercy instead. That is why, the tale says, Guangong's face is red, from all the crying he did. According to the second, which, I note, also found its way into my field notes, some Chinese believe that Guangong became the Jade Emperor, promoted to the position during the 19th century.

The effect of these tales, considered as superscriptions, is to further humanize Guandi. The awe-inspiring general starts out as a simple beancurd hawker. He may have inhuman self-control; but, like other men, he is subject to sexual temptation. He can cry until he is red in the face. He may, like the founder of a new Chinese dynasty, rise from humble origins to the highest power in the land. But as Robbie Burns once said, "A man's a man for a' that." This god remains approachable.

The opposite is true of another superscription described by Duara.

> In 1914 the president of the Republic, Yuan Shikai, ordered the creation of a temple of military heroes devoted to Guandi, Yuefei, and twenty-four lesser heroes. The interior of the main temple in Beijing, with its magnificent timber pillars and richly decorated roof, was impressive in the stately simplicity of its ceremonial arrangements. There were no images. The canonized heroes were representedby their spirit tablets only (1988: 779).

Here there is no mention of *ling*, no humanizing detail. The message is clear and unequivocal, a pure and uncompromising assertion of the value of loyalty.

Neither wholly abstract and dehumanized nor dynamically *ling* in appearance, the seated Guang Di on the altar of the Yokohama Guandi Miao falls between these extremes, nicely positioned for a god who is both an epitome of classic virtue and willing to lend a worshipper a hand with a traffic accident, a business problem, or passing a school entrance exam. What happens to the god, however, when his image is globalized?

When Liu analyzes the historical and cultural background to Chinese popular religion in Taiwan, he frequently employs a style of functional analysis that anthropologists associate with Malinowski. The central premise is that Chinese emigrants to Taiwan, struggling to reach and then to carve out new lives on the island found themselves in uncertain and frequently dangerous circumstances. They venerated gods who offered supernatural aid: Mazu, for saving them from the dangers of the four-day sail from the mainland to Taiwan; Tu-di-gong for protecting against storms, drought or other threats to the harvest; Bao-sheng-da-di for protection against and cure of illness.

In this context, Guandi stands out as the epitome of values essential to social order: 仁 (*ren*, benevolence), 義 (*yi*, righteousness), 禮 (*li*, propriety), 智 (*zhi*, wisdom), and 信 (*xin*, honesty). His legendary strictness in keeping his promises has made him a favorite deity of businessmen as well as soldiers. His lack of association with any particular set of material dangers may, in addition, make him especially apt as a symbol of morality elevated above the sorts of worldly concerns that motivate worshippers looking for *ling*. It is thus, I suggest, that since the Qing dynasty, we have found him paired with Confucius, with his *wu miao* (military temples) built alongside the *wen miao* (temples of culture) in which Confucius is venerated. It is thus, too, I suggest, that of all the gods in the popular pantheon, he is the one being celebrated globally as a symbol of Chinese culture.

Divine Body Language

At this point we should all be ready to concede of Guandi what Robert Weller (1994) has said about Chinese religion and ritual in general. The forms are familiar. The possible meanings ascribable to them seem endless. They resemble the chemicals suspended in saturated liquids, ready to precipitate in a multitude of forms depending on what is added to them.

Are we left, then, with a generalization of Adam Chau's conclusion about his Longwanggou case in Shaabei?

> No "interpretive community" has emerged out of the cacophonous and "saturated" jumble of texts to present clearly "precipitated" meanings and ideological or theological statements (2006:97).

Let us look once again at the tangible qualities of the statue of Guandi at which our tourist is looking and compare them with other images, first of Guandi and then of other deities.

Google searches for "Guandi, " "Guangong," and "Guanyu" yield thousands of images. In most of those clearly identifiable as god statues, we see what we might call "sedate dynamism." In the seated figures the god seems alert but relaxed. He strokes his beard. His feet are planted on the ground, but his legs are spread but not rigidly squared off. In standing poses the right leg is thrust forward.

The significance of these poses emerges in contrast with other deities. The Jade Emperor is represented sitting four-square, looking straight ahead, his hands joined in front of his chest (Figure 7). In some communities, he is represented only by a tablet bearing his title. He is seen as "too awesome and too powerful to be represented by an image....Among the Fukienese in particular, his spirit was believed to reside in the ash of the main incense pot on the primary altar table in the temple dedicated to him, and not even a tablet is permitted" (Stevens, 1997: 53).

Other spirits who are typically represented by tablets include ancestors and Confucius. In the case of Confucius, we know that until 1530 sculptural images of the Sage were found in state-supported temples all over China and, "the icons' visual features were greatly influenced by the posthumous titles and ranks that emperor conferred on Confucius and his follows," treating them, in this respect, like Daoist and Buddhist deities. This treatment aroused the ire of Neo-Confucian ritualists, who led a successful campaign to replace images with tablets and posthumous titles with the designation "Ultimate Sage and First Teacher" (Murray, 2009: 371).

Compared to the Jade Emperor, Guandi seems more relaxed, more human. But compared to other, more dynamic, images, his statues seem sedate. Consider, for example, Zhen Wu, Lord of the Dark/Profound Heaven, possessor of spirit mediums, who is barefoot, with his feet resting on the snake- tortoise who symbolizes the North, the most Yin of all directions (Figure 8). We have noted the legend that describes Guandi as a tofu maker before he became a soldier. A similar legend describes Zhen Wu as a butcher and the snake-tortoise as his intestines, torn out in an act of repentance for killing so many living things while plying his butcher's trade. Guangong is sometimes depicted standing, but his statues are never so dramatically dynamic as those of Nazha, the Third Prince, whose statues depict him standing on his wheels of fire and wielding his spear (Figure 9). In some images, Guangong appears to be frowning, but his face is never so distorted as those of, for example, the goddess Mazu's demonic attendants *Shungfenger*, Fair Wind Ears, and *Chianliyan*, Thousand-Mile Eyes (Figure 10).

With these examples I have, I would argue, briefly sketched an iconographic continuum that stretches from tablets inscribed with text to demonic or once-demonic figures whose dynamic poses or expressions express more humanized, more magical forms of divine power. The statues of Guandi mentioned here represent authority humanized, accessible to human sentiments, but fundamentally righteous. But what of other superscriptions more tailored to the modern world?

Guangong Globalized

Google searches turn up a number of images from manga and video games in which the pre-divine Guanyu, the hero from The Romance of the Three Kingdoms is depicted as a warrior superhero. He glares with intent fury at enemies outside the frame. His robe is slipped off one or both shoulders to reveal a heavily muscled body. In some his pose is similar to that of Nazha on Taiwanese altars. He is shown swooping down thrusting with his halbred. Here, however, I turn to another superscription, Guangong (not, we must note Guandi), as a symbol and salesman for China and Chinese culture.

I refer here to another website, World Guangong Culture (世界關公文化, http://www.guangong.hk/). Here, the hero deified as Guandi (Emperor Guan) is presented as Guangong (Honorable Guan). *Di*, a Chinese character associated with divine or imperial status, has been replaced by *gong*, which, while formerly the the highest of five orders of nobility and translated "Duke," is now a common honorific, applied, for example, to a father-in-law.

First up in the list of dignitaries whose statements appear on the site is PRC President Hu Jintao, who says,

> In current era, culture has increasingly become the important source of national cohesion and creativity. In addition, it has increasingly become the important factor of the comprehensive national power competition.

He does not mention Guangong by name.

Next is Lui Chun Wan, chairman of the board of directors of the World Guangong Culture Promoting Association, who, after reviewing Guangong's history, concludes that,

> We believe that the rich and colorful Guangong Culture will become a strong force to unite the Chinese people from home and abroad!

There is, however, no mention in his comments of miracles, of magical response, of *ling*. In this superscription, however, Guangong is not reduced to a title on a tablet, an impersonal abstraction.

The standing image of Guangong chosen to brand the World Guangong Culture Promotion Association shows the god standing and striding confidently forward (Figure 11). In this conspicuously cleaned up version of more traditional depictions of the deity, all traces of armor and glittering gold have been removed. The green of the robe is a paler, more subtle hue than the the blue or green of the more traditional representation. The overall green tone of the image may reflect, I speculate, current "green" concerns with the state of the global environment.

While he does carry his halberd, this version of the god has a warm, modern look, more like a prosperous businessman striding forward to shake your hand than a model of warrior virtues. The "magic" in this image is no longer the traditional *ling* but instead, I suggest, the economic miracles to be expected from doing business with China.

Beyond China

As we return to where we started, it is, I believe, important to recall that our tourist is looking at the statue of Guandi in a Chinese temple in Yokohama. Our analysis so far has included only Chinese data. Our tourist's question, however, is motivated by the contrast between what she sees at the Yokohama Guandi Miao and what she has seen elsewhere in Japan, especially when visiting Shinto shrines. There the gods are invisible, posing the question why Chinese temples are filled with god statues, full-figured anthropomorphic representations of gods, while Japanese shrines are not.

Some might question whether an anthropologist should consider such a question at all. Isn't it wrong, especially when studying religion and ritual, to rip what we see from its cultural context? Isn't this the kind of speculation for which such 19th century predecessors Sir James Frazer, the author of *The Golden Bough*, were so roundly condemned by such critics as Sir E. E. Evans-Pirchard who called their work telling "If I were a horse" stories?

But no, this is not what our 19th century predecessors were up to. Frazer and his contemporaries were constructing speculations about the prehistoric origins of religion, a topic for which the direct evidence is very slim, indeed. What I propose here is to extend the method that Robert Weller describes when, having shown that Wolf's thesis that Chinese gods are bureaucrats is, at best, only party true, then goes on to say,

> At a deeper level these cases force us toward some position like Wolf's: that Chinese religious interpretation moves hand in hand with social experience (1996: 21).

The classic Durkheimian vision in which religion mirrors society may be too simplistic. We now recognize that,

> Religion is not a reflex of Chinese social structure, or even of class, gender, or geographical position. It is instead part of an ongoing dialogue of interpretations, sometimes competing and sometimes cooperating (1996:21).

We can, however, go a step further and recognize that the on-going dialogue that Weller describes extends beyond the borders of China. Chinese ideas and images have been absorbed and adapted throughout East Asia and, in some cases—one thinks of Chinese medicine, martial arts, fengsui, the Yin and the Yang—have spread worldwide, carried now by film, video games and the Internet as well as overseas Chinese and other East Asian diasporas. To explore these transmissions and transformations in search of pan-human patterns is far from telling "if I were a horse" stories. It is, instead, the sort of thing that historians do all the time when engaging in comparative research within or across regions or eras, a task that can now be grounded in a rich and growing body of scholarship. In the case of China, we are not dealing with speculation about what happened in prehistory. If anything, we confront the opposite problem; the relevant literature is enormous compared to the number of scholars who research it (McCreery, 2008: 304-305).

In this context, there is, I would argue, much to be said for embracing the "methodological fetishism" that Arjun Appadurai (1986:5, cited in Brown, 2009:142) ascribes to material culture studies. Brown's "Praesentia" (2009: 177-194) and Michael Taussig's "In some way or another one can protect oneself from the spirits by portraying them" (2009: 195-207) offer numerous opportunities for close comparison with Lin Wei-Ping's findings concerning the consecration and localization of god statues in Wan-nian. Closer attention to Chinese god statues reveals not only a richly detailed iconography but also general principles that have broader implications. They make inescapable the larger question: Why are Chinese gods, like the gods of Hindu India and ancient Greece and Rome, Christian saints and Christ himself represented in human form?

The *kami* venerated in Japanese shrines are concealed from their worshippers. Only priests may see the sacred regalia in which they reside when invited to participate in Shinto ceremonies (Nelson, 1997). We have seen that when held in greatest awe, the Jade Emperor is also invisible: a feature he also shares with the gods of the Old Testament, Calvin and the Holy Koran.

What we see here in tablets, books and other non-anthropomorphic forms of material representation is, I would argue, a precise analogue to Maurice Bloch's description of ritual language as a language deliberately impoverished to force particular interpretations (cited in McCreery, 1995: 158). Abstraction and formalization assert unimpeachable authority. Conversely, however, concrete representations, and especially those that take a full-figured anthropomorphic form, render the gods approachable, transforming them into patrons with whom it is possible to form particularistic relationships in which both emotion and exchange can be used to secure the gods' favor.

In this paper we have seen anthropologists whose eyes are focused beyond what they see, on theories that purport to explain how Chinese culture or society works. We have seen collectors, whose iconographic perspectives draw our attention back to the visual evidence that our eyes provide and noted the diversity of stories that add meaning to what we see. The author has sketched one dimension of a visual grammar, a continuum that extends from authority abstracted in inscribed tablets to power expressed in near-demonic forms.

There are no final answers here. If, however, we open our eyes to the tangible qualities we find in Chinese god statues, we will, I suggest, be able to write thicker descriptions, descriptions that challenge our theories and demand more subtle ones, theories that may, at the end of the day, enable us to situate Chinese religion more firmly in relation to religion as a human phenomenon.

References

Appadurai, Arjun (1986), "Introduction: Commodities and the Politics of Value," in Arjun Appadurai, ed., *The Social Life of Things: Commodities in Cultural Perspective.* Cambridge: Cambridge U. Press.

Brown, Peter (2009) "Thing Theory, " in Fiona Candlin and Raiford Guins, eds., *The Object Reader.* London: Routledge, pp. 139-152.

Brown, Peter (2009) "Prasentia, " in Fiona Candlin and Raiford Guins, eds., *The Object Reader.* London: Routledge, pp. 177-194.

Byrne, David and Charles C. Ragin, eds. (2009), *The SAGE Handbook of Case-Based Methods.* Sage Publications, Ltd.

Chau, Adam Yuet (2006) *Miraculous Response: Doing Popular Religion in Contemporary China.* Stanford:

Stanford University Press.

DeGlopper, Donald (1974) "Religion and Ritual in Lukang," In Arthur Wolf, ed., *Religion and Ritual in Chinese Society*. Stanford: Stanford University Press.

Feuchtwang, Stephan (2001) *Popular Religion in China: The Imperial Metaphor*. Richmond, England: Curzon Press.

Feuchtwang, Stephan (2006) "Miraculous Response: Doing Popular Religion in Contemporary China." In *Journal of the Royal Anthropological Institute*. 12:4:978.

Geertz, Clifford (1973) *The Interpretation of Cultures*. New York: Basic Books, Inc.

Gell, Alfred (2009) "The Technology of Enchantment and the Enchantment of Technology, " in Fiona Candlin and Raiford Guins, eds., *The Object Reader*. London: Routledge, pp. 208-228.

Katz, Paul R. (1995) *Demon Hordes and Burning Boats: The Cult of Marshal Wen in Late Imperial Chekiang* (Suny Series in Chinese Local Studies) New York: State University of New York Press.

Katz, Paul R. (1996) "Enlightened Alchemist or Immoral Immortal? The Growth of Lü Dongbin's Cult in Late Imperial China," in Shahar and Weller, eds., *Unruly Gods: Divinity and Society in China*. Honolulu: U. of Hawaii Press, pp. 70-104.

Lin Wei-Ping (2008) "Conceptualizing Gods through Statues: A Study of Personification and Localization in Taiwan," *Comparative Studies in Society and History*, Vol. 50, No. 2: pp. 454-477.

Liu Senhower (劉文三) (1981) *The God Statues of Taiwan*

(台灣神像藝術). Taipei: Yishuchia Press.

McCreery, John (1990) "Why Don't We See Some Real Money Here? Offerings in Chinese Religion. *Journal of Chinese Religion* 18:1-24.

McCreery, John (1995) "Negotiating with Demons: The Uses of Magical Language. *American Ethnologist* 22:1:144-164.

McCreery, John (2008), "Traditional Religions of China" in Ray Scupin, ed., *Religion and Culture, An Anthropological Focus*, 2nd edition. Upper Saddle River, New Jersey: Pearson Prentice-Hall.

Miller, Daniel, ed. (1998) *Material cultures: Why some things matter.* Chicago: Chicago University Press

Murray, Julia K. (2009) "'Idols' in the Temple: Icons and the Cult of Confucius." *The Journal of Asian Studies* 68:2:371-411.

Nelson, John K. (1997) *A Year in the Life of a Shinto Shrine.* University of Washington Press.

Sangren, Steven (1987) *History and Magical Power in a Chinese Community.* Stanford: Stanford University Press.

Shahar, Meir and Ropert P. Weller, eds. (1996), *Unruly Gods: Divinity and Society in China.* Honolulu: U. of Hawaii Press.

Stevens, Keith (1997) *Chinese Gods: The Unseen World of Spirits and Demons.* London: Collins & Brown Ltd.

Taussig, Michael (2009) "In some way or another one can protect oneself from the spirits by portraying them, " in Fiona Candlin and Raiford Guins, eds., *The Object Reader.* London: Routledge, pp. 195-207.

Weller, Robert P. (1994) *Resistance, Chaos, and Control in China: Taiping Rebels, Taiwanese Ghosts, and Tiananmen.* University of Washington Press.

Wolf, Arthur, ed. (1974) *Religion and Ritual in Chinese Society.* Stanford: Stanford University Press.

Figures

Figure 1: The Yokohama Guandi Miao (Exterior)

Figure 2: Sengen Jinja (a Shinto Shrine)

Figure 3: Guandi on the altar of the Yokohama

Figure 4: Japanese Buddha

Figure 5: Shinkoyasu Jinja (Interior)

Figure 6: Guandi at the Yokohama Guandi Miao

Figure 7: The Jade Emperor

Figure 8: Xuantianshangdi

Figure 9: Nahza, The Third Prince

Figure 10: Thousand-Mile Eyes

Figure 11: Guangong on the Guangong World Culture

Chapter 8

AN AMAZONIAN QUESTION OF IRONIES AND THE GROTESQUE: THE ARROGANCE OF COSMIC DECEIT, AND THE HUMILITY OF EVERYDAY LIFE

Joanna Overing

The place of humour

My strongest memories of Piaroa people of the Venezuelan Amazon Territory involve experiencing their humour. The ludic was vital to their everyday life. These were people who were lovers of slapstick and witty, outrageous play on words. There was their punning, their satire and irony, where the use of the apt and mischievous trope was given especially high value. It was through hilarity that I felt I actually understood my Piaroa teachers. It was then that I felt at one with them.

I will dwell upon the connection between this love of slapstick, the apt pun and their egalitarian antipathy to hierarchy, rules and regulations. To begin to understand this link between a love of laughter and the feeling for social and political equality of both men and women, it is necessary to consider the absurd grotesqueries of creation time hubris, which the Piaroa shaman unfolds through his singing narrations of mythic time, as he conducts his daily healing ceremonies. My main interest is in this telling of the monstrous modes of power set loose in creation time by the creator gods – and of course their repercussions. We find that the stress upon the grotesque in these healing narratives is strongly related to the shaman's thorough understanding of the dangers in the present day of the monstrous modes of power unleashed by the gods when they created the world. It is through exploring these mighty, but highly dodgy, powers of creation time that we (as anthropologists) can begin to understand their connection to the rich social philosophies of folly that are attached to the egalitarian practices of Piaroa people as they interact in 'today time' sociality.

Along the way, I shall unfold the two diseases of folly and madness that Piaroa people may experience in the course of everyday life. The names of these two illnesses are *ki'raeu* and *ke'raeu*. The former, *ki'raeu*, was a comparatively minor disease of social irresponsibility which could lead to such errant behaviour as crazy laughter, promiscuity, wandering at will – and also diarrhoea. Sufferers of such symptoms are considered victims, led to their waywardness (such as their excessive use of orifices) by the social irresponsibility of others who perhaps taunt, or are unduly arrogant toward, them. The taunter blatantly displays a lack of regard to familial matters and good etiquette, which leads their victim into a state of minor madness.

Ke'raeu – in contrast to *ki'raeu* – is a much more serious threat to the social fabric: its symptoms involve more violent display, such as accompanies the madness of hubris, paranoia, extreme arrogance – and also murder. As happens today, characters in mythic time also fell foul of both illnesses, with behaviour becoming truly grotesque when *ke'raeu* seriously set in. We find a major irony here. These stories speak of the original violent creation, acquisition and stealing of grotesque powers that would allow for the culinary arts. However, it was these very toxic powers that led eventually to the creation of beautiful, but dangerous culinary skills that enable Piaroa people today to achieve the sort of life that they could consider to be human.

Sociology, Political Anthropology

It is important to note that my exploration of Piaroa understandings of the grotesque and other modes of power is intended as a foray into political anthropology. For instance, I find that certain comparisons of modes of power can be highly enlightening. For example, in Greek myth, Zeus, who becomes sovereign of the whole universe, gets away with hubris and excessiveness, while Wahari (the creater god of Piaroa people) does not. Why this difference? To answer such a question, we need to widen our horizon of concerns greatly to understand its importance. Obviously, the cultural context (for instance, the aesthetics of living together) and histories (within which modes of power are enacted) vary considerably with regard to matters of social and political value. It is certainly legitimate to question the worth of comparing the political values of a Greek city state with those of an Amazonian village. On the other hand, with our horizons expanded, we might well find gold. In comparing the political concerns of the citizens of Thebes with those of a Piaroa village I discovered that they shared a number of egalitarian values and practices. For instance, in both cases it is particularly the women, as chorus, who take responsibility for unfolding to the people the irresponsible actions of a tyrant – or a shaman – gone mad.

Perhaps we need to understand that an aesthetic of living may well play a large part within most political agendas. For quite a long time political anthropology has been deeply in need of new sociological ways of thinking, talking, examining – and most importantly imagining.

Exploration of this kind is needed to open up sociological categories and ways of thinking and even to begin to understand the extraordinary political repercussions (and lessons) emerging from the respective fates of these two creator gods – Zeus and Wahari. The former is king of hierarchy, teaching its 'wonderful attainment'. As for Wahari, it originally was his desire to create for his world a moral order comprised of equals. However, it was his plight that he was foiled in following through with his plan. On the other hand, he did succeed in creating a people who held tight to his original dream of creating a moral order of equals. They also had the intelligence to understand how difficult it is to actually achieve this state of existence – one capable of creating beings who were actually *human*.

Modes of Power

I shall begin by sketching some of the basic characters within Piaroa cosmology and the *modes of power* attached to each:

First there is Tapir/Anaconda: This monstrous, almighty, subterranean Tapir/Anaconda let loose all those mighty powers that eventually allowed for an animated existence on earth. The great granite outcrops of the ancient Guianese landscape are the result of his defecation: Lying beneath the earth, he propelled his waste upwards, like worm casts, to sit on Earth's surface. His granite shit became the source on earth for all 'life force' of a sensual sort: it thus plays a crucial role in the empowerment of each Piaroa individual: the casing for their beautiful, interior 'beads of life' is made of these potent defecatory granite upcastings of Tapir/Anaconda. It is this casing that allows for their 'life of the senses' and thus all of their physical capacities. When the terrifying and violent Tapir/Anaconda wandered along the earth's surface, s/he wreaked mayhem in his/her wake.

Next there is Kuemoi: Tapir/anaconda was the father of **Kuemoi** who became the Master of Rivers and Lakes. Tapir/Anaconda grew Kuemoi within the womb of the Mistress of the lake, feeding him with wildly poisonous hallucinogens from the rust of the sun and the centre of sky down of the sun. Through these hallucinogenic powers from the dreadful heat of the sun, *Kuemoi became the father of all cultivated food. He was the creator of all those forces that belong to the culinary arts*: gardening, hunting, curare, cooking fire. He is also a tyrannical, grotesque, little madman and is portrayed as a diabolical buffoon, raucously laughing with each plot he hatches, shrieking in outrage when foiled: he stamps his feet when foiled: *a figure of high comedy*, not tragedy. When overtaken by total madness, he runs endlessly around in circles. (He reminds me of Robert Nye's depiction of the devil in *Merlin*: "He grins like a fox eating shit out of a wire brush; the Devil is 'snoring as loud as a pig'; 'he giggles and he writhes'"). This is the hilarious, absurd and mockable side of wickedness.

The main aim in life for Kuemoi is to gobble up as many beings of the domain of the jungle as possible. Coming out of water, he was the evil cannibal predator of all beings of the jungle. He stalked all jungle beings as food. He lusted after their meat. He devoured them raw, he ate them cooked. To catch them used cunning and an odious use of guile and sorcery. He was the master of horrid traps! The king of stealth! The trap he enjoyed most was his own daughter, 'Maize'. When she was sleeping, he filled her womb with piranha fish and electric eels - as a seductive trap for the handsome young men of the jungle, who then became his meal at night. He created all creatures nasty to jungle beings, each as a trap to catch them for a meal: the jaguars and all other cats, ticks, biting insects, the stingray, poisonous snakes. He is the father of opossum and electric eel, the grandfather of bat, vulture, quarrelling, sting ray and boils.

He was the owner of what the Piaroa call the *'crystal boxes of tyranny, treachery, and domination'*. He epitomizes excessive power – the power of the true tyrant. Kuemoi released all the horrors from these boxes of primordial powers full blast into this world. Kuemoi was the owner of the *'crystal boxes of Night'*. It was he who in great glee released night and all its dangerous creatures into earthly space. All of these vicious beings are Kuemoi's *weapons*. In fact *all of Kuemoi's creations* serve as his weapons, *including the culinary arts*. All have powers either to kill or to poison. He transformed himself during his escapades as jaguar, vulture, mudfish or anaconda.

Through all this he achieved the clothes of physical might. A small, but monstrous two-headed figure, Kuemoi had one head to eat meat raw, and one to eat meat cooked. Kuemoi is the archetypically evil figure of creation time – and its most ridiculous. This very *foolish god who has all the knowledge of the culinary arts* speaks nonetheless to a highly sophisticated theory of ethical behaviour and to the side of human nature (as the Piaroa perceive it) that gives all human beings the potential for odious and wicked behaviour. A deep cruelty drove Kuemoi and the use of his might. The power of his thoughts, that had their source in the poisonous hallucinogens he took, though sufficiently mighty to create the culinary arts, continually *poisoned his will*. Overtaken by total madness, Kuemoi *always acted without reason. He had no dignity*. Evil here is clearly associated with knowledge and thus with too much power. Kuemoi had far too much of both. He ever experienced an extreme poisoning of his emotions (the disease that the Piaroa call *ke'raeu* – paranoia, hubris, the desire to murder). *This condition of suffering poisonous unmastered knowledge is firmly attached to an imagery of madness and buffoonery*. The political lesson is clear.

Then there is Wahari: The greatest adversary of Kuemoi in creation time was **Wahari**, the Master of the Jungle, and the creator god of the Piaroa. As such, Wahari was the opposite side of the coin to Kuemoi's evil – at least at the start of creation time. Wahari, who was also created through Tapir/Anaconda's efforts, was fed on different hallucinogens from those given Kuemoi. Wahari was given the power of earthly space, of the day, light and sociality (although in the end it all went wrong). He with his brother, worked together to create many of the aspects of terrestrial space that made it habitable. They took the sun and moon from their homes beneath the earth, and jumped with them into the sky to give themselves light by day and night. Wahari created air, breeze and the skies for the comfort of the earthly creatures of his domain. He created all branch animals and birds of the jungle. The hummingbird, eagle hawk and the lapa were the most important manifestations of his power. They were his transformations, his thoughts and as such his sons. He used the force of the hummingbird to fly above and beneath the earth in his flying canoe. He, like Kuemoi, had mighty powers of transformation. He too had the power of cunning, guile and the arts of trickery, combined with mighty sorcery.

But Wahari had the benevolent desire to create a good life for his inhabitants of the jungle. He wanted to provide them with the civilised conditions for a human life on earth, including the culinary arts, and the capabilities for civilised sociality and social virtue. He spoke the principles of a moral social life for his people. Certainly at the beginning of creation time, *he was the god of unity and accord*, including that which should hold within the family. But Wahari strongly wanted to capture the culinary arts from his father-in-law, Kuemoi. With this desire began a treacherous cosmic comedy of errors. None of Wahari's benevolent desires were accomplished in creation time – and that is its tragic irony. The narrations tell how Wahari begins mythic time with the gift of social finesse, but the moment he tries to trade with Kuemoi, cosmogenesis becomes a bag of tricks, a high comedy (then tragedy) of errors. The genre of the bawdy grotesque slips in the end to true tragedy.

Creation Time Hubris and its Landscape of Monsters

This we can gather through the tales about creation time and the shaman's skilled performance of the hilarious, bawdy, grotesque episodes of mythic time through which the ludicrous conditions of being human

215

are disclosed. The narrations disclose the subtle lessons of two-edged folly – that which is good, engendering health and well-being, and that which is disastrous. Erasmus' sermon on Lady Folly would fit well here.

Creation time, much as with Sophocles' Oedipus cycle, moves from a kind of naughty irony, filled with crazy jokes such as reversing heads and buttocks or grabbing a penis hovering in the air in order to create men. They also tell of mistakes that lead to intentions backfiring, for example when putting up the sun and moon, and in the antics of monkeys. Finally, a more grotesque, dark place of the *tragedy of hubris* emerges, where excess pride, arrogance, greed tend to lead to the ruin of the transgressors. We here find similarities with Foucault's reading of Sophocles' Oedipus, whereby the downfall of Oedipus is caused not by innocence, but a monstrous excess of knowledge, and too much power. This rings true with the experiences of Wahari. There are also similarities to the often erratic destiny and suffering found in the historical tyrants of Sophocles' time, with their tendency to rely on their own *solitary* knowledge, rather than solving problems by conversing with 'the people' and other 'knowledgeable' advisors. Such lack of regard can lead easily to 'real' tyranny, which is associated with the tendency to excess. This in turn leads to the hubris and asociality of tyrants who misuse power. In dwelling on these problems, classical Greece comes up with democracy as a solution.

All of the vignettes from the shamanic narrations below come from the cycle on the origin of the craziness disease, *k'eraeu*. This disease gives you delusions of grandeur and paranoia. It is the 'fall down' disease, the 'go round and around disease', the 'twirling circles' illness. *K'eraeu* is the most deadly illness you can get and the most destructive malady of folly imaginable. It leads to *deranged intentionality*. You can die from it and with it you are very likely to damage and kill others.

Here is the history: Creation time becomes the battleground between the two powerful creator gods,

Wahari and Kuemoi, and ends with a cannabilistic war of all against all. Wahari tries to trade with Kuemoi, to acquire his powerful hunting spells and powers for the cultivation of plants; in turn, Kuemoi tries to poison Wahari with his powerful hallucinogenic drugs, in order to capture and eat him. So Wahari stealthily tries to steal from Kuemoi the means to civilised life. He tries to rob all the edible fruits and vegetables from Kuemoi's great tree of life. But suffering from the poisons of Kuemoi's spells, Wahari instead becomes desperately ill, thirsty; he lusts after women and spends many years chasing after foreign beauties. *He becomes insufferably arrogant*, destroying all of his personal relationships with kin. He sells his sister to the Master of White Man's Goods for 6 boxes of matches; he sodomises her, an event that leads to the birth of his son Diarrhoea, whom he tries to kill. He suffers hubris: his mockery infuriates his relatives, who take revenge, by further zapping him with Kuemoi's disease, *k'eraeu*, the craziness illness: his head hurts, he runs in circles. It makes him want to kill. The terrible twirling circles of *k'eraeu* really captures Wahari: maddened, he announces that all of his own creations (people) will suffer this disease. He wanders in the world, lost, arrogant, beautiful. However, he returns again and again to steal Kuemoi's powers for civilised eating. He manages to steal Kuemoi's daughter (after cleaning her womb of piranha fish). Next comes a god-awful series of battles between Wahari and Kuemoi, where they both indulge in villainy, thievery, trickery, deceit and disguise, traps and general mayhem. In hilarious episodes, Wahari often outwits Kuemoi because he foresees his intentions. He manages to give Kuemoi diarrhoea and causes him to rape his own daughter (Wahari's wife). Kuemoi runs round and round in circles.

Wahari becomes crazier and crazier as he becomes increasing zapped by Kuemoi's poisons. On one occasion Wahari becomes locked in the midst of a *k'eraeu* circuit comprised of the narrow translucent streams of *k'eraeu* descending from four of Kuemoi's mountains. He then falls into Kuemoi's trap of poisoned hunting charms, filled with vulture down, sky rust, centre of the sky down. He goes off hunting and then fishing, through yet other traps set by Kuemoi, and manages to kill, not a deer, but his much beloved old grandmother. He cries and wails at this mistake.

Wahari then decides to create his own culinary arts:

He tries to create his own fire, his own sweet and wild fruits and hunting paraphernalia, but he fails badly, These are tales usually told with rather hard-edged slapstick comedy. Each and every creation was false and perverse because of Kuemoi's poisoning of his will, making Wahari crazy. At one point he tries to kill his own brother. The more he tries to create the culinary arts, the more Wahari proclaims *his own* greatness – as master of the universe, the jungle, and the rivers. It was his *hubris* that created the forces of a *monstrous, perverted culinary arts*. His 'fire' blossomed as skin disease, burns, and boils, a fire that scorched but could not cook; his cures backfired on the user and became the miscarrying of women and the bleeding of adults from the mouth, the anus, the vagina; his hunting charms became paralysis, his fish hooks, sore throat... All these useless, poisonous creations became the diseases *that human beings suffer today* and not the useful artefacts for civilised living that Wahari so desired for them. These creations today *impregnate* human beings with disease. As in Greek myth, life for human beings is not easy; the gods made it so.

How do humans receive all these horrors? This is the story:

It was when Wahari invited most of the people beings of the jungle to a great feast. He gets them drunk and then transforms them into animals, to become game for him to hunt and eat. He takes away all their powers for thought and intentionality *and gives them instead all of his perverse creations*. The animals will not suffer them, but instead they will pass them on to human beings. Piaroa people thus *do* receive Wahari's artefacts, but in the form of diseases given to them by the animals.

Wahari, the star of mythic time, becomes *its worst villain*, all due to his mistakes and his arrogance.

Today, human beings (ironically) have to use the dangerous forces for the culinary arts that were originally let loose by Kuemoi, not Wahari. All of Wahari's efforts turned out to be useless. In fact, it is only earthly human beings who can use the powers created by Kuemoi. There are all sorts of dangers there for folly (their intentions can so easily be poisoned by Kuemoi's deadly powers). Today, human beings must, through *everyday hard work*, manage the culinary arts on their own, transforming the ugly and dangerous powers for the hunt and the gardens into beautiful forces, safe for a civilised life. They must cleanse their vegetables and fruit from the poisons of Kuemoi and all their game and fish from those of Wahari. And, they must deal with the fact that the game they eat is really human in origin.

The relation between the culinary arts and the arts of conviviality:

This everyday work of the culinary arts and civilised sociality is at the same time accomplished through a good deal of practice in the comic arts. Indeed the practice of the arts of conviviality become a sign that the powers they use are those of civilised eating, a practice which keeps hubris at bay. *The wisdom of folly is highly valued.*

On the other hand, there is no resolution of the great conflicts of mythic time. The villainy of the ludicrous, ironic, treacherous practices of creation time generate the ambiguous conditions for the humans who live today on earth – civilised eating, civilised sociality – are all to be acquired at great cost, with great difficulty, with great suffering, and with a good dash of treachery. We who use the powers of the cannibal god, Kuemoi, can also be poisoned into greedy, arrogant behaviour. The domesticated Piaroa can hardly separate themselves in any absolute way from the animal other. As human beings they are hardly innocent. This takes us to the genre of the grotesque, that genre that retains to the bitter end its unresolved conflicts and ambiguities.

The Genre of the Grotesque: the mythic narratives and the unresolved incongruities of history:

Mythic imageries of the grotesque and the absurd are not unusual. The French scholar, Vernant, speaks of the robust, multi-layered imagery of mythic narrations, their hilarity and the intellectuality attached to them. And, we may add, their strong connection to particular social philosophies, to distinctions of moral worth, to treasured ways of doing things. He calls for deeper cross-cultural comparison of mythic styles (with which I strongly agree). Is there a particular style of mythic presentations? I suggest that the genre of the grotesque is one such widespread style. The powers sufficiently mighty for creation are typically violent dramatic stories, as we see from Vernant's own disclosure of the ancient Greek mythology, and ours from Amazonia.

The story of creation time is one of poisoned intentionalities, of cosmic follies: it is a story of greed, hubris and mental derangement.

The genre of the Grotesque is calculatingly used by the narrator of Piaroa myths in unfolding, disclosing, evoking the deep absurdities of human existence and its pre-conditions as played out in creation time. Wisdom depends on understanding the message of the grotesque. We need to pay attention to such messages.

The 18th and 19th centuries had a pejorative view of the grotesque, judging it a vulgar species of the comic, deprived of the serious. In general it was viewed as a genre of ludicrous exaggeration, a genre of the fantastic. However, more recent responses (Kayser 1963, Thomson 1972) have understood it otherwise, stressing its power to speak to *reality*. They note that its explosive force serves to make us see the real world anew. It jolts one into a transformation of perspective on what reality might be.

Some relevant points with regard to this re-assessment of the genre of the grotesque to our understanding of the mythic narration performances are the following:

1) The genre of the grotesque (also read as the genre of mythic narrative) is *more attached to realism than fantasy*. It is extravagant, but not fantastic. However strange the grotesque world is, *it is also our world*. The mythic narration, in partaking of this genre, has as its first and foremost aim to express *the problematic nature of existence, and its preconditions*, to unfold the absurdities of our life, its ambivalences, as played out originally in the ironic grotesquery of creation time.

2) *The comic is necessary for the genre of the grotesque to work*. There is its playfulness and its terror, its confusion and interplay of heterogeneous elements: the monstrous and the ludicrous; humans, animals, and vegetables. There are its paradoxes and ironies (the creator of fire devouring meat raw), and also its shock tactics (Wahari eating stew discovers he is eating his own son). We react to the slapstick experience of such horror with glee, as opposites continually clash. We laugh at the tale of deceit, trickery, mischief, hubris, illness, death, cannibalism, treacheries, greed, general mayhem. Part of the glee comes from the question ever rising over 'who are the victims? who the victimisers?

3) There are the physical deformities, the (bawdy) bodyliness of it all (see Bakhtin). We have the 2-headed god of culture; the huge sexual organs, male and female (Think of Cronus' enormous member). Wahari, creator of people, transforms himself into the monster supreme deity beneath the earth, the dangerous chimerical Tapir/Anaconda, preying intently on his own kinsmen.

4) The most distinctive trait of the grotesque, according to Thomson (1972), is the unresolved nature of grotesque conflict, separating it out from neighbouring genres (e.g. the absurd). In Piaroa

myth, this grotesquery of the origin of culture is never resolved – Wahari did not succeed (Zeus did, but earthlings didn't). Thus, the forces for creation continue into today as the uncleaned product of the deadly hallucinogens that the creator god of the culinary arts withdrew from the rust of the sun andthe heart of the armadillo. The gods were creators and as such, killers.

5) The emotional and intellectual tension continues through the story: *it is one of poisoned and poisonous intentionalities*. Despite the human capacities of Piaroa people (their capabilities for the culinary arts, for reasoned intentionality and therefore sociality), *there remains this deep ambiguity to being human*. For *as humans they are hardly innocent*. Their reflections upon alterity recognise that the violence of foreign politics demands from the start an unleashing of poisonous forces from themselves not so very different from those of exterior others – or the gods (Overing 1996).

Ironic practices of the everyday

How should we as anthropologists interpret the Piaroa reactions to their absurd universe? We have then the ironic performances/rituals of everyday life among an egalitarian people who love their freedom and also their sociality. These are a people who are very fond of the comic; they find the practice of folly essential to their well-being: a very Amazonian way of thinking. My interest is how such a cosmogenesis and the philosophy of the absurd that comes from it (as understood by the Piaroa) are linked to their social psychology and to their egalitarianism. As we know, our own social theory of the comic is indeed weak, as too that of the grotesque.

For insight, we might be wise to turn to the likes of Vico on the political use of tropes (the more hierarchical people's values the more literalness is approved of) and Kenneth Burke on true irony being attached to *a deep humility with regard to our own frailties*. We need to think about an irony that does not make us 'superior' to the enemy, for we have some of the same attributes as he/she – and indeed we are indebted to this enemy. (For Piaroa, *the gods are cannibal predators, and so are the Piaroa themselves*).

Perhaps it is with lessons from the Taoist Monks (e.g. see Peter Berger) that we might begin to *understand the comic as a mode of knowledge*. Thus perhaps the Amazonian case is not totally alien. Let us look at the connections:

1) The role of the jokester shaman leader has much in common with the raucously laughing Taoist Monk. For both, *the comic is a mode of knowledge*.
2) The humour of both is forthcoming from a profound sense of the *incongruities (lack of reason) of the universe, and of human behaviour within it.*
3) There is a strong use of tropes. According to Peter Berger, the Ch'an/Zen way of teaching is through parables, through riddles, and *most solutions are in the form of jokes.*
4) What is more, *a self-mocking humility is taught.* The Piaroa shaman is the teacher of this attitude of the world – he starts with the children when they are five years old. Success in the ability of *not* taking oneself seriously is a good test of whether liberating, true learning has taken place, one that is *conducive to the deconstruction of reality*, with the disclosure of all its incongruities – albeit the shaman's job, but to a lesser, yet important extent by each individual.

Berger lists these components of a comic philosophy (as followed by the Taoists):

1) The diagnosis of the world as a mass of incongruence
2) The radical *debunking of pretensions of grandeur and wisdom* (the breeder of hubris)
3) A spirit of mocking irreverence

4) A profound discovery of and appreciation of freedom

Such a list fits as well the attitudes and teachings of the Piaroa shaman who teaches of the importance of humility – in light of the enemy within – and stresses at all times the craziness of the expression of anger and arrogance, true signs of a tyrannical temperament destructive of the accomplishment of a human sort of life. These are the lessons of the two diseases of craziness: *k'iraeu and k'eraeu.*

These are also philosophical insights that lead to a stress on the immense importance to sociality of the accomplishing affective comfort. The hierarchical and the literal are both too direct for affective comfort and well-being. The hierarchical and the literal can too easily and treacherously poison intentionality.

The comic, the social and the creation of a counterworld

Finally, a word on the notion of comedy as a counterworld and as 'anti-rites'. See M. Douglas and others on the notion that jokes are an intrusion of the comic into everyday life. **They see jokes as 'anti-rites'**, rebellious of ordained patterns of social life. They understand the comic as a *temporary* suspension of social structure!

However, for many Amazonian peoples, *folly lies at the heart of the social.* Far from the comic as an intrusion into everyday life, the view is that the human social condition can only be accomplished through the spirit of folly. Through an understanding of an ironic, grotesque cosmogenesis, Amazonian peoples tend to stress the value of playing out in social life a sociable 'humble irony'. For example, with Piaroa, ludic practices allow for sociable living and working together. They enable the bringing up of children, feeding them, curing them, and most important, teaching them the arts and decorum of Folly. In other words, ironic practice allows them to deal with the poisonous forces within that are at the same time conducive to a human way of life. *These are a people who recognise well the happiness of foolery, its poetics and also its necessity, its health-giving properties.*

In Amazonia often the achievement of the social forms a counterworld that protects against all those absurdities of the universe. Thus the ironic practices: a spirit of mocking irreverence, a debunking of all those pretensions of grandeur and wisdom, but coated with a good dose of well-considered humility in the face of it all. For those absurdities not only always intrude upon the everyday, they also rest within each person, corporeally so to speak. At any moment, and you never know, anyone can suffer **k'iraeu** (promiscuity, crazy laughter...) and any shaman could be attacked by **k'eraeu** (paranoia). This is the misery of cosmic Folly. It is the comic as a mode of knowledge that provides insight into this downside of folly: by knowing it, and practising in its light, we can, for a time at least, fool the cosmic comic incongruities of existence and of this world on earth. The latter being an environment created by means of poisonous, deadly hallucinogens.

References

Bakhtin, Mikhail (1968) *Rabelais and his World*, Cambridge, Mass: MIT Press.

Berger, Peter (1997) *Redeeming laughter: The Comic Dimension of Human Experience*, New York: Walter de Gruyter.

Douglas, Mary (1975) *Implicit Meanings*, London: Routledge and Kegan Paul.

Fernandez, James & M.T. Huber eds (2001) *Irony in Action: Anthropology, Practice, and the Moral Imagination*, Chicago: the University of Chicago Press.

Kayser, Wolfgang (1963) *The Grotesque in Art and Literature*, Bloomington.

Meyer, Michael (1995) *Literature and the Grotesque*, Amsterdam: Rodopi.

Overing, Joanna (2000) 'The efficacy of laughter: the ludic side of magic within Amazonian sociality', in Overing & Passes (below), *The Anthropology of Love and Anger*.

Overing, Joanna (2006) 'The Stench of Death and the Aromas of Life: Poetics of Ways of Knowing and Sensory Process among Piaroa of the Orinoco Basin', *Tipiti, Journal of the Society for the Anthropology of Lowland South America*, Volume 4, numbers 1& 4, June & December.

Overing, Joanna & Alan Passes eds (2000) *The Anthropology of Love and Anger: the aesthetics of conviviality in Native South America*, Routledge.

Thomson, Philip (1972) *The Grotesque*, Methuen & Co.

Zijderveld, Anton (1963) *On clichés: The supersedure of meaning by function in modernity*, Routledge & Kegan Paul.

Note

1. Paper originally presented in Santiago Chile, July 2003.

Chapter 9

HOW KNOWLEDGE GROWS:
AN ANTHROPOLOGICAL ANAMORPHOSIS

Alberto Corsín Jiménez

> *'the most admirable operations derive from very weak means'*
> *– Galileo Galilei (1968: 109)*

> *'Not just judgments about analogy but judgments about proportion inform any organization of data.'*
> *– Marilyn Strathern (2004 [1991]: 24)*

> *'A strange thing full of water'*
> *– Michel Serres (1995: 122)*

I open with a myth of origins:

All political thought evinces an aesthetic of sorts. Dioptric anamorphosis, for instance, was the 'science of miracles' through which Hobbes imagined his Leviathan. An example of the optical wizardry of seventeenth century clerical mathematicians, a dioptric anamorphic device used a mirror or lens to refract an image that had deliberately been distorted and exaggerated back into what a human eye would consider a natural or normal perspective. Many such artefacts played with pictures of the faces of monarchs or aristocrats. Here the viewer would be presented with a panel made up of a multiplicity of images, often emblems representing the patriarch's genealogical ancestors or the landmarks of his estate. A second look at the panel through the optical glass, however, would recompose the various icons, as if by magical transubstantiation, into the master's face.

Noel Malcolm has exposed the place that the optical trickery of anamorphosis played in Hobbes' political theory of the state (Malcolm 2002). According to Malcolm, the famous image of the Leviathan colossus that furnishes the title-page of Hobbes' book came as an inspiration to Hobbes following his encounter with a dioptrical device designed by the Minim friar Jean-François Nicéron. Nicéron's design involved a picture of the faces of twelve Ottoman sultans which, on looking through the viewing-glass tube, converged into the portrait of Louis XIII (Malcolm 2002: 213). Seduced by the structural symbolism through which such optical illusions could be used to represent *relations* between political persons (e.g. between the state and its subjects) (Malcolm 2002: 223), Hobbes commissioned an iconographic representation of similar effects for the title-page of his book. Here the image of the colossal Leviathan rises over the landscape energized by a mass of small figures. These morph by congregation into the body of the monarch, that hence takes a life of its own. A projection onto a one-dimensional surface of the dioptric trick, the figure of Leviathan aimed to capture the political innovation of Hobbes' theory of representational personification. For Hobbes, the aggregation of the political will of multiple individuals into an overarching sovereign person brought about a political transubstantiation: the Many became the One, which contained, but also transcended, the Many. This is why for Hobbes the theory of (political) representation is a theory of duplicity and duplication: it calls for the critical capacity to see oneself as both the creator of a political object (the body politic) and its subdued servant; both a distant outsider to the body and in partial identity with it. This entails, as Malcolm puts it, 'a curious structure of argument that requires two different ways of seeing the relation between the individual and the state to be entertained at one and the same time.' (Malcolm 2002: 228)

Building on the implications of Malcolm's analysis for our theories of the state, Simon Schaffer has recently offered a phantasmagorical reinterpretation of the place of optical illusionism in political perspectivism (Schaffer 2005). For Schaffer, the dioptric capacity to 'see double' is in fact but a first step towards the cancelling of all visions but the sovereign vision. According to Schaffer, dioptrics enables this parallax shift because it rationalizes as illusory all political perspectives that do not conform with the One: outside the body politic all visions are but the visions of political phantoms (Schaffer 2005: 202; on parallax shifts see Žižek 2006). In seventeenth century politics this was easily accomplished, according to Schaffer, because outside the rule of sovereign law – as Hobbes noted – lay only a chaotic state of nature, shaped by mistrust, fear, witchcraft accusations and the mischievous play of invisible phantoms. The rise of Leviathan exterminated the invisible, neatly aligning, in a supreme gesture of political illusionism, the planes of the natural and the phantasmagorical.

* * *

This paper offers anthropological insight into a certain fashion of Euro-American intellectual practice, namely, the operations through which knowledge comes-unto-itself as a descriptive register (of other practices). I am interested in the cultural epistemology that enables knowledge to become an enabler itself: what the growth of knowledge – or its rise as an expression of enablement – looks like. What does knowledge need to grow 'out of' for such an escalation to become meaningful or, simply, visible?

The making visible of knowledge as an object of growth has an anthropology to it.[1] It involves playful operations with social ideas of size and vision, and is materialized in a practical epistemology where the optical plays an intriguing culturally salient role[2]. Optics makes size an effect of exploration. It makes things big and small in different proportions, intensities and shapes. It provides a form or carrier for the expansions and contractions in/of knowledge. There is a seductive analogy between how knowledge has been rendered a mode of enablement in some Euro-American social theory and the perspectival technique known by art historians as anamorphic illusionism. (This should not be taken as pejorative: an illusion can be both hopeful and delusive.) As a praxis or craft of optical deformation, the anamorphic offers a useful *imago* for the cultural comportment of some aspects of Euro-American knowledge (De la Flor 2009).

As will come evident throughout, a source of inspiration for what follows has been the work of Marilyn Strathern. Of her own experimentation with narrative and analytic strategies in *Partial Connections*, she described the use she made of the imagery of the fractal (Cantor's Dust) in that book as 'an artificial device' that allowed her to 'experiment with the apportioning of "size" in a deliberate manner.' (Strathern 2004 [1991]: xxix) My interest in the anamorphic lies likewise in its use as a tool for making explicit how social theory and critique size themselves – that is, how 'size' has become an idiom for what theory does.

A rather obvious and yet rarely acknowledged route through which the imagination of 'size' has made its way into the sociological canon is via the descriptive and analytical purchase afforded by relations of magnitude known as 'proportions'. The analogy between enablement and escalation that I drew above – the image of knowledge as an expression of escalating enablement – is a case in point. There is an important and not-always acknowledged current in Euro-American social theory and philosophy that refracts the work of knowledge through the operations of a proportional imagination. Proportionality becomes the enabling mechanism of knowledge: how knowledge escalates out of itself.

Take the Leviathan. Hobbes' iconographic choice makes the Leviathan appear as a supreme trickster figure, at once enabling and concealing its own source of agency. The state's power figures as an aesthetic effect: the effect of a parallax shift, the alignment of two perspectives in one optical illusion. Importantly, the illusion is held in place through the work of a proportional imagination: 'the relation between the individual and the state', as Malcom puts it, is tricked into view and held stable as a proportional artifice. The One and the Many stand in a political relation to each other *because* of their proportional relationship. As a symbolic form, the meaningfulness and 'comparability of phenomena rests on preserving proportion or scale.' (Strathern 1990: 211) Nicéron's dioptric lens generates the perspective from which knowledge of the political surfaces. 'The political' emerges as a modern theoretical object thanks to the effect of the anamorphic artifice: it is what the world looks like from the point of view of the lens. Anamorphosis situates and aligns the world of political theory for us.

The anamorphic operates a second effect on the workings of knowledge, which I shall call 'reversibility'. Reversibility describes the double and simultaneous vision required to grant theoretical status to an object. When commenting on the illusionary character of Hobbes' Leviathan, Malcolm described it as 'the curious structure of argument that requires two different ways of seeing the relation between the individual and the state to be entertained at one and the same time.' (Malcolm 2002: 228) The *relational* character of sovereign power emerges thus as another effect of the anamorphic artifice. It is a produce of having to hold *simultaneously* an internal and external vision on the images of the twelve sultans and Louis XIII's emblem. Not without reason, Simon Schaffer described the methodological exigency underpinning our encounter with the phantom qualities of the Hobbesian body politic as 'seeing double' (Schaffer 2005). Moving in and out of the dioptric lens – performing the anamorphic – lends political theory its relational purchase.

The rest of this paper explores the hold that proportionality and reversibility have over the make-up of social theory. It may be read as an exploratory foray into the cultural analytics of some aspects of Euro-American knowledge,[3] and in this sense as an investigation into the novel anamorphic devices through which contemporary social theory may be generating its escalatory effects. Some comments are also made in passing about the contemporary economy of knowledge as, itself, an anamorphic configuration.[4]

$$* * *$$

Let me start with a rich and evocative account of how architects visualize their building projects by sociologist Albena Yaneva. Her field site is the Office for Metropolitan Architecture (OMA), the workplace of the famous Dutch architect, Rem Koolhaas; and her focus is the work carried out by architects at OMA during the design and development of a number of models for the new exhibition hall at the Whitney Museum of American Art in New York (Yaneva 2005). Yaneva writes from a self-confessed social studies of technology perspective, and indeed declares that in her account 'the architectural office will be studied in the same way that STS has approached the laboratory.' (Yaneva 2005: 869)

The ethnography starts from the premise that 'knowing through scaling is an integral aspect of architectural practice' and the author sets as her task to describe ethnographically the so-called enigma of the 'rhythm of scaling' (Yaneva 2005: 870, 868). The scales that Yaneva takes to task here are differently sized models of the Whitney building project. Architects in OMA work with two scale models of the projected building: a small-scale model, which is quickly put together by architects to provide a sketchy and abstract materialization of the basic concept guiding the project, and which includes a number of site constraints, such as urban and local zoning regulations or client requirements; and a much larger scale model, which is used to fine-tune the small model by fleshing-out its concrete details.

The small and large models are set up in two adjacent tables and architects spend a good amount of time moving from one table to the next, "'scaling up', 'jumping the scale, 'rescaling' and 'going down in scale'", in the vernacular terminology used by Yaneva's informants (Yaneva 2005: 870). In moving between tables and models, architects spend a considerable amount of time working with an instrument known as a 'modelscope', which is used to explore the inside of the small model. By inserting a miniature periscope into the model, architects redeploy themselves as human users of the building. 'The modelscope', an architect tells Yaneva, 'gives you a view that is like the scale of that model. So, you get to express the space at that scale. It gives you the opportunity to move around spaces you ordinarily can't get into and to see how they look... We are able to see how space is inside.' Yaneva further notes that 'minimized to the scale of the tiny model, [the architect] is exploring these microscopic spaces like in Gulliver's travels, he 'enters' the spaces and experiences them.' (Yaneva 2005: 876) Having cruised the inside of the small model, architects then assemble to discuss possible changes in the architectural layout of the building, which are later given concrete expression in changes made to the large model.

The scoping in and out of the small and large models is a recursive process: 'Scaling up', writes Yaneva, 'is immediately and reversibly followed by scaling down.' (Yaneva 2005: 883) However, as times goes by, the larger model inevitably amasses more information and detail than the smaller one, for it is to the larger model that the insights gained from exploring the small model eventually get transported and where they get reflected. Thus, the larger model grows in power and information by gathering the produce of the recursion. But importantly, Yaneva insists, this does not mean that the design involves a linear or evolutionary movement from the small model to the large model. The small model is not a pre-condition, or an evolutionary antecedent, for the revelation of proper and useful knowledge at the level of the larger scale model. Rather, the design is simultaneously present in the small and the large, the before and after of every recursion, the scoping in and out through which architects multiply the versions and the trajectories of the design. According to Yaneva, the shape the project finally takes emerges gradually as a form of extended and ubiquitous co-presence in the time and space of all such scalar operations. As 'it passes through these trials,' she says, 'it becomes more and more visible, more present, more material, real. 'Scaling' is not a way to fit into reality; rather, it is a conduit for its extraction.' (Yaneva 2005: 887)

There are two points I would like to make about the architects use of scaling as a method of knowledge and design. One is the extraordinary ease with which it sits next to *Gulliver's Travels*. The second is what this figure of scale takes for granted.

It is certainly worth noting how Jonathan Swift and Yaneva resort to a similar imagination of size to make their arguments carry force. For both size is important; it helps render certain insights valuable and visible. In fact, literary theorist Douglas Lane Patey has described *Gulliver's Tales* as 'laboratory experiments based on difference of size' (Patey 1991: 827), much like Yaneva describes her ethnography of architecture as a laboratory study in the 'rhythm of scaling'.

Of course, Swift's use of size has long attracted the attention of literary theorists for its satirical effects. It is satire that size aims for. I want to suggest, however, that one may explore the use of size in Swift not for its effects on something else, but for its effect on itself – that is, on its own self-apprehension as a body of knowledge. Size, then, as a vehicle for making knowledge an adequate expression of itself.

There is a wonderful episode in *Gulliver's Travels* that captures something of what I am hoping to convey here, namely, the extent to which knowledge comes in different sizes. At Brobdingnag, the land of the giants, Gulliver is taken to court for the diversion of the Queen and her ladies. Impressed by Gulliver's demeanour, the King, 'who had been educated in the Study of Philosophy, and particularly Mathematicks', suspects of Gulliver being 'a piece of Clock-work... contrived by some ingenious Artist.' He therefore sends for three great Scholars to examine Gulliver's shape and make-up. The scientists all agree that Gulliver 'could not be produced according to the regular Laws of Nature'. However, an opinion that he was an 'embrio' was rejected, as was his characterisation as an 'abortive Birth'; nor could he be a dwarf, because his 'Littleness was beyond all degree of comparison; for, the Queen's favourite Dwarf, the smallest ever known in that Kingdom, was near thirty Foot high.' (Swift 2002 [1726]: 86-87) Thus, 'After much debate', the scholars finally sentenced that Gulliver

> was only *Relplum Scalcath*, which is interpreted literally, *Lusus Naturae* [a freak of nature]; a Determination exactly agreeable to the Modern Philosophy of *Europe*, whose Professors, disdaining the old Evasion of *occult Causes*, whereby the Followers of *Aristotle* endeavour in vain to disguise their Ignorance, have invented this wonderful Solution of all Difficulties to the unspeakable Advancement of human knowledge. (Swift 2002 [1726]: 87)

The episode is emblematic of Swift's mordacity, and in particular his dislike of the new Modern science of the Royal Society, epitomised here in the figure of the three scholars. For Swift, modern science falls trap to tautology (circular and self-explanatory arguments, such as something being a 'freak of nature') inasmuch as ancient science did. But the episode is further remarkable for its defence of size as comparative epistemology. Gulliver does not survive comparison, not against dwarves, embryos or abortive births, so he is in the last instance catalogued as a freak of nature. Not even the use of a 'Magnifying-Glass' can help the scholars reach an agreement on what Gulliver may be. They size him up and they size him down, only to conclude that he is not a product of nature.[5] Thus, for Lane Patey, 'Swift's play with perspective (relative size and its implications)' ultimately enacts the question: 'what is there in us that survives comparison – what that cannot be rendered ludicrous, shameful, or disgusting when magnified to Brobdingnagian proportions or shrunk to Lilliputian?' (Patey 1991: 826) Said differently, in Brobdingnag country, Gulliver lacks ontology because he is out-of-proportion with the world.

My second remark on architects' use of scaling as a method of knowledge builds on this question about size and the proportionality of the world. In Yaneva's account, what is at stake is how the project grows and consolidates its own size, or how it finds in the small and large models different capacities to deploy different aspects of the design. The qualities of the design are therefore allowed to emerge through the recursive travelling between models of different size. Thus, the scale that dominates is that of size. I want to suggest, however, that Yaneva's ethnography provides some room for speculating about an alternative scale; to imagine the architects looking into the models for certain qualities other than those of *adjustment to size*. For example, when the effect that a giant red escalator has on the interior of the exhibition hall is examined through the modelscope, the architects agree that the escalator needs to be moved to a different spot within the hall. We are left in shades as to what exactly motivates the relocation, although Yaneva intimates that the 'scaling team engages in a dialogue... [about] dispositions, objects they see inside the model, spatial transitions, material properties of the foam [used to build the model], proportions and shapes.' (Yaneva 2005: 875) Things do not quite fit together for the architects, but it is no longer clear that this fit is a question of scale. Thus, the adjustment that the architects appear to be looking for now seems to aim for a different kind of harmony, or an equilibrium of different proportions.[6]

Adjustments to scale

In an age of computer technology, the use that OMA's architects make of the use of scale models may appear a little surprising for those of us who are new to the field of architecture. But in fact, as historian of architecture Paul Emmons has shown, the use of scale and scalar drawings has played a fundamental part in architectural practice throughout history (Emmons 2005). For example, from 'the middle of the second millennium BCE,' writes Emmons, 'a statue of Gudea, leader of the City State of Lagash in present day Iraq, is seated with a building floor plan resting on his lap. Also on the tablet are a stylus and a scale rule, showing fine divisions of the finger measure.' (Emmons 2005: 227). Like Yaneva, in his historical survey Emmons draws too an analogy between the use of scale in architecture and Swift's *Gulliver travels*, and the 17th century scalar imagination at large. Thus, he compares Swift's use of scale with that of Voltaire's in *Micromégas*, and identifies further in Robert Hooke's *Micrographia* a locus of general influence for the period. Hooke, who was a Surveyor for the City of London and designed himself a number of buildings along with his friend Christopher Wren, 'transferred his familiarity with scale from architectural drawing to the microscope.' (Emmons 2005: 231) Published in 1665, *Micrographia* described Hooke's use of a microscope to make observations of miniature aspects of the natural world, such as fly's eye or a plant cell. The book became an immediate best-seller of its day.

Of interest for our purposes here is Hooke's mode of use and relationship to the microscope. Emmons cites a passage in the *Micrographia* which echoes in fascinating ways how Yaneva's architects scooped in and out of the small and the large scale models. 'Hooke organised his microscopic observations', writes Emmons, 'progressively from simple to complex, like a geometer ascending from point, line, plane to volume and the chain of being from mineral to vegetable and animal. He began with observing the point of a pin under the microscope... He next analysed a dot made by a pen, and in a scalar reverie imagined this dot as the earth in space.' However, Hooke was also aware that this amassment of detail – from the simple to the complex – required a second operation to remain epistemologically productive. He went at quite some effort to keep the observations made *inside* the scale of the microscope at a par with those made *outside* the microscope. As Emmons puts it, 'Hooke explained his method determining the microscope's scale of magnification by looking with one eye through the microscope as the other naked eye examines a ruler, *simultaneously engaging both scales*.' (Emmons 2005: 231, emphasis added) This simultaneous engagement of both scales echoes the parallax shift of Hobbes' Leviathan: an illusion of epistemological and political efficacy enabled by the dimension of reversibility at work in the anamorphic. I shall come back to this point later.

Emmons concludes his observations on the historical importance of scale for architecture by commenting on architects' contemporary use of computer software to generate 1:1 or full scale CAD projections of architectural designs. For Emmons, the use of CAD technology emulates a Cartesian approach to the generation of objects, where things can be described or plotted through systems of notational or algebraic relations. Thus, the use of CAD-enabled full scale drawing 'makes it more likely that the designer looks at the image as an object rather than projecting oneself into the image through an imaginative inhabitation. Scale sight is not an abstraction; it is achieved through judging the size of things in relation to ourselves.' (Emmons 2005: 232) His 'handbook advise', then, is to 'learn to think within a scale rather than translate from actual measure.' (Emmons 2005: 232) Against Cartesianism, for Emmons, the 'empathetic bodily projection' of scale is 'critical to imagining a future edifice.' (Emmons 2005: 232)

Of Emmons' description of the history of architectural practice there are two aspects that I would like to hold in view. The first deals with the proportionality of architecture as a skill and trade; the second, to which I shall return later, with the deployment of the 'double vision' that is entailed in the practice of scoping in and out of scale.

Emmons' concern is with current architectural practice, where scale fares as a context-free metric, and advocates instead a return to 'judging the size of things in relation to ourselves.' This form of empirical judgment echoes what Yaneva called a 'rhythm of scaling': an iterative re-proportional exercise through which the world sizes its ontology (its human and non-human landscape) to a proper shape and form.

In fact, architectural practice provides in this context an interesting place for seeing not only the work of proportionality at play, but its recurrent entanglement in larger debates about the epistemic structure of scientific knowledge. David Turnbull, for example, has described how in the absence of knowledge about structural mechanics the use of proportionality in medieval times enabled the construction of imposing and majestic Gothic cathedrals such as Chartres. According to Turnbull,

> In the absence of rules for construction derived from structural laws problems could be resolved by practical geometry, using compasses, a straight-edge, ruler, and string. The kind of structural knowledge which was passed on from master to apprentice related sizes to spaces and heights by ratios, such as half the number of feet in a span expressed in inches plus one inch will give the depth of a hardwood joist.... This sort of geometry is extremely powerful; it enables the transportation and transmission of structural experience, makes possible the successful replication of a specific arrangement in different places and different circumstances, reduces a wide variety of problems

to a comparatively compact series of solutions, and allows for a flexible rather than rigid rule-bound response to differing problems.... Essentially it enables a dimensionless analysis precluding the need for a common measure. Geometrical techniques in this case provide a powerful mode of communication that dissolve problems of incommensurability that the use of individual measurement systems might otherwise have. (Turnbull 2000: 69)

Turnbull is interested in the constitution of what he calls 'knowledge spaces'. These are the 'kinds of spaces that we construct in the process of assembling, standardising, transmitting and utilising knowledge' (Turnbull 2000: 12). Western science is in this respect no different from other knowledge systems, such as indigenous or amateur knowledge systems. What distinguishes the epistemic robustness of technoscience, rather, is its development of a corpus of techniques and protocols that enable knowledge to move and travel beyond localised sites of production. The further knowledge can travel, the more coherent and robust its epistemic make-up. This is why for Turnbull one can imagine the architectural site of a cathedral in no different terms from those of a laboratory (Turnbull 2000: 66-67). All that it takes is identifying an analogical 'scalar' denominator: something that can operate the changes in scale required for knowledge to cohere and travel. For Turnbull, in the context of medieval cathedral building this task was performed by the 'template':

Three major 'reversals of forces' are achieved with this one small piece of representational technology; one person can get large numbers of others to work in concert; large numbers of stones can be erected without the benefit of a fully articulated theory of structural mechanics or a detailed plan; and incommensurable pieces of work can be made accumulative (Turnbull 2000: 68).

Turnbull's focus on proportionality as a tool for sense-making provides a vivid example of the terms through which knowledge is said to 'grow' as an epistemic object. The work of proportionality suffuses knowledge with an ontological structure. In Turnbull's account this is actually so in two senses. On the one hand, proportionality is what masons used to calculate the fit between spaces and heights. The proportion is the vehicle for lending the world a certain height, length and width. But the imagery of proportionality is also what underpins Turnbull's very own analytical explanations. Thus, in an echo of the Galilean epigram that heads this paper – 'the most admirable operations derive from very weak means' –, Turnbull writes of how the use of the template by masons enabled 'one person... [to] get large numbers of others to work in concert'. This is a truly Archimedean metaphor, where a sociological effect is made visible by imagining agency as a leverage of sorts.

Architectural optics of volumes

The movements in size, the dynamics of aggrandizement and miniaturisation that Turnbull describes as characteristic of the epistemic work of science, are nowhere rendered in so vivid a style as in Bruno Latour's historical ethnography of Pasteur's microbiology. According to Latour, amongst Pasteur's greatest achievements is his translation of the interests that nineteenth century farmers and veterinarians had in the anthrax bacillus into the discourse and practices of bacteriologists. This Pasteur accomplishes by becoming himself a 'microbe farmer': by removing a cultivated bacillus from the 'outside' real world of farming and veterinary science and isolating and culturing it 'inside' a sanitised laboratory space. Whereas in the former the 'anthrax bacilli are mixed with millions of other organisms' and therefore practically invisible to the scientific gaze, in the latter 'it is freed from all competitors and so grows exponentially', 'growing so much' that it 'ends up... in such large colonies that a clear-cut pattern is made visible to the watchful eye of the scientist.' (Latour 1983: 146) The inside:outside::visible:invisible equation creates and enables different zones of empowerment and agency for different actors. Thus,

> the asymmetry in the scale of several phenomena is modified: a micro-organism can kill vastly larger cattle, one small laboratory can learn more about pure anthrax cultures than anyone before; the invisible micro-organism is made visible; the until now interesting scientists in his lab can talk with more authority about the anthrax bacillus than veterinarians ever have before. (Latour 1983: 146)

Translation works therefore as a sort of rebalancing mechanism, where Pasteur stands as fulcrum: the messy and cloudy world of outside farming and veterinary diseases is funnelled through the inside of Pasteur's laboratory to crystallise and make visible a new balance of powers. Pasteur's laboratory becomes a lever for a new distribution of power. In Latour's succinct formulation:

> The change of scale makes possible a reversal of the actors' strengths; 'outside' animals, farmers and veterinarians were *weaker* than the invisible anthrax bacillus; inside Pasteur's lab, man becomes stronger than the bacillus, and as a corollary, the scientist in his lab gets the edge over the local, devoted, experienced veterinarian. (Latour 1983: 147)

In these and other accounts Latour uses the imagery of scale to produce sociological explanations. He sizes objects and agencies up and down vis-à-vis each other to make certain sociological effects visible. A similar appraisal of the Latourian project has been offered by Simon Schaffer, who has remarked on the extent to which 'The model of the lever plays a fundamental role throughout Latour's *oeuvre*: scientists achieve astonishing reversals of force by rendering lab objects commensurable with the forces of the world, then manipulating the former to shift the latter.' Schaffer notes how in his descriptions Latour chooses an 'Archimedean point' around which he then proceeds to effect an 'inversion of scale' letting certain beings (human or nonhuman) 'move forces apparently more powerful than' them (Schaffer 1991: 184).

Latour is certainly aware of the choice of imagery through which he fleshes-out his epistemology. Of his Pasteur article, 'Give me a laboratory and I will raise the world', he writes that 'I used in the title a parody of Archimedes's famous motto' because '[t]his metaphor of the lever to move something else is much more in keeping with observation than any dichotomy between a science and a society.' (Latour 1983: 154) His point, quite rightly, is that the reception and endorsement of Pasteur's scientific advances by French society cannot be explained by a simple dichotomic framework of Science-Society encounters. Rather, one needs to attend to the different strategies and practices through which a variety of partisan interests are recruited and converted into laboratory skills and techniques, and vice versa, the way in which the laboratory and its infrastructural equipment gets deployed and travel outside the laboratory walls *sensu stricto*. In other words, the way in which Pasteur becomes a farmer and farmers becomes Pasteurians.

Notwithstanding this declaration of epistemological self-awareness, what remains intriguing is the long lineage of proportional epistemologies to which this style of sociological reasoning and argumentation belongs. In *We have never been modern* Latour comments on the Hobbes-Boyle controversy by observing how Hobbes insisted on denying what was 'to become the essential characteristic of modern power: the change in scale and the displacements that are presupposed by laboratory work.' (Latour 1993: 22) For Latour, the laboratory performs for modernity the role of a 'theatre of measurement' or instrument for size-making, and indeed it is the self-explicitation of size that in his own work becomes his analytic trademark. His sociology fares as a sociology of size, or rather of the fluctuations of size.

The term 'theatre of measurement' is Michel Serres' (1982). It is used by Serres to describe 'the scene of representation established for Western thought [by ancient Greeks] for the next millennium.' It marks the 'instauration of the moment of representation' by philosophy, an instauration brought about through the use of 'a perspectival geometry, of an architectural optics of volumes' (Serres 1982: 92). This is a wonderful phrase that captures much of what I have been dwelling on up to this point. Serres' argument builds on the tale of Thales' measurement of the height of the great pyramid. Thales accomplishes this feat by placing a post in the sand. As the sun sets, the triangular shadows cast by the pyramid and post are then compared. In so doing, Thales invents thus 'the notion of a model' (Serres 1982: 86):

> By comparing the shadow of the pyramid with that of a reference post and his own shadow, Thales expressed the invariance of similar forms over changes of scale. His theorem therefore consists of the infinite progression or reduction of size while preserving the same ratio. From the colossal, the pyramid, to the small, a post or body, decreasing in size *ad infinitum*, the theorem states a logos or identical relation, the invariance of the same form, be it on a giant or a small scale, and vice versa. Height and strength are suddenly scorned, smallness demands respect, all scales and hierarchies are demolished, now derisory since each step repeats the same logos or relation without any changes! (Serres 1995: 78)

Steven Brown, who has commented on the originality of Serres' oeuvre for social theory at large, glosses Serres' analysis thus:

> Here truly is the 'Greek miracle' – one man dominates a mighty pyramid. In this 'theatre of measurement' invented through the simple act of placing a peg in the sand, it is as though everything

changed place. The weak human overcomes ancient hewn stone, the mobile sun produces immobile geometric forms... There is an interaction or communication between two diverse partners (Thales, Pyramid) which involves a switching or exchanging of properties (weak/strong, mortal/durable). (Brown 2005: 220)

We are back, then, to the Archimedean image of the leverage. The world's intelligibility holds itself together through an image of ontological balance. Whatever the world turns out to be – however and wherever we locate its sources of agency – this will always 'net-out' as an exchange of equations: weak/strong, mortal/durable, cathedral/template, gigantic/infinitesimal, etc. The use of a proportional imagination allows social theory to net-out its descriptive projects in ontological fashion.[7]

Proportions in perspective

Of course, in some sense, the importance of proportionality for architectural, and indeed socio-spatial reflection at large, has always been a matter of perspective – of optics. The origins of perspective in the fifteenth century have long been traced back to the renaissance of classical proportionality. As Martin Jay has observed, 'Growing out of the late medieval fascination with the metaphysical implications of light - light as divine *lux* rather than perceived *lumen* - linear perspective came to symbolize a harmony between the mathematical regularities in optics and God's will.' Pictorial and aesthetic preoccupations shifted from a religious interest in objects to 'the spatial relations of the perspectival canvas themselves. This new concept of space was geometrically isotropic, rectilinear, abstract, and uniform.' (Jay 1988: 5-6) Thus, famously, for Erwin Panofsky Renaissance perspective realised reflexivity as a spatial gaze (Panofsky 1993 [1927]). The difference between classical and renaissance perspective is one in the mode of occupying space and imagining spatial relations. In the Renaissance, the perspective marks a mode of taking the world in by looking through it. This is different from the classical disposition of bodies in space, which remains anchored in the physical mimesis of experience and bodily movement (Iversen 2005). We may say that Renaissance perspectivalism introduces epistemological gradients to the way we look at the world: perspective does not drive us to a singular epistemological residence. There are differences between 'looking at' and 'looking through' something; the movement of the gaze through space – the achievement of depth and the skewing of vision through off-centred displacements – generates different sorts of friction. In this context, rather than, or beyond its comprehension as a geometrical or symbolic form, the way Panofsky did, perspectivalism may be seen instead as a 'general capacity for producing effects' (Damisch 1997 [1987]: 41, my translation).

What kind of effects are those the deployment of perspective produces? Very early on in the theorisation of perspectivalism, Renaissance writers already described Brunelleschi's architectural use of perspective (for it is Brunelleschi who is widely acknowledged for discovering the technique of perspectivalism), for its very special effects on making objects *diminish in size*. Hubert Damisch cites Antonio Filarete's famous *Trattato di archittettura*, where the use by Brunelleschi of a mirror to help frame the lineaments of whatever the architect needs to represent is praised for 'making easily observable the contours of those things closer to the eye, whilst those that are farthest away will diminish proportionately in size.' (cited in Damisch 1997 [1987]: 68) The observation is common: Antonio di Tucci Manetti, an early biographer of Brunelleschi, likewise describes perspective as a 'science which requires to determine well and with reason the diminutions and augmentations... of things close and afar' (cited in Damisch 1997 [1987]: 70-71). An acknowledged novelty of perspectivalism, then, seems to lie in the cultural salience lend to the technical capacity for making *variations in size visible*. Moreover, size becomes an effect of scoping: a consequence of zooming-in and out of representation. A spectator can enter a picture's plane so long as she can keep certain proportions in place. The world inside the painting is therefore made to appear geometrically co-extensive with the world outside. An ontological continuity between pictorial and world space is obtained through the friction and play entailed in making things big and small.

In its original formulation, the question of perspective raised yet another cultural complex with epistemological significance, namely, the problem of reflexive *distance*. The experiment or demonstrations for which Brunelleschi is regarded as the discoverer of perspective involved two paintings of the Baptistery of St. John and the Palazzo de' Signori, both long lost. The only eye-witness account describes the Baptistery painting as being executed on a small wooden panel. Once the painting was accomplished, Brunelleschi drilled a small hole in the panel at the point which would represent his equivalent viewpoint on the Baptistery's plane (the vanishing point). He then invited spectators to peer through the hole from the back of the panel at a mirror held in front to reflect the painting. (In passing, let me draw attention to the emphasis that Filerete's account of the drawing places in how it is the sharp use of 'one eye' that will best bring to life the full power of the perspectival illusion (Damisch 1997 [1987]: 69).) It remains uncertain whether Brunelleschi realised he needed to control the viewing distance for spectators to replicate his original point of view on the Baptistery (Damisch 1997 [1987]: 98; Kemp 1990: 13, 344-345). What Brunelleschi's experiment did accomplish, however, was to throw into relief the significance of *distance* as an epistemological figure. There is a proper distance between our holding the world in view and the world's presentation or disclosure of its forms. A subtle shift is introduced: between the point of view on the world and the *relational variance* through which the view obtains.

Anamorphosis

The relation between perspectivalism and proportionality assumed a number of forms from the fifteenth to the seventeenth century.[8] In keeping with the optical trope, Martin Jay has identified at least three scopic regimes of modernity: Cartesian perspectivalism, of the symbolic kind analysed by Panofsky; the so-called art of describing, where the viewer is drawn to the surface or material qualities of objects and not their relational disposition in space; and, finally, baroque or anamorphic modernity (Jay 1988). It is with the latter that I am concerned here.

Anamorphic illusionism deployed the epistemological power of relational variance to its full. Anamorphic projections of objects are distorted such that it takes the use of a special device or manoeuvre to have the object restored to its original form. Remember the Leviathan and Nicéron's dioptric device. Sometimes it is the use of a special kind of lens that does the trick of reconfiguration; sometimes the observer is required to skew her vision, for example, by approaching the picture at a particular angle. As Lacan famously argued, vision is here confronted with a blind spot of conscious perception (Lacan 1979). The object stares back from a point of view that remains oblique to us. In the Brunelleschian demonstration, what is excluded is *the other eye*: the eye that does not look through the peephole and yet which is reflected back from the vanishing point. This one-eyed optics is intriguingly reminiscent of Hooke's microscopic vision, where one eye holds the scale of the miniature in view whilst the other is focused on the scale of representation. It further echoes the 'seeing double' at play in the Leviathan's optics. An eye is constructed that is therefore simultaneously internal and external to vision.[9] The eye becomes the optical metaphor through which the body is made visible as a conduit of dis/proportional relations: the bodies of the architect, the micrographer and the perspectival illusionist holding the world to account by virtue of a 'double vision'. Double vision foregrounds thus the body as a figure of scale between the natural and the social worlds. In Margaret Iversen's formulation, 'The real in the scopic field is formed when the eye splits itself off from its original immersion in visibility and the gaze as *objet petit a* [as unattainable object of desire] is expelled.' (Iversen 2005: 201) A split eye that signals in turn the birth of the Baroque as an aesthetic of the uncanny: an aesthetic 'which consisted in making something visible, in being a pure apparition that made appearance appear, from a position just on its edges' – and which citing Paul Klee, Christine Buci-Glucksmann describes as 'to see with one eye and consciously perceive with the other' (Buci-Glucksmann 1994 [1984]: 60).

Under the scopic regime of the anamorphic, then, the illusions of knowledge undergo a transformation from a concern with proportionality to an obsession with reversibility – with the illusions of double vision – the eye that sees inside/outside itself. It is indeed in these terms that Deleuze described too the anamorphic as the condition of possibility of the Baroque age – and by extension of our neo-Baroque contemporary. In his lectures on Leibniz about the rise of perspectivalism in the development of projective geometry Deleuze asks, recalling Leibniz's thought, 'What produces a point of view?', to which he answers, 'That regional *proportion* of the world that is clearly and distinctively expressed by an individual in relation to the totality of the world that is expressed confusingly and obscurely.' (Deleuze 2006 [1980/1986/1987]: 37, emphasis added, my translation) However, in his book on the expressiveness of Baroque thought as a philosophy of curvature and sensuous shadows, which represents Deleuze's mature reflections on Leibniz (Deleuze 1993), this very same thought is rendered somewhat differently: 'every point of view', writes Deleuze there, 'is a point of view on variation. The point of view is not what varies with the subject... it is, to the contrary, the condition in which an eventual subject apprehends a variation (metamorphosis), or: something = x (anamorphosis).' (Deleuze 1993: 20)

What is at stake in the holding of the world as an

ontological infinitude of variance, Deleuze realizes in editing his lecture notes on Leibniz for publication, is not the movement of proportional changes through which the world transforms itself, but the condition of variance itself: 'The infinite presence in the finite self is exactly the position of Baroque equilibrium or disequilibrium.' (Deleuze 1993: 89) What is of interest to Baroque thought, therefore, is no longer the proportions through which the world holds itself together, but the distortions and disproportions (the shadows) that call for its deformation (anamorphosis).[10] It is the anamorphic, the politics of the gigantic and the exaggerated – of variance as a sense of amplitude, expansion and/ or subsequent contraction – that characterises and is worthy of commentary in modernist thought. The anamorphic becomes the distinguishing characteristic of modern society.

The economy of knowledge

Let me change registers for a moment and turn to the knowledge economy.

Much has been written about it so I will be very selective today on the aspects I want to focus on. My concern is the relatively recent discourse on knowledge as a social product. It is the explicitly 'social' dimension of knowledge that I am interested in here.

Prompted by recent developments in intellectual property law, legal theorists and information and knowledge economists have turned to the Internet for understanding the emergence of new distributed and collaborative platforms for the production and consumption of online media. There is a sense in which the velocity of distribution, circulation, modification and consumption of new media by an expansive community of users imprints the nature of such an exchange economy with a distinctive 'social' dimension (Benkler 2006; Lessig 2008). The social is here identified with a sense of expansion, velocity and online presence. This is a relational economy of knowledge where the social is the outcome of people being partners in the exchange of knowledge for one another. We may push the analogy by saying that if there is no knowledge and no exchange, then, in this economy, there is no sociality – or at least no *productive* sociality (Shirky 2008). It appears that knowledge, economy and the social are therefore conceptualised as some kind of substitutes for one another. Karin Knorr-Cetina and Alex Preda have described this allegedly mutual transparency of knowledge, economy and the social to each other as being founded on (again using an optical metaphor) a 'specular epistemology' (Knorr-Cetina & Preda 2001: 34). The work that the specular performs here reminds us of Emmons' rendition of CAD-enabled full scale architectural drawing, where a computer-generated object is presumed to map transparently, one-to-one, to the future edifice. Architects work with the model *as if* it was the real building. Thus, both the specular and the 'as if' function seem to operate with an underlying principle of substitution which *regardless of the changes in scale* does not neutralize the importance of size. The computer-generated building is scale-free but it is sizeable nonetheless; as Michel Serres said of Thales' accomplishment, it 'expresses the invariance of similar forms over changes of scale.' (Serres 1995: 78) Social theory and philosophy thus no longer need scale to deliver impressions of size. We could say that the substitution has effected a sort of proportional equivalence that allows one to stop thinking of size in terms of scale but which retains a sense of dimensionality. In the context of the new economy of knowledge, this is patently obvious: knowledge has a size because the economy has a size and because society, naturally, has a size too!

Such specular epistemology points to a second characteristic of those approaches to knowledge that take for granted its sociological condition, as if knowledge were indeed a sociological object *per se*. Knorr-Cetina distinguishes between 'interiorized' and 'exteriorized' theories of knowledge. The former focuses on knowledge as something to be wrought and struggled with, sometimes with care, often with effects that are distressing, maybe even painful. Knowledge is something that is put together through time and whose permanency and stability is often transitory and contingent. Exteriorized theories of knowledge, on the other hand, see knowledge as a ready-made object upon which other forces exert their pressure. Knowledge is here imagined as an object of sorts, a commodity or resource to be transacted, stored, managed or appropriated in different ways. The idea that knowledge can be put to work alongside other objects of political economy, such as governance, interdisciplinarity or user-centred designs, partakes of the specular epistemology described above, because insofar as knowledge is treated as a self-contained object it can sit comfortably next to other political objects. 'Knowledge' and 'governance', for example, are specular to each other because arguments can be made about one *as if* refracted or optically accommodated through the other. They function as proportionate forms for each other.

If exteriorized theories of knowledge treat knowledge as an 'unspecified 'it'', ready to be grasped and deployed in policy circles, interiorized theories, on the other hand, bring 'into focus knowledge itself, breaking open and specifying the processes that make up the 'it''. (Knorr-Cetina & Preda 2001: 30) In her study of the cultures of contemporary science (molecular biologists and physicists), Knorr-Cetina has unpacked some the processes that interiorize knowledge as an epistemic form (Knorr-Cetina 1999). Her focus is what laboratory work does to scientific knowledge: the reconfiguration of objects and human relationships that take place in laboratory settings. According to Knorr-Cetina, what laboratory work accomplishes in essence is the adaptation and reconfiguration of natural processes and objects to suit the spatio-temporal requirements of scientists. In a laboratory a scientist can resist the natural tendencies and properties of an object in at least three ways: (i) she 'does not need to put up with an object *as it is*, it can substitute transformed and partial versions'; (ii) she 'does not need to accommodate the natural object *where it is*, anchored in a natural environment', and; (iii) she does not need to 'accommodate an event *when it happens*'; she can 'dispense with natural cycles of occurrence and make events happen frequently enough for continuous study.' (Knorr-Cetina 1999: 27) Under such conditions

> Laboratories recast objects of investigation by inserting them into new temporal and territorial regimes. They play upon these objects' natural rhythms and developmental possibilities, *bring them together in new numbers, renegotiate their sizes, and redefine their internal makeup...* In short, they create new configurations of objects that they match with an appropriately altered social order. (Knorr-Cetina 1999: 43-44, emphasis added)

The image of re-combinatorial and re-configurating processes draws of course on a familiar genealogy in science and technology studies. The 'partial versions' that are substituted for natural objects in laboratory experiments echo for example the 'partial connections' that relate difference in Donna Haraway's famous cyborg assemblages (Haraway 1986: 37). Manipulating a laboratory object's internal rhythms and developmental possibilities is not unlike what a cyborg's prosthetic extensions realize by way of supplementary or accelerated capacities. The experimental and the cyborg both operate as scale-shifting devices: they bring about enhancements that are of a different order of magnitude to their original state. 'The one component is of different order from the other, and is not created by what creates that other. They are not built to one another's scale.' (Strathern 2004 [1991]: 39) They both create extensions beyond a 1:1 equivalence. Importantly, as Strathern points out, such enhanced capacities work because the partial versions 'are neither proportionate to nor disproportionate from one another.' (Strathern 2004 [1991]: 36) There is a displacement, an extra-effect, that echoing Deleuze we might describe as a 'variation (metamorphosis), or: something = x (anamorphosis).'

There is also central place warranted to bodies in cyborg politics. In a cyborg world... people are not afraid of their joint kinship with animals and machines, not afraid of permanently partial identities and contradictory standpoints. The political struggle is *to see from both perspectives at once* because each reveals both dominations and possibilities unimaginable from the other vantage point. Single vision produces worse illusions than *double vision* or many-headed monsters.' (Haraway 1990: 196, emphases added)

The architect, the micrographer, the illusionist, the microbiologist... and the cyborg. The eye becomes the optical metaphor through which the body is made visible as a conduit of dis/proportional configurations. Double vision foregrounds the *political* body as a figure of scale of natural and social relations.

Conclusion

If I may sum up my argument to this point, I have tried to elucidate the terms of a proportional analytic underpinning in profound ways modernist social theory and philosophy. This is characterised by the work of scale and size as modes of explicitation of knowledge. The point is worth underscoring: it is not that knowledge takes a size (which in a very crass sense it certainly does) but that it becomes self-explicitated as an epistemic object in terms of size and scale, and in particular through movements of aggrandizement and/or miniaturisation. The epistemic productivity of knowledge appears in this context as being premised on an analytic of what may be described as a play of scopic deformations. The figure of anamorph, I have suggested, may work as both an epistemic and political *imago* for these kind of effects.

The anamorphic provides us also with an interesting commentary on anti- or non-modernist social theory, or in the words of Martin Jay, with the point of view afforded by a scopic regime that operates at the margins of modernity, within the vicinity of its material wreckages.[11] A point of view, then, apprehended as such from its own displaced remainders. Anamorphism is what modernity looks like when residual vision (the other eye) pushes its discarded bodies centre stage. When the object, that is, stares back. In this sense, if there is a form of aesthetic elicitation that takes the point of view of the non-modern for granted (including non-human persons and objects), that would certainly be the anamorphic. We may therefore say that the anamorphic is the analytics that elicits 'perspectivism' itself as an analytic; the analytic that allows an object-centred epistemology to come into view.

In a beautiful image, Michel Serres has described Thales inauguration, his emplacement of the peg in the sand, as 'a strange thing full of water': the creation of a 'logos-proportion' capable of providing accounts of 'objects whose appearance and birth are independent of us and which develop by themselves in relation to other objects of the world': things that are born from air, fire or water, and that do not attend to the laws or rules of kings or gods. The Nile floods to which Thales was a witness washed away the fields' crops and his 'proportion' came to the rescue of, indeed, a strange world full of water: a world which demanded a new logos to measure the land, re-establish the cadastral register, net-out the outstanding balances between creditors and debtors (Serres 1995: 122).

Today the proportion has dried-up the world again. In their examination of the status and place of atlases in the history of objectivity (and the wider history of epistemology), Lorraine Daston and Peter Galison have searched for a type of explanation that is 'on the same scale and of the same nature as the explanandum itself.' In their own words,

> If training a telescope onto large, remote causes fails to satisfy, what about the opposite approach, scrutinizing small, local causes under an

explanatory microscope? The problem here is the mismatch between the heft of explanandum and explanans, rather than the distance between them: in their rich specificity, local causes can obscure rather than clarify the kind of wide-ranging effect that is our subject here... Looking at microcontexts tells us a great deal – but it can also occlude, like viewing an image pixel by pixel. The very language of cause and effect dictates separate and heterogeneous terms: cause and effect must be clearly distinguished from each other, both as entities and in time. Perhaps this is why the metaphors of the telescope and the microscope lie close to hand. Both are instruments for bringing the remote and inaccessible closer. But relationships of cause and effect do not exhaust explanation. Understanding can be broadened and deepened by exposing other kinds of previously unsuspected links among the phenomena in question, such as patterns that connect scattered elements into a coherent whole. (Daston & Galison 2007: 36)

Although they surreptitiously subscribe to the language of scale and the playful operations of scopic deformations, the call to attend the problems of 'The mismatch between the heft of explanandum and explanans', as they put it, is of course a call to re-describe the weights that inhere in the forms of the explainer and the explained; in other words, a call to creatively re-imagine the dis/proportions that exist in the languages of social-scientific explanation. We need, they are suggesting, forms of explanation that escape our proportional imagination. It is about time a flood washed ashore a new strange thing full of water.

Notes

1. On the importance of visualisations for the history of science, see Wise (2006)

2. On materialized epistemologies see, for example, Pamela Smith's work on 'artisanal epistemologies' (2004) and Peter Galison on the 'epistemic machinery' of elementary particle physics (1997).

3. The praxicology of the anamorphic recalls Don Ihde's description of the *camera obscura* as an 'epistemological engine', involved in the Renaissance configuration of knowledge as something instrumentally generated. For Ihde, the camera obscura operates two optical transformations with epistemic effects:

> The first is one of escalation — from Alhazen's observation of an optical effect; to da Vinci's camera as analogue for the eye; to Locke's and Descartes' analogue of camera to eye to mind — by which the camera is made into a full epistemology engine. The second is the inward progression of the location where 'external' reality, itself an artefact of the geometry of the imaging phenomenon, interfaces with the 'inner' representation. For da Vinci, the interface of external/internal occurs "in the pupil"; for Descartes, it is the retina; and, still continuing the camera epistemology, contemporary neuroscience locates it in the brain. (Ihde 2000)

What Ihde calls 'escalation' describes the kind of relation of magnitude that I have called proportionality. The movement between internal and external domains corresponds to my use of the term reversibility.

4. I should add that an interest in the laboratory runs through the essay as a possible *topos* of our contemporary anamorphism.

5. The disputation is reminiscent of the 'relation of a child which remained twenty six years in the mothers belly' which Monsieur Bayle published in the *Philosophical Transactions* in 1677 (cited in Daston & Galison 2007: 68) and which exemplifies the general fascination with the anomalous and the disproportionate that inflects the

Enlightenment's epistemic way of life. Size figures thus as a contemporary epistemic quality.

6. Phillipe Boudon makes a distinction between architecture and architecturology (the study of architecture as a conceptual practice). According to Boudon, architecture confronts scale not as a given but as an epistemological 'shift': architects encounter scale and proportionality as something to work *with* rather than *upon* (Boudon 1999). Scale is something that one does to a project, rather than a geometric or physical constraint; it is a 'mode of shifting' one's conceptual take on an architectural challenge (Boudon 1999: 10). Thus, the criteria employed to relocate the giant red escalator in Yaneva's account above, would fare as one such 'mode of shifting'. It would provide an answer to the question, 'how does the architect give measurement to space?', which is, for Boudon, the architecturological question par excellence (Boudon 1999: 15).

7. The netting-out of ontology accomplishes *purity of form*: the birth of logos or reason as pure relationality. Thus, Serres observes how

> Thales demonstrates the extraordinary weakness of the heaviest material ever worked, as well as the omnipotence, in relation to the passing of time, of a certain logical structure: of the logos itself as long as we redefine it, no longer as a word or statement, but, by lightening it, as an equal relation; even softer because *the terms balance each other*, obliterate each other so that all that remains is their *pure and simple relation*. (Serres 1995: 78, emphasis added)

The ontological robustness of logic, then, appears in this context as the result of a proportional equation. Proportionality is prior to relationality. The world endures as an intelligible object for as long as we can provide some kind of proportionate account of it.

This proposition sets the place of 'measurement' in reason

in a new perspective. Andrew Barry, for example, has brought attention to the central role of the history of measurement in mediating and configuring the relationship between science and political economy (Barry 1993). For Barry, the instrumentation of measurement has been key to generating political metrologies: 'measurement and other forms of scientific representation have been deployed in the regulation of social and economic relations over large 'geographical' areas of space.' (Barry 1993: 464) In his account this is a relatively recent historical phenomenon, in that 'If measurement has become a central resource for the regulation of space, it has only been so to a great degree since the mid-nineteenth century - the period in which science has become articulated with the moral, political and economic objectives of imperialism; and more recently with those of transnational industry and government.' (Barry 1993: 467) My suggestion here, however, is that measurement has been integral to how all forms of epistemic knowledge have conceptualised themselves in the modern age. (Note that Serres' account is of course a modern account.) Measurement, or what I call proportionality, is the shape that modern knowledge takes every time it gets actualised.

8. For example, the relation between perspective and proportion inflected the manufacture of objectivity in scientific practice too. Lorraine Daston and Peter Galison have commented on the case of Bernhard Siegfried Albinus, professor of anatomy at Leiden, who produced 'several of the most influential eighteenth-century anatomical atlases' (Daston & Galison 2007: 70). In their words,

> worried lest the artist [who drew the illustrations under Albinus' guidance] err in the proportions, Albinus erected an elaborate double grid, one mesh at four Rhenish feet from the skeleton and the other at forty, the positioned the artist at precisely the point where the struts of the grids coincided to the eye, drawing the specimen square by square, onto a plate Albinus had ruled with a matching pattern of "cross and straight

[*sic*] lines." This procedure, suggested by Albinus's Leiden colleague, the natural philosopher Willem 's Gravesande, is strongly reminiscent of the Renaissance artist Leon Battista Alberti's instructions for drawing in perspective (Daston & Galison 2007: 73).

9. David Topper has argued against what he calls the 'postmodern' use of anamorphosis for sustaining subjectivist or relativist epistemological positions (Topper 2000). In his rendering, a postmodern account of anamorphosis would emphasize the either/or version of an image: either you see the twelve sultans or you see Louis XIII. Instead, he makes a cognitive argument about the dual nature of visual perception. With James J. Gibson, he suggests that human perception can hold the 'concurrent specification of two reciprocal things' or 'in-between perceiving' (Topper 2000: 118, 116). A classic example is our holding together in one integrated vision the flat-depth distinction between a painting's surface and the surfaces of the objects represented inside the painting (Topper 2000: 117). Notwithstanding the fact that some anamorphs are so distorted that their viewing for the first time will require a wholesale surrendering of 'concurrent' perception, I think his argument about 'in-betweenness' is nonetheless part and parcel of the historical analytic of reversibility: the mode of knowledge that can hold simultaneously internal and external expressions of itself.

10. The place of the uncanny in thus intuited in the work of optics. Andrea Battistini recalls in this respect an early observation of Emanuele Tesauro, who 'marked the maximum wit of the optical emblems, "which, for *certain proportions of perspective*, through strange and ingenious appearances, make you see things that you do not see."' (Battistini 2006: 19, emphasis added)

11. Hence the baroque's obsession with still life and material carcass.

References

Barry, A. 1993. The history of measurement and the engineers of space. *The British Journal for the History of Science* 26, 459-468.

Battistini, A. 2006. The telescope in the baroque imagination. In *Reason and its others: Italy, Spain, and the New World* (eds) D.R. Castillo & M. Lollini. Nashville: Vanderbilt University Press.

Benkler, Y. 2006. *The wealth of networks: how social production transforms markets and freedom*. New Haven: Yale University Press.

Boudon, P. 1999. The point of view of measurement in architectural conception: from the question of scale to scale as a question. *Nordic Journal of Architectural Research* 12, 7-18.

Brown, S.D. 2005. The theatre of measurement: Michel Serres. *The Sociological Review* 53, 215-227.

Buci-Glucksmann, C. 1994 [1984]. *Baroque reason: the aesthetics of modernity* (trans.) P. Camiller. London, Thousand Oaks and Delhi: Sage Publications.

Damisch, H. 1997 [1987]. *El origen de la perspectiva [Spanish translation of L'origene de la perspective]* (trans.) F. Zaragoza Alberich. Madrid: Alianza Editorial.

Daston, L. & P. Galison. 2007. *Objectivity*. New York: Zone Books.

De la Flor, F.R. 2009. *Imago: la cultural visual y figurativa del Barroco*. Madrid: Abada Editores.

Emmons, P. 2005. Size matters: virtual scale and bodily imagination in architecture drawing. *arq: Architectural*

Research Quarterly 9, 227-235.

Galilei, G. 1968. *Opere* XI. Florence: Barbèra.

Galison, P. 1997. *Image and logic: a material culture of microphysics*. Chicago: The University of Chicago Press.

Haraway, D. 1986. Primatology is politics by other means. In *Feminist approaches to science* (ed.) R. Bleier. New York: Pergamon Press.

Haraway, D. 1990. A manifesto for cyborgs: science, technology, and socialist feminism in the 1980s. In *Feminism/Postmodernism* (ed.) L.J. Nicholson. New York and London: Routledge.

Ihde, D. 2000. Epistemology engines. *Nature* 406, 21.

Iversen, M. 2005. The discourse of perspective in the twentieth century: Panofsky, Damisch, Lacan. *Oxford Art Journal* 28, 191-202.

Jay, M. 1988. Scopic regimes of modernity. In *Vision and visuality* (ed.) H. Foster. Bay Press.

Kemp, M. 1990. *The science of art: optical themes in western art from Brunelleschi to Seurat*. New Haven and London: Yale University Press.

Knorr-Cetina, K. 1999. *Epistemic cultures : how the sciences make knowledge*. Cambridge, Mass.: Harvard University Press.

Knorr-Cetina, K. & A. Preda. 2001. The epistemization of economic transactions. *Current Sociology* 49, 27-44.

Lacan, J. 1979. *The four fundamental concepts of psychoanalysis* (trans.) A. Sheridan. Hardmondsworth: Penguin.

Latour, B. 1983. Give me a laboratory and I will raise the

world. In *Science observed* (eds) K. Knorr-Cetina & M. Mulkay. London: Sage.

Latour, B. 1993. *We have never been modern*. Harlow: Longman.

Lessig, L. 2008. *Remix: making art and commerce thrive in the hybrid economy*. New York: The Penguin Press.

Malcolm, N. 2002. The title-page of Leviathan, seen in a curious perspective. In *Aspects of Hobbes*. Oxford: Oxford University Press.

Panofsky, E. 1993 [1927]. *Perspective as symbolic form* (trans.) C.S. Wood. Cambridge, Mass.: The MIT Press.

Patey, D.L. 1991. Swift's satire on "science" and the structure of Gulliver's Travels. *ELH* 58, 809-839.

Schaffer, S. 2005. Seeing double: how to make up a phantom body politic. In *Making things public: atmospheres of democracy* (eds) B. Latour & P. Weibel. Boston, Mass.: The MIT Press.

Serres, M. 1982. Mathematics and philosophy: what Thales saw... In *Hermes: literature, science, philosophy* (eds) J.V. Harari & D.F. Bell. Baltimore, MD: John Hopkins University Press.

Serres, M. 1995. Gnomon: the beginning of geometry in Greece. In *A history of scientific thought: elements of a history of science* (ed.) M. Serres. Oxford: Blackwell.

Shirky, C. 2008. Gin, television, and cognitive surplus: a talk by Clay Shirky. In *The Edge*.

Smith, P.H. 2004. *The body of the artisan: art and experience in the scientific revolution*. Chicago: The University of Chicago press.

Strathern, M. 1990. Negative strategies in Melanesia. In *Localizing strategies: regional traditions of ethnographic writing* (ed.) R. Fardon. Edinburgh: Scottish Academic Press.

Strathern, M. 2004 [1991]. *Partial connections*. Walnut Creek: AltaMira Press.

Swift, J. 2002 [1726]. *Gulliver's Travels*. New York and London: W. W. Norton & Company.

Topper, D. 2000. On anamorphosis: setting some things straight. *Leonardo*, 115-124.

Turnbull, D. 2000. *Masons, tricksters and cartographers: comparative studies in the sociology of scientific and indigenous knowledge*. London and New York: Routledge.

Wise, N. 2006. Making visible. *Isis* 97, 75-82.

Yaneva, A. 2005. Scaling up and down: extraction trials in architectural design. *Social Studies of Science* 35, 867-894.

Žižek, S. 2006. *The parallax view*. Cambridge, MA, and London: The MIT Press.

Chapter 10

LANCE ARMSTRONG:
THE REALITY SHOW (A CULTURAL ANALYSIS)

Lee Drummond

Seven successive Tour de France victories, anointed four times as Sportsman of the Year by the United States Olympic Committee, countless other awards, a mound of books, magazine exposés, and newspaper articles accusing and defending Lance Armstrong of wrongdoing, a small army of lawyers launching suits and counter-suits, multimillion-dollar endorsement deals, and it all came crashing down around him that fateful day in January 2013 when he walked out and took his seat on the set of the most sacred shrine of the American conscience: The Oprah Winfrey Show.

The show is America's Confessional, and Oprah the Grand Inquisitor. In front of millions, under the blazing studio lights, she can extract confessions of sins concealed for years by the most distinguished among us. From best-selling authors of bogus books to repentant celebrities, Oprah has them in tears, telling all between car-giveaways and painkiller commercials. The CIA could have saved all the expense and bad press over its secret prisons and waterboarding – just trundle Khalid Sheikh Mohammed out on stage and Oprah would have had him singing like a canary in time for top-of-the-hour cable news.

And what about the audience for Lance's confession, those couch potato voyeurs who experience life as a bizarre combination of talk shows, reality TV, cable news breaking stories, sitcoms, and HBO/Showtime movies, that is to say, what about *us* – the great American public?

With her dramatic unveiling of Lance's charade, Oprah bestowed the ultimate gift on that audience, better even than those fabled car-giveaways. For a few brief moments, before we had to return to our troubled, occluded lives, she allowed us to experience a true, pure feeling, hot as a poker, bright as a laser: the *righteous indignation* that wells up inside the American breast when we encounter a fundamental betrayal of trust, a scam far worse than Bernie Madoff's (who merely stole from the rich), a con that subverts the balance of the way things are and are supposed to be. Lance was our ultimate athlete-hero, and in many ways our ultimate American Hero of recent times, far more impressive and sponge-worthy than a Super Bowl quarterback (for all the weeks of hype, really just a flash-in-the-pan, forgotten until next season), a muscle-bound home-run slugger, or an unlikely sort-of-black president with a lawyer's golden tongue. Day after day, year after year, mile after torturous mile, Lance wore that yellow jersey, the leader's emblem of the Tour de France. And – the sweetest treat of all – this gaunt, determined young Texan from the outskirts of Dallas wore it proudly through throngs of spectators right there in that citadel of anti- American snobbishness: France.

Lance's betrayal of the public trust was especially painful because he was the ultimate underdog, the hero-image we Americans somehow manage to embrace while riding roughshod over the rest of the world. It was a modern miracle that he should have been on that bicycle seat at all, that he should even have been alive. At twenty-five, with his reputation as a top cycling competitor already established, he was diagnosed with advanced testicular cancer, a cancer that had already spread to his brain and lungs. Following surgery and chemotherapy he was given less than a 50-50 chance to live. Survival, let alone a return to sports, seemed a remote possibility. Yet with excellent physicians and an innovative regimen of chemotherapy, he not only survived but three years after his surgeries won the first of his Tour de France victories. His is a remarkable story, perhaps the most impressive come-from-behind living legend of American history. And, cruelest of ironies, all made possible by that fount of life-giving, life-extending wonders, the pharmaceutical industry, which was later to strike him down.

Lance Armstrong was an athletic prodigy, endowed with remarkable stamina from childhood and, quite probably, from birth. While still in junior high school he became attracted to endurance sports – swimming, running, bicycling – and, seeing a poster for an "Iron Kids Triathlon," entered the competition. He won. He was thirteen years old. Two years later he was ranked first in the under-19 category of the U. S. Triathlon. At sixteen, he became a professional triathlete. In 1988 and 1989, aged 18 and 19, he held the title of national sprint-course triathlon champion. Two years later he became a professional in the world of international cycling competition, and put together an impressive series of victories which culminated in his first Tour de France win in 1999. The scandal that erupted around him in later years should not detract from the remarkable gifts of a truly exceptional human being. Rather, it adds to the tragedy: that one so gifted should feel he needed an edge to remain on top.

But . . . It is precisely at this point, when our moral compass seems fixed on a steady bearing, that it is necessary to question the basis of our certitude, to question whether we inhabit a neatly partitioned social world in which some deeds and people are good, some evil, and in which we know for a certain fact when someone – Lance Armstrong in this case – crosses the line, goes over to the Dark Side. Oprah, with her enormous audience of other right-thinking Americans, does not question the premise that good and evil are clear to all, necessary anchors to secure us in a rapidly changing, often bewildering world. Nor does anyone in her parade of penitents appear to question that premise; they know the secret wrongs they have done and, under the blazing studio lights and Oprah's doe-eyed gaze, confess all to the Grand Inquisitor. It is necessary to ask, in short, whether Lance Armstrong's deeds violated all that is good and decent in human life or whether, just possibly, those deeds actually cast their own inquisitorial light on our basic values. In the very midst of the public firestorm of outrage, it is necessary to ask whether Lance is so awfully bad. [Do you perhaps recall the old joke circulating during the trial of Lyle and Erik Menendez, two enterprising teenagers who took a drastic shortcut to their inheritance by doing away with their parents in their Beverly Hills mansion: "So we shot-gunned Mom and Dad – was that so awfully bad?"]

When one begins to turn the Inquisition back on itself, to consider what the Lance Armstrong affair reveals about our basic values, it is at once apparent that Americans have quite specific expectations of their athletes. By far the most important, and general, of these is that the star athlete displays his God-given *physical* talent: he performs feats of *natural* prowess before the stadium throngs, the crowds lining the race course, the multitudes of those couch potatoes slumped in front of their giant flat screen HD sets. Not to get too Lévi-strauss on a readership that has mostly turned its back on the master, Americans believe in a fundamental division between Nature and Culture. And the star athlete is the embodiment of The Natural (as played by Robert Redford). His body is his temple, and anything he does to defile that temple is dealt with harshly by bureaucratic agencies established to identify any violation of that ideal. [And by high school football coaches who forbid beer – and even sex – for their

Friday-night wonders] Drug tests have become the norm in professional sports: the football or basketball player who tests positive for cocaine or other mind-altering drugs faces suspension. Gone are the days when Mickey Mantle could walk up to the plate drunk as a skunk and swing for the bleachers. But far worse than these debilitating drugs is the use of drugs intended to improve performance: steroids and blood-doping chemicals of all sorts are part of a growing pharmacopeia of the Great Satan of professional athletics, the dreaded and despised *performance-enhancing pharmaceuticals*. These evils subvert the Natural Order of things.

The Lance Armstrong affair has put one little bureaucracy in particular in the spotlight: the U.S. Anti-Doping Agency. Created in 2000 to enforce strictures on drug use by Olympic athletes, its lab-coated inquisitors conduct their studies under the Agency's slogan, "Inspiring True Sport." Examining their goals in some detail is at least as revealing of American values as reading those fanciful documents, *The Declaration of Independence* and the *Constitution*, drafted by a small group of wealthy white slave-owners in the late-eighteenth century:

> To be the guardian of the values and life lessons learned through true sport. We hold the public trust to:
>
> **Preserve the Integrity of Competition** — we preserve the value and integrity of athletic competition through just initiatives that prevent, deter and detect violations of true sport.
>
> **Inspire True Sport** — we inspire present and future generations of U.S. athletes through initiatives that impart the core principles of true sport — fair play, respect for one's competitor and respect for the fundamental fairness of competition.
>
> **Protect the Rights of U.S. Athletes** — we protect

the right of U.S. Olympic and Paralympic athletes to compete healthy and clean — to achieve their own personal victories as a result of unwavering commitment and hard work — to be celebrated as true heroes. (www.usada.org)

". . . to compete healthy and clean . . ." The self-righteous obtuseness of the mediocrities who formulated these goals does justice to Ward Cleaver, that all-knowing disciplinarian who dispensed his sage advice every week to keep The Beaver in line.

What is wrong, misled, or, frankly, stupid about the pretentious goals of the U. S. Anti-Doping Agency? Why should we not look to them as an admirable statement of a fundamental morality that all the world, particularly the world of professional athletics, should embrace?

The principal problem with those goals is that they fail to recognize that the dichotomy Nature / Culture embraced by Americans is in fact an elaborate cultural construct, a contrivance which owes little to the joint physical and social endowments of a human being. The crucial fact the lab coats ignore is that there has never been a "natural" man or woman "to compete healthy and clean" in anything. Our bodies are the product of some three million years of an evolutionary process which mixed – and often mangled – discrete physical abilities, technical expertise, and social skills. If it possesses any distinguishing feature at all – and that is quite debatable – what we choose to call "humanity" is a loose and ever-shifting assemblage of biology and culture. For a few technocrats to stroll into this rats nest and begin to dispense ill-formed opinions in the guise of scientific findings is laughable, and terribly sad.

But even if we set aside these big-picture considerations drawn from paleoanthropology and cultural anthropology, the antics over at the U. S. Anti-Doping Agency appear quite limited in scope. Let us begin by granting their premise that professional athletes should be required, under penalty of exclusion from their sport, to refrain from tampering with their "natural" abilities through "unnatural" performance-enhancing measures. This proves to be a slippery slope.

For starters, how do the lab coats identify precisely which chemicals are to be placed on their Index of forbidden drugs? The American pharmaceutical industry is a multibillion-dollar enterprise devoted to creating more and more new drugs (which they tout as being far more effective than their earlier products, whose patents soon expire and fall prey to cheap generic replacements). In tandem with America's official "war on drugs" (and we all know how well that's going), the FDA and other bureaucracies like the Anti-Doping Agency face the impossible task of keeping up with, let alone regulating the flood of new drugs hitting the market every year. Where the general public is concerned (the trodden masses without its own army of lobbyists in the Gucci Gulch corridors of Congressional office buildings), the best these agencies can do is require the giant pharmaceutical corporations to issue disclaimers and warnings when they showcase their products in commercial spots on Oprah and the evening news: "Feeling depressed? Take our new anti-depression pill! It'll make you feel great! . . . Well, actually, it may make you want to kill yourself. But, hey, your doctor will prescribe it!"

Closely related to the challenge posed by new pharmaceutical drugs is the burgeoning group of vitamins, minerals, and other "nutritional supplements" which, because they are deemed "natural," fall outside the purview of the FDA and similar agencies. When Mother June sent The Beaver down to the corner grocery store to pick up a few things for supper, her shopping list didn't include items such as acai, ginkgo, kava, bilberry, satvia, or senna. There are thousands of these substances, whose effects on the human body are known only vaguely. And when used in their purified or processed form and in an enormous variety of combinations, it is anyone's guess what their short or long-term effects may be. Suppose that Lance and other professional athletes, rather than raiding the medicine chest, paid a visit to the local herbalist, who gave them a god-awful tasting brew compounded of berries from the New Guinea highlands, roots from the Amazonian forest, leaves from the Manchurian steppe. After a few weeks of hooking down this stuff, they went out and did amazing things on the race course or playing field. Would our little band of inquisitors at the USADA hastily revise their regulations and go forth to strip medals, return prize money, and generally insure that athletes "compete healthy and clean"? We are a little further down that slippery slope, and picking up speed (but hopefully without any "unnatural" lubricants!).

And here's another curve ball – no ~~shit~~ spit: Suppose Lance *et al* decide to frustrate the lab coats who routinely sample their urine and blood for tell-tale traces of proscribed substances. Instead, they find a few medical technicians of their own, physicians and therapists at the vanguard of an established and expanding field: ultrasound treatment. Long used to reduce inflammation, relieve osteoarthritis, and promote post-surgery healing, innovative ultrasound treatment is found by these pioneers to strengthen muscle growth and significantly improve stamina. A few weeks of regular treatment have all the *performance-enhancing* effects of steroidal and blood-doping chemicals, but without the unpleasant side effects (you can still get it up!). Natural? Unnatural? Permissible? Proscribed? If the officials decide such treatments confer an unfair advantage, what will they say about deep-tissue massage? Whirlpool baths? The slope grows steeper.

On a not altogether whimsical note, we may extend this inquiry to a quite different scenario. Rather than take a risk with any physical means of improving their games, suppose that "Slammin" Sammy Sosa, Mark McGwire, and Barry Bonds discovered a remarkable sports hypnotist. Under deep hypnosis, they were told over and over, "You are a very good long-ball hitter. You will hit many home runs. You may now wake up and head for the ball park. But first, that will be five hundred dollars." They then proceeded to hit record numbers of home runs and garner an impressive list of rewards until the whiskey-bloated lawyers in Congress, finding it unfashionable to hunt Communists, hauled them in for forced testimony that forever tarnished their outstanding careers.

Taken together these examples seriously undermine the moral certitude exuded by USADA bureaucrats, Oprah, her vast audience, and the "wrongdoers" themselves. Still, we are just coming to what is by far the slipperiest part of our downward rush, as represented by the *equipment* and *facilities* which are integral to athletic competition. Virtually every athletic event (perhaps excepting only nekked female mud-wrassling, which has not yet been designated an Olympic event, *tant pis*) involves the use of complex, manufactured artifacts in a specialized, often fantastically expensive setting such as the ball park or Olympic stadium. Kevin Costner's *Field of Dreams* is built on a tract of bulldozed urban blight rather than an Iowa cornfield, and only after the city fat cats have stuffed a whopping bond issue down the throats of the rube citizens.

Even a seemingly simple *mano-a-máquina* arrangement like a man on a bicycle is hedged around by a host of technical and financial matters. The bicycle itself is not two centuries old; before that the particular combination of physical ability and mental toughness required to win a Tour de France was likely expended harvesting crops in a seigniorial manor. Today's racing bicycle is a piece of cutting-edge technology, the product of advanced metallurgy, engineering, and aerodynamic tests conducted in a wind tunnel. Lance Armstrong's bicycle (rather, bicycles since he required a stable of them for a single Tour de France) was a $10,000 machine with incredible lightness and tensile strength. That *machine* was essential to his victories. Its importance cannot be overstated. Suppose that somewhere in Bulgaria, Romania, or Something-or-other-istan there lives a strapping farm lad with the metabolism of a

Galapagos turtle and a dream of himself in the yellow jersey leading the pack through the tortuous course of the Tour. The only bicycles available to him, however, weigh twenty-five pounds and have tires that would fit a light truck. Unless some wheeler-dealer promoter spots the lad and plucks him out of his rural oblivion, he will grow old picking beets and riding his two-wheeled clunker around the town square.

Even when an athlete's equipment is minimal, as, say, with a Speedo suit worn by an Olympic diver or swimmer (but not *too* minimal – none of those scandalous Riviera codpieces for our Natural Man), the *facilities* required for the sport are monumental. Greg Louganis, the Olympic diving sensation of the 1980s, grew up in southern California around swimming pools, trampolines, and diving coaches (he was later to become yet another star penitent on The Oprah Winfrey Show). The Olympic diving pool for the ten-meter platform and three-meter springboard where Louganis launched his remarkable aerial displays is at least sixteen feet deep, not exactly Mom and Dad's backyard above-ground Target special. Had Greg grown up in Bayou country as one of the *Swamp People*, learning how to dive off the dock of granddaddy's crawfish hole, he is unlikely to have perfected his signature reverse 2½ pike.

These examples could be compounded endlessly, and all underscore the crucial fact ignored by the narrow-minded lab coats of the USADA that their so-called "true sport" involves the seamless meshing of physical ability *and* technical expertise. It is almost certainly true that these technocrats are kept too busy compiling lab reports and giving legal testimony to keep up with the vastly more interesting scientific discoveries in the field of paleoanthropology. Tool use has long been thought to be a distinctive feature of the human species: long before language evolved to anything like its present state early hominids were feeding and protecting themselves with the help of stone tools. The human body and nervous system (including the brain) evolved to promote tool use; such is our Natural Man. Moreover, it now appears that, contrary to previous anthropology textbook wisdom, stone tool use actually *preceded* the appearance of the entire *Homo* genus. The earliest stone tool users (and possibly makers) were not humans at all, but an australopithecine lineage that flourished over three million years ago. The most famous member of that lineage (whose claim to natural-ness might now be challenged by the USADA!) is Lucy (in the sky with diamonds). Her conspecifics, *Australopithecus afarensis*, were using stone tools to butcher carcasses some half-million years before the appearance of the *Homo* line (http://www.nytimes.com/2010/08/12/science/12tools.htm l). Human evolution was in large part a consequence of tool use, not the reverse.

* * *

Hurtling down this slippery slope, we at last plunge over the edge of a vast precipice (like James Bond in the adrenaline-pumping opener of *The Spy Who Loved Me*) into a dark and bottomless sea. We have encountered and must now face (sink or swim!) a stunning paradox: An athlete's physical body is in fact *less* natural than the implements / tools / machines he employs to display his skill. For the ancestors of those artifacts *created* his body millions of years before all the recent hype about biotechnology engineering a race of cyborgs. The human body is basically a particular sort of artifact, which we happen to find very special (since we inhabit one).

How might this revelation affect our deeply rooted belief that Nature and Culture are fundamentally separate? If that dichotomy now appears far too nuanced and convoluted for bureaucratic dullards to comprehend, let alone regulate, what are we to make of our strong feelings, our love, of the athlete? If not a display of unblemished physical perfection, what is it about "true sport" that we celebrate, even worship?

Ironically a clue to the answer to these questions is to be found in the very language of those who regulate athletics: their goal is to detect and banish the use of "performance-enhancing drugs" because they seek to insure the *integrity of performance*. Anyone can ride a bicycle, but only a very few can ride at speed over the two thousand miles of jumbled terrain of the Tour de France. We like to see people who can do things very well.

But only certain things. Warren Buffet is an exceptional performer when it comes to making money, but we don't throng the streets of Omaha to catch a glimpse of its Oracle. And we don't award him any gold medals (since he already has most of the gold). Nor do we celebrate the people skills and networking abilities of those we send to Congress; in fact, we'd much rather tar and feather that lawyerly vermin.

What we value about *performance* is intrinsic to the meaning of the word: it is an activity involving display and focused attention. The performer, as an individual or member of a small group or team, behaves before an audience in a way that engages, excites and rivets the attention of that audience. He is the catalyst essential to transforming the humdrum doings of daily life into an *event*.

We have been hurled over the edge of a slippery slope into the sea below, but we now find ourselves in troubled waters. If we as right-thinking, fair-minded Americans insist or acquiesce in our government and its lackeys regulating the performers among us, what are we to think about the highly discrepant treatment we apply to those individuals? Performers come in all stripes. We bestow attention, even adulation, and riches on them based on their ability to engage and excite us. Some accomplish this on the playing field, some on the race course, some on the three-meter board and still others on stage, film, CD, or even, to invoke a rapidly disappearing world, through the written word. Yet if it is superb performance we value, why should we apply different standards to the outstanding performers among us? Particularly now that we have seen how intractable the Nature / Culture opposition is, and in deference to the cherished American value of fair play, should we not demand that all our performers adhere to the same standards of conduct?

Perhaps, to the delight of the bureaucrats in the USADA, we should greatly extend their mandate, tasking them with the responsibility of insuring that all our performers are "healthy and clean" exemplars to the general public and, especially, to our young people who emulate them.

Yet as the inquisitors begin their new assignment, they immediately encounter some deeply disturbing material. Having decided to begin their new studies with the performance-arts equivalent of Olympic gold medalists and, their arch villain, Lance Armstrong, they compile CDs, DVDs, and journalistic accounts of a musical group which over the decades has provided the most successful spectacles of any type of performance, including sporting events such as the Super Bowl. That group goes by a whimsical name: The Rolling Stones. The lab coats confirm persistent and shocking rumors that a prominent member of that group, one Keith Richards, is often under the influence of a variety of controlled substances and, horror of horrors, sometimes performs on stage while in that condition. Moreover, they learn that the leader of the group, a Mick Jagger, is said on occasion to do the same, prancing around the stage like the drug-crazed maniac he apparently is. Considering the blatant disregard these performers show for their bodies and, far worse, for the multitudes that idolize them, the USADA must act swiftly. Using their expanded authority, they act to strip The Rolling Stones of every musical award the group has received over the past half-century. And the bureaucrats, supported by a phalanx of lawyers, take steps to impound and seize the fortune the group has amassed through its illegal activities. They embark on the daunting task of removing the group's songs from YouTube and other social media while confiscating any CDs and DVDs it locates in stores and online.

Having sniffed out this flagrant violation of our basic

values, the lab coats are distressed to find that the stench goes far deeper than contemporary musicians caught up in the narcissistic drug culture. Additional research documents that major figures in literature were anything but "healthy and clean," and, even more alarming, that their work is tainted by unmistakable signs of their substance abuse. On reviewing the novels and short stories of Ernest Hemingway the investigators find that all exude the strong bouquet of liquor, and that the blood-alcohol content of his later work in particular should be incorporated in its titles: *Islands in the Stream (of Rum)* for example. Fearful of the harmful effect Hemingway's conduct may have on the millions of Americans required to read his poisonous books in school, the authorities make every effort to eradicate that influence by seizing copies of his books and expunging references to him in textbooks. And just as they did with Lance Armstrong and his trophies, they strip Hemingway of his Nobel Prize.

As the expanded USADA digs deeper into the field of literature, they find other cases that require their inquisitorial attention. They discover that the nation's youth, already the victims in a raging war on drugs, are subjected throughout middle school and high school to the poetry of an especially pernicious figure: the notorious opium addict, Samuel Coleridge. Like Hemingway, Coleridge not only made no secret of his drug abuse but wove it into the body of his work with dark, disturbing images. In the *Rime of the Ancient Mariner*, which millions of our children are required to read at a young and impressionable age, we find deeply troubling passages:

> Alone, alone, all, all alone,
> Alone on a wide wide sea!
> And never a saint took pity on
> My soul in agony.
>
> The many men, so beautiful!
> And they all dead did lie;
> And a thousand thousand slimy things

Lived on; and so did I.

I looked upon the rotting sea,
And drew my eyes away;
I looked upon the rotting deck,
And there the dead men lay.

I looked to heaven, and tried to pray;
But or ever a prayer had gusht,
A wicked whisper came and made
My heart as dry as dust.

* * *

All in a hot and copper sky,
The bloody sun, at noon,
Right up above the mast did stand,
No bigger than the moon.

Day after day, day after day,
We stuck, nor breath nor motion;
As idle as a painted ship
Upon a painted ocean.

Water, water, every where,
And all the boards did shrink;
Water, water, every where,
Nor any drop to drink.

The very deep did rot: O Christ!
That ever this should be!
Yea, slimy things did crawl with legs
Upon the slimy sea.

About, about, in reel and rout
The death-fires danced at night;
The water, like a witch's oils,
Burnt green, and blue, and white.

Coleridge's final outrage, which prompts the lab coats to drastic action in removing his name from the record of world literature, is that he actually composed a large part of one of his most famous poems, *Kubla Khan* while in an opium stupor. Even Coleridge's decadent English contemporaries were scandalized by his audacity in publishing his hallucinations as poetry. Clearly, such behavior is unacceptable to anyone who values the integrity of performance.

* * *

The integrity of performance. At this point in our inquiry it is difficult to know just what that phrase might mean. Readers will appreciate that the previous pages have been an exercise in *reductio ad absurdum* (although an occasional reader with ties to the Moral Majority might endorse these arguments to the letter!), a fixture of philosophical and mathematical thought since the pre-Socratics. If we approve the punishments meted out to Lance Armstrong for his use of performance-enhancing drugs, then we must condone punishment for other exceptional performers who have done the same. If that course of action is untenable, then our treatment of Lance Armstrong is seriously in error. Something is deeply amiss in the American socio-logic.

To begin to understand what that might be, it is necessary to employ the classical *reductio* argument in a way that departs from the formal proofs of Russell and Quine. In the matter before us there is no unambiguous truth-value: [It is not the case that A implies B and A implies not-B] does not apply. The law of contradiction, a bulwark of traditional philosophy, is of no help here. Why? It is because the Lance Armstrong affair, like every cultural phenomenon, obeys a "logic" that owes far more to Camus than to Russell. What most Americans accept as unquestionably true – the need to assure that athletic performers be "healthy and clean" – is shot through with ambiguity and irresolvable conflict. Our moral compass is not fixed on a true course because there is no true course; an unflinching examination reveals that compass to be spinning haphazardly from one point to another. Any certain truth one proposes is therefore incomplete and mistaken, and to insist on it, particularly by legislating it, is an absurd undertaking. It is a page from Camus' *Rebel*, not Russell's *Principia*.

It seems the only honest approach for a cultural analysis of the Lance Armstrong affair and, by extension, American society in general, is to identify key *dilemmas* at the heart of our set of basic values. [For a detailed presentation of this proposal, see Chapter 3, "A Theory of Culture as Semiospace" of *American Dreamtime*, available at www.peripheralstudies.org]. Any credo put forward as a guide for behavior, especially the all-too-common odious variety which regulates and punishes, is inevitably skewed, a one-sided distortion of an underlying absurdity.

The key dilemma (or "elemental dilemma," following James Fernandez) in the Lance Armstrong affair is the irresolvable conflict posed by an extraordinary individual being both an autonomous actor *and* a social being subject to the laws and standards of a group composed of highly diverse but mostly ordinary individuals. We value his exceptional performance yet at the same time insist that he conform to rules set by all-too-unexceptional people who want to live in a mediocre world.

The unhappy marriage between the individual and society is a fundamental feature of human life, but it is particularly strained in the United States. Only in Camus' world would the slave-owner Thomas Jefferson draft what is arguably the best-known sentence in the English language: "We hold these truths to be self-evident, that all men are created equal . . ." Founded on absurdity, American society over the past two-plus centuries has become a land of irresolvable contradictions (we are the logician's excluded middle, the "or" symbol in the *Principia* proposition: $*2 \cdot 11 \vdash p \lor \sim p$

Nowhere is this more evident than in the matter of *competition*. Created equal, everything in life urges us *to get ahead*. Of course, it is impossible to get ahead without leaving others behind. During the first decade of the 21st century financial inequality in the United States has returned to the extremes reached during the boom-and-bust era of the late 1920s that precipitated the Great Depression:

The Wealth Distribution

In the United States, wealth is highly concentrated in a relatively few hands. As of 2010, the top 1% of households (the upper class) owned 35.4% of all privately held wealth, and the next 19% (the managerial, professional, and small business stratum) had 53.5%, which means that just 20% of the people owned a remarkable 89%, leaving only 11% of the wealth for the bottom 80% (wage and salary workers). In terms of financial wealth (total net worth minus the value of one's home), the top 1% of households had an even greater share: 42.1% ("Wealth, Income, and Power," G. William Domhoff <http://www2.ucsc.edu/whorulesamerica/power/we alth.html>).

If competition for wealth and social status has now largely played out, with one per cent of Americans owning nearly half of the country's financial resources, we non-one-per-centers are left with a burning need that has no real-world economic outlet. How can one hope to get ahead when the odds are so terribly long?

It seems that American culture has generated two complementary responses to the agonizing problem of increasing inequality and wage-servitude in this land of golden opportunity: spectator sports on a massive scale; and television reality shows. While politicians of a declining Roman republic of the 2nd century BC devised the scheme of "bread and circuses" to keep their masses from rising up in protest at their corrupt regimes, the American establishment has hit on a more stringent plan: forget the bread and concentrate on the circuses.

Sporting events have lost most of their former appeal as local affairs in which ordinary people could participate: While kids still play ball in vacant lots on occasion (when they aren't exercising their thumbs on their iPods) and while a few oldsters still slog around softball diamonds in community parks, much of the participatory nature of sports has lapsed. Instead, enormous Colosseum-like structures have been erected in our cities, and every four years an entire sports complex – a sprawling athletic village – is built to host the Olympic Games. Those kids still playing Little League baseball are inculcated, sometimes violently by dads frustrated by their own mediocrity, with the hallowed American value of competition. Yet only a tiny fraction of those kids wind up in the big leagues, The Show that mesmerizes the herd made up of their former teammates who did not make the cut. Baseball, our unofficial national pastime, has been transformed almost beyond recognition over the past several decades. Billionaire owners trade millionaire players in a 21st century slave market and send them out to play in immense stadiums erected as municipal shrines at taxpayers' expense, stadiums with roofs, climate control, and Astroturf for grass. Games played at night under batteries of lights with near-freezing temperatures outside have become the norm for the World Series (the exigencies of cable TV coverage demand it). And the playing season, already long, has been extended to pump up the bottom line. The team itself has become a specialized corporate unit. The boys of summer have become the designated hitters and base runners of November.

Even with their new corporate structure and big-screen HDTV appeal, however, spectator sports have taken a back seat to a phenomenon that has exploded at the heart of American popular culture: reality shows. In a sense, MLB, the NFL, and the NBA serve up sports programming that is itself a genre of reality television, since they are unscripted displays of American competitiveness in action. But the definitive shows that have completely transformed American television are much more recent than corporate-based sports. Productions of the 1970s such as *The Dating Game, The Newlywed Game*, and *The Gong Show* prepared the way for shows of the late 1990s and 2000s that took the television industry and the American public by storm. The phenomenal success of the now-iconic shows

Survivor and *American Idol* have ushered in a new viewing environment with a myriad of shows that feature *competition* as the supreme value in virtually every facet of American life. Participants in these shows do not simply go on vacation to exotic locales (*Survivor*, *The Amazing Race*), enjoy singing and dancing (*American Idol*, *Dancing with the Stars*), work at advancing in the world of business (*Apprentice*), form romantic attachments (*The Bachelor* and *The Bachelorette*), or even, in what may well be the most pernicious of these shows, play the little-girl game of dress-up (*Toddlers & Tiaras*). JonBenét's body lies a-mouldering in the grave. Participants do none of these real world things; instead they engage in contrived and cutthroat competition to see who can do reality-show things best, who can be *the winner*.

As traditional religious faith and church attendance wane even in this land of Puritan ancestry, it would not be an exaggeration to suggest that reality television has become the new national religion, one that engages and excites tens of millions of viewers and keeps the most popular shows at the top of rating charts. From week to week, we can't wait to see who gets voted off *Survivor* and who the nasty judges of *American Idol* send home in tears. It is a "religion" based, not on Christian love or Islamic orthodoxy, but on raw, unbridled, in-your-face competition. However, the bitter irony of reality television is that the situations and made-for-television personalities and dramas of the shows are hopelessly artificial, distorted and contrived versions of competitive life in an American society which has already picked the winners – that tiny one per cent who own and control the bulk of the nation's resources. The reality of American life, its stark inequality, racial hatred, rampant gun violence, perpetual war, untreated medical conditions, prisons (for-profit!) bursting with a population that dwarfs that of Solzhenitsyn's Gulag – none of this is touched on in the breadless American circuses that enthrall us. For all too many of us, the multitudes that make up the shows' audiences, actual life is incredibly alienating and painful, and so we eagerly grasp at a fictional reality composed of the basest stereotypes and passed off as genuine.

In *The Future of an Illusion* Freud lays out a formidable and chilling argument in which he describes monotheistic world religions as a collective case of a self-delusion neurosis, a neurosis cultivated by people incapable of facing life's problems without a cognitive / affective crutch. And in *Civilization and Its Discontents* he extends that argument to civilization as a whole: human society is a fabric of palatable lies, woven over the ages to disguise irresolvable conflicts within each individual psyche. Here is the reality which our new national religion, reality television, does everything to conceal.

In its tentative encounter with its host culture – ourselves – American cultural anthropology has paid insufficient attention to these fundamental arguments which come to us brilliantly presented in the work of Camus and Freud. Instead, that faltering academic discipline has preferred virtually to ignore Camus' penetrating analysis of modern society and to dismiss Freud and the psychoanalytical approach as inadequate to the task of the description and analysis of social action (and incidentally has tarred Lévi-Strauss' profound thought with the same brush). Although anthropologists may occasionally speak of cultural analysis as cultural criticism, that discussion is generally confined to economic and political topics. But the problem before us goes deeper; it goes right to the heart of the system of basic values we profess to embrace. As suggested above, a close analysis of those values reveals them to be shot full of contradiction and ambivalence. Rather than pursue that line of thought rigorously, cultural anthropology as it has developed in the United States tends to put a happy face on social life, taking as its program the elucidation in meticulous detail of the symbolic composition of culture – essentially an exercise in hermeneutics which celebrates the intricate structure of its subject, and not the discordant systems of non-meaning integral to the key dilemmas of American and any culture.

It is much nearer the truth to regard culture, not as a treasure trove of a people's vital essence, but as a disease, a virulent outbreak which infects and poisons its carriers. To approach culture from this perspective requires the anthropologist to examine and dissect it with the cold, analytical precision of the pathologist. It requires Nietzsche's coldness, which he advocated repeatedly to little avail. [For applications of this idea, see *Culture, Mind, and Physical Reality: An Anthropological Essay*, and *Shit Happens: An Immoralist's Take on 9/11 in Terms of Self-Organized Criticality*, available at www.peripheralstudies.org] In its advanced pathological state, it is essential that the anthropologist approach his analysis of American society as a pathologist would a diseased organism, seeking out the specific toxins and tumors which are in the process of destroying it.

In that analysis, a particularly malignant tumor attached to vital organs of our society is the body of reality shows; these sap whatever creative energy survives in a sadly diminished America. Those shows are so virulent because they tap directly into the core tissue of American values: to tame the wilderness through individual effort; to make something of oneself starting with the very little available to the immigrant; or again, in a phrase, *to compete and win*. It is often said that American society owes its distinctive character to the experience of pioneers and settlers faced with a vast frontier which they had to conquer or die in the attempt. [See the classic work by Henry Nash Smith, *Virgin Land: The American West as Symbol and Myth*] If the grand design of American culture may be described in this way, then one might suggest that the historical theme is repeated in the host of reality shows now inundating the airways. That suggestion would come with a crucial disclaimer, however, which we owe to Marx's famous observation in *Eighteenth Brumaire*:

Hegel remarks somewhere that all great world-historic facts and personages appear, so to speak, twice. He forgot to add: the first time as tragedy, the second time as farce.

The tragedy of America is part of the larger tragedy of the Americas. It is the story of genocide and environmental degradation on an unprecedented scale, perpetrated by European explorers and colonists turned loose on the New World, turned loose and intent on enriching themselves, on *winning* regardless of the cost in human lives and established ecosystems:

> The discovery of America was followed by possibly the greatest demographic disaster in the history of the world. [*The Native Population of the Americas in 1492*, William M. Denevan, ed., 1992]

The extent of the carnage and catastrophe was not widely acknowledged for centuries after the event, although lone and immediately discredited voices were raised from the beginning (the work of Bartolomé de las Casas being an outstanding example). It might be hoped that the mistake would have been corrected by the young discipline of cultural anthropology, which in the United States came of age through exhaustive studies of Native American societies. [See the impressive volumes of the *Bureau of American Ethnology*] To its lasting shame, however, the foremost authorities on those groups, Alfred Kroeber, dean of American anthropology, and Julian Steward, editor of the canonical *Handbook of South American Indians*, grossly underestimated the indigenous population of the Americas. In a flagrant display of professorial arrogance, Kroeber and Stewart dismissed population figures of thirty-five to fifty million advanced by Las Casas and other scholars as the inflated and fanciful work of non-specialists. Instead, Kroeber proposed a figure of 8.4 million and Steward 15.6 million. ["Native American population." *American Anthropologist*, n.s., vol. 36, no. 1, pp. 1-25. Alfred Kroeber, 1934; Julian Steward, *Handbook*] With their influence in the field, those numbers were not seriously challenged for decades. They provide a jarring contrast with the best current estimates of indigenous population at the time of Columbus' arrival: 54 to 75 million. [see Denevan] Tens of millions perished from smallpox, measles, influenza, and massacres, and the response by anthropologists was to count moccasin beads and record the quaint customs of the few survivors.

On a smaller scale, the tragedy of America unfolded in an especially agonizing manner: in the Rocky Mountain west with the coming of the mountain men and their exploitation by the first of the robber barons, John Jacob Astor and his American Fur Company. Perhaps no figure in American history or legend is imbued with the independence and supreme competence of the mountain man: living by his wits in a wild and hostile land, he survived hunger, bitter winters, and Indian attacks. And not only survived, he triumphed. In the best American tradition, he *won*. At least for a couple of decades. Even before the beaver began to run out and European tastes changed to silk, legendary mountain men like Jim Bridger, John Colter, and John "Liver-Eating" Johnson (most definitely *not* the individual portrayed by Robert Redford in *Jeremiah Johnson*) felt the pressure to abandon their independent lifestyle in favor of a more regimented existence as employees of a fur company. It was a fundamental change in a nascent American culture: the freest of men became pawns in a new world of big business crafted by Astor and later robber barons such as Leland Stanford and Cornelius Vanderbilt. Astor and the others had learned the secret of capitalist alchemy: how to change the blood and sweat of others into gold for themselves.

With the advent of reality television, the tragedy of America has returned as farce. Astor and the robber barons have given way to an even more crushing economic force: multinational corporations which sponsor television shows carefully designed by media giants to bring in the circus audiences with their consumer dollars (an insidious refinement of the early Roman political palliative, with the masses now supplying bread for their masters). The most popular shows, *Survivor* and *American Idol*, have replaced immensely brave and talented personalities like Bridger and Johnson with shallow caricatures of heroes and heroines who submit themselves to the abuse of the shows' directors and judges in return for a shot at fame and fortune. It is a pathetic charade of competition in which even the supreme American value, winning, has lost its meaning, become a minor ripple in the onrushing torrent of 24/7 cable news. Who were last year's winners of *Survivor* and *American Idol*? Or the year before, or the year before that? No one knows; no one cares; it doesn't matter at all; the circus opens tonight under the big top/screen with a new cast of stunted, superficial characters ready to endure any humiliation for a moment of glory. And we, the American multitudes, will be glued to our sets.

In what Nietzsche might have called an example of world-historical irony, one season of *Survivor* managed to take things beyond farce into sheer travesty and thereby expose a fundamental but contingent premise of American culture: competition and reward are inseparably linked. Who could disagree with that premise, which is the basis of the American experience from grade school to the grave, the underlying force at school, at work, at play, and, in its distilled essence, reality television? You compete, win, and are rewarded with trophies, money, adulation. You compete, lose, and are rejected and forgotten.

As with all previous seasons, *Survivor* embraced this premise in its 2009 installment: *Survivor: Tocantins – The Brazilian Highlands*. Set on the Tocantins River, a tributary of the Amazon in north-central Brazil, the show followed its usual format of dividing the sixteen contestants into two "tribes," thus underscoring its adventure theme of primitive life in exotic locales. The names selected for the two tribes were Jalapao, after the region of Brazil where the show was filmed, and Timbira, the name of an actual tribe of Brazilian Indians whose survivors lived about a hundred miles from the *Survivor* camp. It would be interesting to know the circumstances behind the selection of the latter name; apparently it was done to add a touch of local color – American contestants playing at being actual indigenous Brazilians. The series unfolded with the usual ridiculous tasks, back-stabbing alliances, hidden immunity idols, the exile island, and elections to vote out unpopular players. The final election ended, as always, with a Sole Survivor, who took the million-dollar prize and became a television personality for a few days. Competition and reward, two sides of a coin.

The travesty perpetrated by the show's directors on an unknowing and uncaring American audience was in selecting "Timbira" as a catchy name for one of the show's "tribes." For everything in actual Timbira life, with its traditional homeland a bare hundred miles away, contradicts the premise of competition-reward etched in American thought and exploited in the *Survivor* series. Had the directors and writers for *Survivor: Tocantins* bothered to do more than superficial background research in selecting a site for the 2009 show, they would have discovered an anthropological classic, *The Eastern Timbira* <http://ia700305.us.archive.org/1/items/timbira/nimuend aju_1946_timbira.pdf>, by one of the foremost ethnographers in the discipline's brief history, Kurt Nimuendajú.

The Timbira are one of several groups associated with the Gê linguistic-cultural stock found throughout central Brazil(others include the Sherente, Shavante, and Apinayé). [In addition to Nimuendajú's monograph, for a thorough discussion of Timbira culture see *The Dream and the Dance: A Comparative Study of Initiatory Death*, available at www.peripheralstudies.org] A prominent institution of these groups, and one elaborated in intricate detail by the Timbira, is the log race. For the race the Timbira form two teams whose membership is based on one of several dual divisions, or moieties, in the social organization of the village (age set moieties, rainy season moieties, plaza group moieties, ceremonial group moieties – theirs is, indeed, an intricate society). The teams travel several miles from the village into the *galleria* forest, where they cut two sections of *burity* palm, each weighing 150-200 pounds. The race begins with a member of each team shouldering the heavy, cumbersome log and running at full speed toward the village. When he tires the log is handed off in mid-stride to a second runner and so on until the exhausted runners reach the village and deposit their logs in designated ceremonial locations. A classic competition with a race to the finish line? A race with winners and losers (hopefully none of whom have ingested performance-enhancing drugs that could be detected by a Timbira chapter of the USADA)? No, on the contrary, the Timbira undertake the grueling competition for its own sake: it is a race in which the purpose is *to race*, not to celebrate a winner and denigrate the losers.

> Log races form the national sport not only of all the Timbira (p. 141 f.), including the Apinaye, but probably of all Northwestern and Central Gê. None of the other numerous observances that characterize the public life of these tribes has so deeply roused the attention of civilized observers. This is primarily because, next to the girls' dances in the plaza, log racing is the most frequently repeated ceremony; further, it stands out for its dramatic impressiveness.

> And now we come to the feature that remains incomprehensible to Brazilians and leads to his constantly ascribing ulterior motives to this Indian game: The victor and the others who have desperately exerted themselves to the bitter end receive not a word of praise, nor are the losers and outstripped runners subject to the least censure; there are neither triumphant nor disgruntled faces. The sport is an end in itself, not the means to satisfy personal or group vanity. Not a trace of jealously or animosity is to be detected between the teams. Each participant has done his best because he likes to do so in a log race. Who turns out to be the victor

or loser makes as little difference as who has eaten most at a banquet (Nimuendajú 1946: 136, 139).

The farce Marx chronicles in *Eighteenth Brumaire* pales in comparison with the travesty of *Survivor: Tocantins*, Had old Karl been around to view the show, it would have had him clawing at his carbuncles and begging for mercy: Stop! No more of the utter absurdity of human existence! (After all, that is supposed to obey the laws of historical determinism, not chaos). Louis Bonaparte, that caricature of Napoleon, doesn't begin to compare with the mediocrities paraded on *Survivor.*

* * *

In its obsession with competition and reward, American culture manages to trivialize athletic activity beyond recognition, to destroy the inherent joy of *doing*. Running or riding a bicycle, along with hitting a baseball, throwing a football, swimming, and skiing may be done for the sheer enjoyment of the activity, of experiencing one's body in concerted motion. Breath-hold diving over a coral reef, open-water swimming in Puget Sound (see Edwin Dobb's brilliant essay, "Immersed in the Wild" <http://www.hcn.org/issues/42.11/immersed-in-the-wild>), skiing a winding mountain trail beneath a stratospheric blue sky, running for miles along a deserted country road, can be, like the Timbira log race, ends in themselves, instances of genuine *re-creation* that transport the individual to another realm of being. That experience is close to the exhilaration described by those 13th century Provençal troubadours, whose *gai saber* or joy-in-knowing/doing Nietzsche commemorated in *The Gay Science*, echoing his own dedication to careful experimentation (*suchen* and *versuchen*) rather than to methodical system-building. To resort to a term no longer fashionable, it is about the *quest*.

It becomes almost impossible for us to capture that sense of exhilaration when our daily existence is subject to a practice that governs American life: *keeping score.*

What did you get on the Chem test? How fast did you run the mile? How did you do on the SATs? What number is on your paycheck? How big is your house? Your car? Even, for God's sake, your dick? (Time to email that order for Viagra – comes in a plain brown wrapper! But, oops, definitely a performance-enhancing drug!). All these questions and countless others like them are distilled in what we do for fun – or have others do for us: sports. Guys who could not manage even to run the bases sit slumped in seats at Yankee Stadium, cradling scorecards they can barely see over their beer bellies, but they *keep score*. The activity itself, the lived experience of superbly conditioned athletes on the field is reduced to a pile of lifeless statistics, the raw material for an endless stream of other numbers that eventually lead to selecting The Winner, the Sole Survivor in American society's reality show of Life.

These absurd questions and activities which permeate and shape all of life in America conceal a monumental irony, a cosmic joke: Our obsessive need to keep score, to identify and reward those who are very good at what they do, may well lead to missing or misinterpreting truly exceptional individuals who fall outside the limited perspectives of the all-too-ordinary individuals who pass judgment on them.

There is a story here, really an apocryphal anecdote (it is an Einstein story and, like most, probably *is* apocryphal). It concerns an organization that is one of the most prominent scorekeepers in the country and, increasingly, around the world: the Educational Testing Service, creator and administrator of the SATs which have impacted the lives of oh-so-many Americans. From an early age children with some intelligence are taught to dread the SATs; they are told that a high score may advance their chances of becoming a professional or a manager of some sort, and thus joining that shrinking middle class (nineteen per cent and going down) which Domhoff described (see above). A low or even average score may doom a child of a family with ordinary means to a difficult life of labor and menial jobs; he will sink into that vast pool of eighty per cent of the population who are just surviving. The story goes like this:

> It seems that when the ETS was just getting organized in the late 1940s, its button-down executives were anxious to determine the effectiveness of the math section in particular – mathematical facts being irrefutable, they wished to calibrate their set of questions so that the test would accurately identify how students performed on a scale of dull to brilliant. Since the ETS was located in the intellectual Mecca of Princeton, New Jersey, someone had a bright idea: just up the road, at the Institute for Advanced Study, there was an individual who was making quite a stir in the world of mathematics and physics, one Albert Einstein. Why not have him take the SAT math test they had just put together? Certainly he would establish a benchmark against which young test-takers could be ranked. So they approached Einstein, he agreed, and they sat him down with the test. Now a major portion of the math SAT tests a student's ability to discern a pattern in a series of numbers. A question would supply a four-number series, say 2-4-6-8 and a multiple-choice set of possible answers, say 16, 24, 10, 1. The student is required to select the answer which best fits the pattern established by the four-number series, in this case the "10." As Einstein went through this section of the test, for each question he thought of an equation that would fit each of the multiple-choice possibilities. Then he picked the answer which gave him what he found to be the most interesting equation – almost always not the answer the test designers wanted.

This little experiment doubtlessly disappointed the ETS executives, but judging from the content of the SAT math test which has been inflicted on students for the past sixty-plus years, its results did nothing to dissuade them from their course of action. Einstein was obviously an anomaly, an oddball, and his toying with their sacred exam could safely be disregarded.

A thought which might have given them pause, but clearly did not occur to the right-thinking, compete-and-win executives of the ETS, is that if anomalies occur in so highly structured a world as theoretical physics, what bizarre deviations from agreed-on, socially acceptable norms might be found in other walks of life? In order to keep score it is necessary to have an authoritative scale, a means of ranking and grading individual performance. But there are in this life those rare individuals whose extraordinary gifts defy ranking; they go off the scales fixed by mediocrities like the executives of ETS. People are different, and a few people are so vastly different that it is senseless to tabulate, to *score* their performance. In a catch phrase from the failed cultural revolution of the late 1960s, now but a sad and haunting memory, there are indeed the haves and have-nots, but there are also the have-something-elses. Those remarkable individuals either go off the charts or, more often and tragically, fall between the cracks of the charts. In that case their exceptional ability, which initially establishes them as stars (or what our punitive society would call "persons of interest") dooms them to censure and sometimes ruin when they allow their exceptional abilities, whether in mathematics (John Nash), chess (Bobby Fischer), engineering (Nikola Tesla), aviation (Chuck Yeager), philosophy (Friedrich Nietzsche), poker (Stu Ungar), or, in the case at hand, bicycle racing (Lance Armstrong), to run afoul of standards of acceptable behavior.

Even if we insist on maintaining scales to rank people, we encounter the next insuperable obstacle: There is not a single scale or even a few which adequately evaluate individual ability. Rather, there is a tangled multitude of scales which cross-cut and often conflict with one another, so that any attempt to implement one hopelessly distorts the over-arching truth of boundless *difference*. As a thirteen-year old Lance Armstrong already possessed an unprecedented combination of raw physical ability and mental determination. Yet everything about his society and his immediate circumstances – he was, after all, named after a star wide-receiver of the Dallas Cowboys; such was his family tradition – led him to embrace organized sport as the means of realizing his potential. And that decision, taken in the context of a judgmental and punitive society, proved his undoing. None of us can experience or perhaps even imagine the tremendous stamina and mental toughness required to stay at the head of the pack of the Tour de France, day after day, year after year, but all too many of us are quite prepared to thwart those remarkable displays, to declare them illegal, not sufficiently "healthy and clean" for the fearful and vengeful herd of non-entities that makes up American society.

A parting thought:

The vast sea of seven billion human beings awash on this fragile planet, those multitudes, are akin to the night sky – dark, without depth or substance, obscure, formless. That sea makes up a background for the stars, each star impossibly isolated from the others, alone, blazing in the dark immensity of space, each with its own history, its birth, evolution, and death. There is no race course, no set of standardized tests, no *contest* of any description that a star must strive to win. The star's light radiates aimlessly, forever, illuminating the darkness of space and imparting to it whatever form it may possess. Here or there its beams happen to strike a random atom, perhaps, on the rarest of occasions, an atom in the retina of a sentient being . . . That is all there is, that is the "career" of the star. Here or there . . . here or there an individual star blazes so brightly that it consumes itself, devours its own matter, reaching the point at which it collapses in on itself in a spectacular explosion, a supernova of cosmic proportions, incinerating or scorching everything around it. Then it sinks into oblivion forever. Lance Armstrong.

Th-th-th-that's all folks!

Chapter 11

RITUAL MURDER

Jean La Fontaine

Ritual murder is a phrase used by many people but what does it actually mean, or imply? To remind you – ritual is a religious performance and embodies authority; its aim is public, the personnel that perform it and, ideally, their actions, are specified and cannot be varied without weakening its efficacy.[1] Its aim benefits those for whom it is performed. Ritual concerns the sacred and it is a truism of anthropology that it also invokes the highest cultural legitimacy, activating spiritual powers, whether they be of gods, spirits, or ancestors, in order to achieve a beneficent result.

Murder is, by contrast, immoral and illegal; it is an act carried out in secret that attracts a severe penalty. In all societies killing human beings is subject to some form of regulation that define what is illegitimate killing, that is to say murder.[2] Murder commonly pollutes the murderer who must be ritually cleansed; the victim's kin incur the duty to seek vengeance or compensation. In Western i.e. Christian doctrine all killing is wrong: thou shalt not kill;

in other societies there may be exceptions to a general rule. These exceptions generally designate categories of person who are virtually rendered non-human by their exclusion. Killing them is not murder. In Bugisu, where I first worked, sorcerers and homosexuals were excluded in this way; killing them was not murder and entailed no blood guilt. Murder then is the opposite of a religious act; it is the prototype of illegitimate action. Murder performed as part of a ritual implies the existence of religious acts which are not legitimate and which are, like murder, illicit and morally wrong. Ritual murder is thus an oxymoron, a contradiction in terms and for any anthropologist this requires investigation.

Several forms of killing may also be referred to as ritual murder. There is also a common synonym, human sacrifice, which is used in much the same sense. What the killings seem to have in common is a link to the realm of spiritual power. One of the aims of this paper is to compare these concepts and show that whereas human sacrifice involved real killings, ritual murder is a much more shadowy concept, invoked often enough to describe grisly events or denigrate particular communities, but never pinned down by reliable evidence. In fact, as I shall argue, the idea of ritual murder is just that, an idea that in Britain represents the epitome of evil and which denotes the alien nature of other people outside what may be known as "the civilised world" or, worse still, the horror of the evil within. In this respect it resembles witchcraft. I shall come back to this.

While it is sometimes said that academics are too prone to spend their time arguing about definitions and distinctions I would argue that such discussions frequently lead to clarification of ideas and this is my aim here. In my approach though, I follow the French historian Muchembled who wrote of the risk carried by an analysis of ideas without taking into account their social context; this is the risk that "the investigator will describe his own mental processes rather than the subject of his research" (Muchembled 1960:141). That he wrote this in an article about witchcraft makes his remarks even more relevant. To avoid this risk I shall consider try to give at least some of the social context of the relevant ethnography.

The impetus to write this paper was given by the reactions evoked by a film in the television series, Dispatches, which some of you may have seen. It concerned a series of murders in Uganda that were referred to both as ritual murder and as human sacrifice, although I would argue that they were neither. This set various anthropologists, myself included, against the film-makers who can be said to represent the general (British) public, although I am aware that journalists are usually believed to be more sceptical than most people.

Professor Pat Caplan wrote an article about this controversy for Anthropology Today (26 (2) 4-7) which provides a useful summary of what happened. The cause of this major disagreement between film-makers and anthropologists was the alleged existence of a rapid increase of killings, particularly of children, who were murdered and then mutilated. It was this that was referred to as "child sacrifice" or ritual murder. In support of their view the film-makers relied heavily on a man who confessed to having killed 70 individuals but to have reformed. He claimed to be mounting a campaign against child sacrifice. Most of the anthropologists did not believe him, recognising the type of Christian leader whose conversion gains added lustre from the contrast with the blackness of former sin, and considering what people say as weak evidence without reliable information on what they do or have done. While the film-makers reported that they had been told by reliable witnesses of multiple killings and mutilations, a Ugandan anthropologist from Makerere referred to the situation as "hysteria" and linked it to the popularity of Nigerian (Nollywood) films in which such killings feature. A series of fairly heated emails were exchanged most of which found their way to Adam Kuper's London Review of Books blog.

Caplan's aim was not to decide either way but to

discuss the two main topics she thought had been raised by the controversy: the first concerned "the interpretation of witchcraft and other forms of alleged ritual killings in contemporary Africa ..." while the second, which I shall not consider, had to do with the media and what she calls 'public anthropology'. She argued that anthropologists are inclined to interpret allegations of witchcraft as ideas and moral values in the classical tradition, implying that this leads them to deny the reality of such beliefs. She does not spell out whether she means that they deny that people actually are witches or that what they do works. She points out that, in an alternative view of 'occult phenomena': "some anthropologists working in Africa have accepted that there has indeed been an increase in allegations of witchcraft, but also in its *material manifestations, including killing and the removal of body parts....*" Here killing for body parts is identified with witchcraft; the other material manifestations are not specified. So, not only is there a dispute between anthropologists and the journalists about what is going on in Africa but there are opposed views among anthropologists. I shall try and show that this situation is in part a confusion of terminology.

I turn now to what we know about killings that are linked with beliefs in occult phenomena and I start with human sacrifice.

Human sacrifice

The killing of a living creature as a ritual offering to a god or spirit used to be termed a blood sacrifice, an old-fashioned term that focuses attention on the spilling of blood. The blood may be important, less in itself, than as a manifestation of the dispatch of a victim's life as offering to the spiritual being or beings to whom the ritual is addressed. Usually a return is expected in the form of good fortune, whether generalised or as the granting of a particular prayer. Blood sacrifice might also be used to cleanse sufferers from sin, prevent misfortune or failure and avert evil. In some cases the blood spilled was human.

However, not all sacrifices entail the spilling of blood; victims were killed in other ways and in some societies, and on some occasions, it was actually important *not* to spill the victim's blood. The reference to blood has been dropped now and we consider sacrifice in general. This is a part of rituals in many parts of the world, though usually the offering takes the form of an animal or even a bird. Most anthropologists in the field in Africa have seen at least one of these sacrifices, usually involving a chicken or a goat. The more valued the creature sacrificed, the greater the honour done the recipient of the offering.[3]

The most valuable of all life is that of a human being and human sacrifice, where it occurred, was the greatest possible ritual gift. Human sacrifice has been recorded in many parts of the world although, as historians have pointed out, executions and other killings of human beings have sometimes been wrongly interpreted as human sacrifice (Wilks cited in Law 1985). The most famous example is perhaps that of the Aztecs, whose human sacrifice allegedly consisted of a heart taken from a living victim.

There is evidence that human sacrifice took place in antiquity in societies, including some in what is now Britain, bordering the Roman and Greek Empires, whose members sacrificed only animals and birds. Rituals including it have been described by outside observers. In Central America the practice of human sacrifice among the Aztecs and Incas was recorded by the invading Spaniards in early modern times and in parts of Africa by the Europeans who came first as traders and then as colonisers. There is most information on human sacrifice in Africa where it has been described in relatively recent times by travellers, missionaries and by officials of the colonising powers, so I will draw largely on that material as summarised in a useful article by the historian Robin Law.[4] There is no doubt that this killing took place as part of public rituals and was considered legitimate.

In Africa, human sacrifice was a practice largely confined to some kingdoms of West Africa, such as Asante, Benin, Dahomey, Calabar and the riverine Ibo, although disregard of human life was much more widespread.[5] Human beings were sacrificed as offerings to gods and to the dead, particularly dead kings and other elite forbears. In the West African kingdom of Dahomey, a regular ritual of remembrance offered to dead kings, known as the Annual Customs, required the sacrifice of human victims to strengthen the dead rulers' spiritual powers and by showing the filial piety, engage them on behalf of his successor. It also demonstrated the mundane power of the ruler and the legitimacy of his position (Law 1985), the former function being explicitly recognised by one such ruler, King Kpengla of Dahomey, who explained succinctly the need for human sacrifice to a European enquirer in the 1780s as follows: "You have seen me kill many men at the Customs. This gives a grandeur to my Customs, far beyond the display of fine things which I buy. This makes my enemies fear me and gives me a name in the bush."[6]

In West Africa, as in ancient China and elsewhere, funerals might entail the killing of human beings to accompany the dead. A great ruler might be buried with his wives and/or members of his entourage to provide him with a suitable retinue in the afterlife. The individuals who were killed were not, strictly speaking, sacrificed, since they were not killed as offerings either to the gods or the spirit of the dead king or ruler. Moreover it is alleged in some cases that the close associates of the dead man volunteered to die, much as Indian widows were traditionally expected to commit suicide on the funeral pyre of their dead husband[7]. Nevertheless, the term human sacrifice may be used to refer to these practices, since the additional deaths were an integral part of the funeral ritual. In parts of West Africa, individuals might also be killed as messengers to the dead in addition to the normal human sacrifices. Fear of the approaching colonial powers resulted in many human sacrifices to avert military disaster.

Killings as offerings to the dead may not seem to Westerners to be sacrifices, in that they are not offerings to gods. However in many African religions, ancestors are holy beings, with spiritual powers to reward or punish their descendants. There may be some recognition of a vaguely conceptualised creator god but as a remote deity, uninterested in human affairs; the ancestors are usually the spirits to whom one appeals for help in trouble. Thus in Dahomey when human sacrifices were made "to water the graves of the ancestors" they were as much part of their religion as other religious festivals. Hence we may call these sacrifices and where the victim was human they were human sacrifices.

Two patterns among the selection of victims can be seen. The victim for sacrifice may be chosen either as a particularly pure or valuable human being: a child, a virgin or a young warrior; alternatively the opposite choice is made; the victim is an outsider: captive, representative of a defeated enemy, or a slave. Slaves might also be bought to be sacrificed, thus avoiding the need to kill a member of the community. However, where the tally of captives and slaves was inadequate, victims might be taken by force from among them.

The Greeks and Romans offered blood sacrifices to their gods but they were never human sacrifices, although both they and the Greeks kept slaves whom they might have sacrificed. In fact the Romans characterised some societies on the margins of their empires as barbarians because they did perform human sacrifices. The failure to draw a distinction between human beings and animals which the existence of human sacrifice implied, was to both Greeks and Romans clear evidence of the lack of civilisation of those people who practised it. Those they conquered, such as the tribes in what is now Britain, were strongly discouraged from the practice. In the early centuries of the Christian Era from which this information comes there were increasing number of Christians within the Roman Empire who believed that the death of Jesus was "a full, perfect and sufficient sacrifice for the sins of the whole world"[8] and it rendered any sacrifice, not merely unnecessary, but a failure of faith. Pagans who offered sacrifices to their gods were barbarians. Thus sacrifice and in particular, what was sacrificed, was a powerful symbol for both communities, dividing them and justifying to each the inferiority of the other.

Human sacrifice is no longer practised, even in those societies where it used to be part of the traditional religious rites. Apart from the disapproval of the Romans, the spread of Christianity in territories taken as colonies by European powers, starting with Spain and Portugal in southern America in early modern times, have rendered it immoral and illegal in many areas where it used to be practised. Islam, spreading southwards from North Africa into Africa south of the Sahara, put an end to the practice in the north of many West African states and further colonisation by the European powers in the nineteenth century has forcibly ended the practice in the southern areas[9]. There may be talk of its revival in independent West African states where it has only been a century or so since the practice was stopped, but the stories are, so far, only unconfirmed rumours. There has been no public revival of the practice. But people persist in associating Africa with human sacrifice. Since the practice is abhorred in Britain it is also seen as ritual murder.

There are also practices that are sometimes confused with human sacrifice or considered to be necessarily linked to it. Cannibalism is not an inevitable consequence of human sacrifice nor are the victims dismembered for use in some other way, although the Aztecs were reputed to eat the hearts of human sacrifices. Some peoples, in many different parts of the world – the Ijo of West Africa are an example – ate parts of their dead enemies as a means of magically taking over their strength. Marshall Sahlins describes with some gusto similar practices in Fiji (Anthropology Today 19 (3) 3-5). Such practices have been referred to as ritual cannibalism, since they have magical and spiritual connotations to the participants. However, in Africa, although animal sacrifices were normally eaten at the end of a ritual, in a feast whose participants were carefully selected for their relation to the spirit (usually an ancestor) in whose honour the sacrifice had been offered, human sacrifices were not eaten. Speaking generally, cannibalism, even as a ritual, was always much less frequent than human sacrifice.

The rationale for eating human sacrificial victims or enemies who had been killed in battle, was that power was thought to be inherent in parts of the human body, even after death. The same belief lies behind the use of body parts in 'medicines'[10] records of which in Africa go back as far as the 17th century. These 'medicines' are magical concoctions but their purposes are purely secular; they are put together by specialists, who charge for their services and they purport to ensure success, wealth and the confounding of enemies. The magicians often referred to as witchdoctors may employ killers to obtain what they need or may kill themselves. The use of human body parts is said to give the 'muti' very great power. This is a form of magic or sorcery, concocted in secrecy for the benefit of the sorcerer's client and of course to increase the renown and wealth of the magician. Universally stigmatised as 'bad' or 'evil' the practice has nevertheless been reported widely in Africa.

The early records of this 'medicine' came from West Africa but it probably occurred elsewhere as well. In modern times, from the end of the twentieth century to the present, murders for the purpose of making medicine (the South African term *muti* may be used) have been reported in large numbers from South Africa and from much of East Africa. The murders of albino Tanzanians for 'muti' were widely publicised in the international press. The acquisition of body parts does not always require killing. Some unfortunate victims have been left alive after limbs have been severed.

The "child sacrifices" in Uganda were killings for such magical purposes. The police reported that some corpses lacked limbs or organs. (Killing was not always necessary; in Kenya recently two men have been arrested for dealing in body parts obtained from a crematorium). But murders for body parts are not offerings to any god or spirit but killings for gain: both the client who orders and the magician/ sorcerer who prepares the 'medicine' profit by the death. While the belief in the power of human body parts may be called magical thinking, as can the idea that albino body parts have greater power than normal African ones, the killing is not part of any ritual. Children and young people may be chosen as victims more often because of their purity and the potential for growth in their bodies, but their selection may be simply the more mundane one of greater ease of capture. We do not know, as everything about these 'medicine' killings is secret until the mutilated body is found. Whereas human sacrifice was performed openly and as part of rituals that were believed to benefit the community, these murders are furtive and hidden, fuelled by individual ambitions and the lust for wealth and power. They are manifestations of continuing belief in the power of magic (or sorcery if you prefer) but not of witchcraft which has never rested on material proof except the misfortunes that are, with hindsight, attributed to it. Killings for 'muti' are openly condemned by members of the communities where they take place but they are not human sacrifices or even ritual murders.

Ritual murder

If ritual murder is not human sacrifice or killing to obtain ingredients for powerful magic, what is it? The term implies a killing to obtain spiritual powers that are not recognised as morally right, but are evil and dangerous. So far from being the same as human sacrifice it is its antithesis.

It is in Western Europe that one finds this idea of ritual murder and it has a long history. In the second century AD, Christians may have despised the religion of their pagan neighbours for the blood spilt in their rituals, but much worse allegations were made against these small dissident groups within the Roman body (Rives 1995). Christians were said to worship their god in secret, performing rites in which there were sexual orgies, often incestuous and cannibal feasts. The central act of the ritual was the killing and eating of a child or baby, perhaps stolen for the purpose. Since the early Christians were forced to conceal their gatherings, meeting in secret, the conviction that they were engaged in shameful acts seemed plausible. In AD 177 in Lyons, a number of Christians were publicly tortured and killed by the Roman authorities and these allegations played a large part in their condemnation. Some of those who died cried out denials of the accusations, proof of the role they had had in these horrible deaths.

When Christianity became the dominant religion in Europe, the idea of secret groups practising ritual murder did not disappear; Christian authorities took over the myth that had earlier been used to justify their own persecution. Like their Roman predecessors they used the accusation of ritual murder to denigrate and persecute opponents. In this case it was those divergent religious communities such as the Waldensians or the Cathars who were designated heretics and accused of it. Centuries later, in a more elaborate development of the story, ritual murder was believed to be carried out by covens of witches, gathering to worship the devil and feast on the flesh of human sacrifice.

They represented the opposite of all that was considered good and their pleasure was to do evil and ultimately to destroy society. The rituals they performed were the opposite of Christian services: they took place at night, not in the daytime and in secret locations, not in public buildings that were known and open to all; most sinister of all, the rites included practices that represented all that was believed to be against human nature: cannibalistic feasts, incest and other perversions. It was these ideas that triggered the infamous witchhunts of early modern Europe.

The picture that I have drawn was built up gradually during the centuries. The people who were accused of ritual murder, or suspected if they were not accused, were people seen as non-believers, outsiders, whose very existence threatened the fabric of society. Belief in hidden conspiracies, secret societies whose members aimed to rule the world, were rife from the eighteenth century onwards. Subsequently Jews, Freemasons, and, in twentieth century America, conspiracies of communists, were seen in a similar light, as people of evil intent, whose aim was to destroy society as it then existed. It is important to recognise the historical depth of our beliefs in a secret and conspiratorial group, the epitome of evil characterised by the ritual killing they are believed to indulge in. The depraved actions of these hidden beings are very similar to those of witches the world over: they commit incest, kill and eat human beings and commit the most lurid crimes. This is part of a cultural definition of evil, just as beliefs in witchcraft as a manifestation of evil, are part of the world view of most Africans (see Pocock, Parkin et al The Anthropology of Evil.[11]

The colonisation of Africa may have suppressed human sacrifice but it allowed for the development in Europe of the myth of ritual murder in another direction. The former existence of human sacrifice in West Africa encouraged the most sinister beliefs about African culture. Events in Africa seemed to confirm these as realistic portrayals. From the end of the nineteenth century onwards there were outcrops of serial killings in different parts of Africa that local people claimed were the work of human beings who had transformed themselves into animals, usually leopards or lions. Given the belief that occurs in many parts of Africa that witches can transform themselves into wild animals for the purpose of killing and 'eating' other human beings, an anthropologist would expect that both the killing and the eating were spiritual rather than actual. However the deaths were real and the death blows appeared to have been dealt by an animal, showing wounds apparently inflicted by teeth and claws, although sceptics claimed that these mutilations might be inflicted by special weapons designed to conceal the fact that the killer was another human being. Given the existence in Sierra

Leone, where the first such cases emerged, of secret societies of witches associated with leopards it was thought that these societies might be to blame and that the killings were offerings to their secret shrines. Some witnesses claimed to have seen leopards attacking the victims, others claimed that the murderers were human beings disguised as leopards. The European colonial servants who were responsible for the areas in which these murders occurred and who shared to a greater or lesser extent existing fantasies about Africa were unable to decide whether the killings were ritual murder or not. But reports of the deaths contributed to a whole genre of literature that embedded the notion of ritual murder ever more deeply into the European imagination.[12]

Ritual murder is still murder and hence a crime. If we treat it as such, we have to consider what the evidence for it is. Over the course of history, many people have been accused of ritual murder and many have been executed for it, but the evidence for their guilt has been unsatisfactory from a modern point of view. Two kinds of evidence have been accepted as 'proof' of participation in ritual murder: first accusations by people who claimed to have suffered the evil attacks and/or to have seen the secret meetings or secondly confessions from the accused, in former times often extracted by torture. Checks as to whether personal malice or pre-existing quarrels were the cause of accusations seem not to have been made although the accused have often claimed that the allegations were the result of malice. Independent evidence or material evidence such as would be demanded in a prosecution today has never existed. Yet the idea persists because it represents in a dramatic form what is the ultimate in inhuman evil and by contrast emphasises what it is to be human.

At the end of the twentieth century people across the world asserted their belief in rituals that included the sacrifice of children as offerings to the devil. In the United States, Britain, Europe, Australia and New Zealand accusations were made. The rituals were said to include a modern sin, that of the sexual abuse of children, but in other respects they resembled the accusations made across early modern Europe and included allegations of human sacrifice and cannibalism. But when investigated, the evidence for the conviction that ritual murder was being perpetrated was very like that of early modern Europe: allegations, often from children, and the 'confessions' of adults who claimed to have been participants. There was no forensic evidence. As one journalist put it, despite modern sophisticated techniques of investigation, police found: "no bodies, no bones, no blood, nothing".

Yet seven years after the ritual abuse panic died down, when a little boy's mutilated body was found floating in the Thames, some of the same people who had publicised their belief in Satanism claimed it as justifying their beliefs. The Catholic Herald proclaimed: "Boy's torso prompts new 'Satanic abuse' fears (March 2002). Was this the proof of ritual murder that had not been available before? It was presented as such in the media. Amazing detective work by the Metropolitan Police traced the child, referred to as Adam, first by the police and later from its use in the media, by everyone in general. Medical science showed the mutilations had been performed after death. The origin of the only garment he was wearing, shorts, were traced by their label. Forensic science indicated from the contents of his stomach where he had originally come from, Nigeria, from a village in the south-east of the country. This is all material evidence on which conclusions may be based and it can only be challenged by similar but contrary evidence.

Yet, despite the good work of the police, they could not show *why* Adam was killed and then mutilated or who did it. Nevertheless his death continues to be cited as evidence for the existence of ritual murder. It was the fact that 'Adam' was found to be African turned attention to the possibility of ritual murder. According to one BBC report, (BBC News July 9th 2002 accessed April 13 2010) police were investigating whether Adam's death "was a West African voodoo killing involving human sacrifice."

The use of the term voodoo is an example of how ignorance about a non-Christian religion can support this myth of ritual murder. Vodun is a religion that developed in the Caribbean among West African slaves, from a mixture of Catholic Christianity and the traditional beliefs preserved in memories of their homeland. Its rituals do not include human sacrifice, but the whites in the Caribbean, for reasons that were partly political, claimed it was devil worship and that evil reputation has clung to it ever since. Voodoo became a term denoting evil magic and ritual practices, even in Africa.[13]

When it was discovered that the child Adam was probably brought to London from Africa, which has for centuries been subject to myths about 'The Dark Continent', certain people hastened to claim that it 'proved' the truth of satanic ritual abuse and of human sacrifice continuing to occur among the 'uncivilised'. The general attitude has been described very nicely by David Pratten who wrote: "...Africa represented a blank space in Europe's collective imagination and could therefore be populated by all manner of invented creatures, sometimes noble, sometimes monstrous, that were the visual and visceral products of European fears and desires" (Pratten 2007:9) Over simplistic ideas about 'leopard societies' and secret organisations that kill for pleasure, have influenced Christian missionaries in Nigeria and kept the idea of ritual murder alive.

While Sanders (2001) has done a good job of pointing out how the continued emphasis on the African provenance of 'ritual murder' has deepened existing prejudices about Africa and Africans, he stuffs all the evidence of British cultural concepts into that vast portmanteau labelled The Other. Unfortunately this neither illuminates nor analyses the ethnographic material that is thus bundled together. What I have tried to do here is to show how British concepts of evil – particularly the ideas of ritual murder and human sacrifice – emerge in the way they think about the African killings. 'Ritual murder' is a European representation of great evil; its historical origin has been demonstrated by historians who have demonstrated its role in generating the Christian pursuit of witches in early modern Europe. It is hardly surprising then that the present rash of accusations of witchcraft against children (which I have no had time to deal with) owes as much to Christian fundamentalist missions as to 'traditional' African ideas of witchcraft. In today's Africa the Pentecostal belief in Satan's demonic servants as the source of the power of witchcraft links the two concepts firmly together into a single contemporary image of the grossest evil.

Beliefs in ritual murder and in witchcraft are similar cultural traditions and both are worthy of anthropological study and of comparison, since if it is to be anything anthropology must be comparative. While I have not attempted this yet, a brief indication of the differences and similarities between the concepts might be a fitting end to this article.

Both the idea of ritual murder and the concept of witchcraft concern activities and persons who do not, as far as we know, exist. While real people may be accused, the evidence supporting the accusations is not rationally founded or supported by hard evidence So we are talking about ideas, not behaviour, but ideas that motivate strong reactions. The actions and the people who perform them represent evil in its most extreme forms. The actions of witches and in ritual murder include the same acts of evil: incest, sexual perversion, infanticide and cannibalism; the cannibalism fills a lust for human flesh, rather than any ritual or symbolic requirement which may surround cannibalism in societies that do undertake it This may be what makes it so evil. In effect, these persons are inhuman and their lack of humanity may be further emphasised by attributing to them nonsensical reversals of behaviour. By opposition then, both concepts define not merely inhuman but human nature, not merely evil but the bounds of what is permissible in human society.

Both concepts also are linked to the distribution of unfortunate events although the power raised by ritual murder is not directed by individuals against their personal enemies. But neither allows for the random event, drawing everything into a framework of human (or near human) causative power. Moreover both concepts embody the possibility of social destruction whether of social life or of interpersonal relations and relate this to the power of evil, whether generated by organised groups or seen in individual malice. Evil can and may destroy the world.

Of course there are differences. In Western society evil is characterised by a group whose individual members act in concert to worship the fount of all evil, their demonic master. Witchcraft is essentially a matter of individuals, although Western witches undertook a collective worship of Satan. While African witches may attend communal feasts, the emphasis usually lies on the debts created by the provision of the flesh, the substance of the feast that create indebtedness between provider and receiver. Hence perhaps the elaboration of differences in behaviour and appearance of witches, the unnatural human beings, that does not appear to characterise participants in ritual murder. Indeed ritual murder does not depend on the people who enact the killing being inhuman, merely evil. Ritual murder, then, brings destructive evil within the range of human possibilities.

Notes

1. Ritual is also used as a technical term in the psychological disciplines to indicate an individual's repetitive behaviour that has meaning but no material effect or purpose. It is usually not public but may be secret without incurring the designation of evil unless it disregards customary rules or breaks the law. Like public ritual it must be invariant and may benefit the performer. I am not concerned with that here.

2. See Bohannan, P. (ed.), 1960. *African Homicide and Suicide*,

Oxford University Press.

3. Evans-Pritchard recorded that Nuer might offer a wild cucumber if no animal were available but that it was clear that this was merely a stand-in and an undertaking to perform the usual sacrifice when possible.

4. See Law, R., 1985. Human Sacrifice in Pre-Colonial West Africa, *African Affairs*, 84 (334) 53–87.

5. Speke records seeing the King of Buganda shoot the head off a passing slave to demonstrate to his European visitor the effectiveness of the guns he had bought from Arab traders.

6. Dapper History of Dahomey, cited in Law p74.

7. Given the pressure of the expectation of the husband's kin and of society in general, it is hard to say that widows who committed 'suttee' as it was called, always died absolutely voluntarily.

8. *Book of Common Prayer* – service of Communion.

9. Historians have pointed out that the fact of human sacrifice was used by some apologists for the slave trade to justify selling slaves because otherwise they might be taken for sacrifice (Law op.cit.)

10. The term denotes a concoction, made by specialists for their clients, which is magically rather than materially effective. It is thus not medicine in a modern Western sense, which is why I use the word in inverted commas.

11. See Parkin, D. (ed.), 1991. *The Anthropology of Evil*, Blackwell.

12. I think it no coincidence that Lawrence Pazder, author with Michelle Smith, first his patient and later his wife, of *Michelle Remembers*, a book which had a considerable influence in generating belief about Satanic Abuse in the USA in the 1980s, had once been a missionary in Nigeria

13. Bettina Schmidt explains vodun as it is properly called. See

La Fontaine, J. (ed.), 2009. *The Devil's Children*, Ashgate.

References

Carrasco, David. 2000. *City of Sacrifice: The Aztec Empire and the Role of Violence in Civilization*, Moughton Mifflin.

Clendinnen, Inga. 1995. *Aztecs: An Interpretation*, Cambridge University Press.

Coggins Clemency and Orrin C. Shane III. 1984. *Cenote of Sacrifices*, The University of Texas Press.

Girard, René. 1979. *Violence and the Sacred*, translated by P. Gregory, Johns Hopkins University Press.

Girard, René. 2001. *I See Satan Fall Like Lightning*, translated by James G. Williams, Orbis Books.

Green, Miranda. 2001. *Dying for the Gods*, Trafalgar Square.

Heinsohn, Gunnar. 1992. The Rise of Blood Sacrifice and Priest Kingship in Mesopotamia: A Cosmic Decree? *Religion*, 22 (2) 109-134.

Hughes, Dennis. 1991. *Human Sacrifice in Ancient Greece*, Routledge.

Hughes, Derek. 2007. *Culture and Sacrifice: Ritual Death in Literature and Opera*, Cambridge University Press.

Hutton, Ronald. 1991. *The Pagan Religions of the Ancient British Isles: Their Nature and Legacy*. Oxford: Blackwell.

Kahaner, Larry. 1994. *Cults That Kill*, Warner Books.

Law, Robin. 1985. Human Sacrifice in Pre-Colonial West

Africa, *African Affairs*, 84 (334) 53–87.

Muchembled, Robert. 1990. Satanic myths and cultural reality. In B. Ankarloo and G. Henningsen (eds), *Early Modern European Witchcraft: Centres and Peripheries*, Clarendon Press.

Pratten, David. 2007. *The Man-Leopard Murders*, Edinburgh University Press.

Rives, James, 1995. Human Sacrifice among Pagans and Christians, *The Journal of Roman Studies*, (85) 65–85.

Sales, R. H. 195.7. Human Sacrifice in Biblical Thought, *Journal of Bible and Religion*, 25 (2) 112–117.

Sanders, Todd. 2001. Save Our Skins: Structural Adjustment, Morality and the Occult in Tanzania. In *Magical Interpretations, Material Realities: Modernity, Witchcraft and the Occult in Postcolonial Africa* (eds) Moore, HL and T. Sanders, Routledge.

Sheehan, Jonathan. 2006. The Altars of the Idols: Religion, Sacrifice, and the Early Modern Polity, *Journal of the History of Ideas*, 67 (4) 649-674.

Smith, Brian, 2000. Capital Punishment and Human Sacrifice, *Journal of the American Academy of Religion* 68 (1) 3-26.

Smith, Brian and Wendy Doniger. 1989. Sacrifice and Substitution: Ritual Mystification and Mythical Demystification, *Numen*, 36, Fasc. 2. (Dec.) 189-224.

Valerio Valeri. 1985. *Kingship and Sacrifice: Ritual and Society in Ancient Hawaii*, University of Chicago Press.

Van Baaren, Th. P. 1964. Theoretical Speculations on Sacrifice, 11, Fasc. 1. (Jan.) 1-12.

Willems, Harco. 1990. Crime, Cult and Capital Punishment (Mo'alla Inscription 8), *The Journal of Egyptian Archaeology*, 76, 27-54.

Williams, Clifford. 1988. Asante: Human Sacrifice or Capital Punishment? An Assessment of the Period 1807-1874, *The International Journal of African Historical Studies*, 21, (3) 433-441.

Winkelman, Michael 1998. Aztec Human Sacrifice: Cross-Cultural Assessments of the Ecological Hypothesis, *Ethnology*, 37 (3) 285-298.

Chapter 12

AN EXTREME READING OF FACEBOOK

Daniel Miller

I welcome the development of internet forums such as the *Open Anthropology Cooperative* and *Medianth*. One question they raise is what we might use such public sites for as opposed to more conventional publications. I guess one answer I have seen is draft papers. Another, which I will explore here, is for taking arguments beyond those likely to be accepted for publication in more conventional media. In this instance I am going to take an actual publication and extract three of its component arguments. I will then take them a bit beyond the form they are given in that publication, simply because I didn't think more extreme readings would be acceptable, and also because, despite being a self-proclaimed extremist (2010:1-11) I am not at all sure if I even agree with them. But like any academic I see an intellectual merit in pursuing such logics, and I would hope that they also suit these public forums as a means for provoking debate.

The publication these excerpts are taken from is called *Tales from Facebook* (Polity April 2011). As it happens, it is a rather unconventional publication in its own right. It consists of twelve portraits of individual Trindidadians written in a similar style to a previous book of mine *The Comfort of Things* (2008) and uses these to consider the impact of Facebook on these individuals, although each also thereby also seeks to make some academic point. These are followed by three short essays. One takes the question of how Trinidadian Facebook is; the second looks at 15 tentative theses about Facebook more generally; and the third, which is summarised in this paper, develops an extended analogy between Kula and Facebook in order to construct an anthropological theory of the latter.

The three propositions I propose to push to more extreme lengths here are as follows:

1)   That Facebook radically transforms the premise and direction of social science.
2)   That Facebook is a medium for developing a relationship to god.
3)   That Facebook, like Kula, is an ideal foundation for a theory of culture mainly because Facebook and Kula are practically the same thing.

I am optimistic that academics will find grounds for disagreement with these three assertions.

Proposition 1: Facebook radically transforms the premise and direction of social science.

SNS (Social Network Sites) are already a major global phenomenon. While some of the initial sites such as Cyworld in South Korea have largely remained regional, Facebook is approaching 500 million users spread right across the world. Where Facebook is banned in China, QQ is used on an average day by 111 million people. Other major populations such as Brazil are dominated by alternative social networking sites such as Orkut, though shifts can be rapid as, for example, currently in South East Asia with the migration in the last year from Friendster to Facebook. Other sites with different functionality such as Twitter and Foursquare are also emerging as potentially highly significant.

The starting point for this proposition is that such developments fly in the face of the central tenets of social science. Foundational to Western social science has been the belief that human societies exhibit a slow but constant trajectory away from what are taken to be an earlier state in which people lived in communities, based around close kinship ties and devotion to immediate social relationships. Whether starting from the writings of Tonnies, Durkheim or Simmel, social scientists have assumed that under such conditions we do not study people just as individuals, but rather each person can be understood as a site of social networking. This became the premise for the development of anthropology. With its emphasis on kinship, any given person was seen primarily through their place in such a network, for example the category of being someone else's `mother's brother'. So, long before Facebook, networking acted as a kind of shorthand for the way social science understood small-scale and traditional societies.

In contrast to anthropology, sociology was principally concerned with the consequences of an assumed decline from this condition as a result of industrialisation, capitalism and urbanism. Still today many of the most influential books in sociology such as Putnam's *Bowling Alone* (2001) or Sennett's *Fall of Public Man*, (1977) along with works by Giddens, Beck and Bauman remain clearly within this dominant trajectory. In all such work there is an assumption that older forms of tight social networking colloquially characterised by words such as community or neighbourhood are increasingly replaced by the dominance of individuals and individualism. My own recent book *The Comfort of Things* based on a single street in London gave strong confirmation to such arguments, since households proved to be largely detached from those who lived nearby and often from all other forms of community or wider social groupings (2008).

How then should social science respond to an extraordinary phenomenon that has arisen within the last decade and most especially during the six years when Facebook has been in existence? When the internet first developed similar claims were made about its revolutionary impact on social science theory. Research by myself and Don Slater (2000) was among the first to show that that while the internet may be hugely important in other ways the evidence for this `reversal' in macro social change towards individualism was very limited. At that time we were keen to pour cold water on any such speculation that the internet somehow flew in the face of conventional social science. We pointed out that just because one could find extensive material on the internet that claimed to represent some sort of community was no evidence in itself. In fact many people ended up putting such materials on the internet precisely because these had been dismissed by all other media and no one took them seriously. A place on the internet could be evidence for how insignificant something was rather than the reverse. Others such as John Postill provide many good reasons for being careful with regard to any glib use of the term community in this regard and Steve Woolgar devoted a whole research project to a sceptical perspective on these early claims (Postill 2008, Woolgar 2001).

However in 2009-10 I carried out research in Trinidad which revealed a very different situation. This is the first work to document what happens when social networking matures into a facility increasingly popular with older people and in countries other than the US. The initial literature on social networking sites (from Boyd and Ellison 2007 through to Kirkpatrick 2010) was based on a period when these seemed to be the plaything of college students (especially in the US), for whom Facebook was invented.

My Trinidad research represents a more mature phase in the development of Facebook. It is based on more than a year participating with many Trinidadians on Facebook itself, supplemented by two months there discussing

Facebook face-to-face with those same participants, including over fifty more formal interviews, most of them carried out with Mirca Madianou, since they overlapped with another research project we are conducting jointly on the impact of new media on transnational communication, with case studies of Filipino domestic workers as well as Trinidadians.

The research in Trinidad demonstrates that there really is a case for saying that SNS reverse certain key trends presumed by most of social science. What had become regarded as the natural attrition of relationships is reversed. Previously we tended to lose touch with groups we once knew well who become replaced by new sets of friends. But almost inevitably the first action in using Facebook seems to be the resurrection of all lost relationships, for example, with ex-school friends or relatives who have migrated. Many of the participants in our study used these networks for several hours a day in order to resurrect what might be seen as a more traditional devotion to close social relationships that do come close to classical ideas of community.

Once this issue arose from the fieldwork, I decided deliberately to target research on people who still live in small villages and hamlets and who are well aware of the nature and character of such communities. It seemed right to let such people comment on the degree to which Facebook was or was not analogous to their own experience of living in a community and in other social networks such as kinship ties.

So let me summarise a portrait of someone who exemplifies this aspect of the research in the book:

Alana is a college student who lives in a kind of settlement that has become quite rare in contemporary Trinidad. Modern Trinidad is a pretty mobile place and one meets relatively few people of any age who live where they were born. Her hamlet, Santa Ana, is quite small. There are around twenty-five houses straddling a ridge in the foothills of the mountains that form a spine pointing north. These houses, with only two exceptions, represent the descendants of the same three or four core families. So by now pretty much everyone in the village is related to everyone else. When it comes to any kind of significant event, such as a wedding or a wake, any remaining lack of relationship is ignored. For all intents and purposes this village is a family writ large. It also has those other hallmarks of community, for example Alana's family have a running feud with their neighbour that has gone on for years. Every time a pause arises that might lead to a rapprochement, it gets extended by disputes about where children shouldn't be playing or when dogs shouldn't be barking.

Alana has two main times when she is involved in Facebook. She was originally persuaded to go on Facebook by a score of younger cousins who like to play the game FarmVille. She admits that this can add up to something like two hours a day of online labour. But the consequence is a thriving online cousinhood that is effective in developing her extended family relations. In order to detach from the family she goes to sleep around 8 pm. She then gets up at midnight and from then to 3 am she is on Facebook with most of her college class. Almost all of them have adopted the same diurnal rhythm. Alana reckons that only about 20% of the subsequent conversation is purely discussion of homework and joint projects.

Amongst my various conversations with Alana, one centres on this question of an analogy with community. What was it like growing up in and continuing to live in Santa Ana? As a student at university she is used to thinking abstractly about such comparisons and concepts. Nor does she have the slightest difficulty appreciating the meaning of community. In her mind there is a clear analogy but in various respects Facebook is not a patch on the real thing. However much one blames Facebook for malicious or ill-informed gossip, Alana feels it doesn't even begin to approach what happens routinely in a small place like Santa Ana. She tells of how, in a community like this, people would look at or the youths in the village, at how their friend's children are growing up,. They wouldn't take time to get to know them, they would just sit and talk about whether a child is neglected or a youth is into drugs. She says `Yeh, it's much much worse. I think people still have some level of respect on Facebook, well at least the people that I socialize with. They wouldn't blatantly put something very offensive. We recently had a stranger that came in. I think he dating a girl out the road and she girl, she pretty young. And she and a guy in the village always had an exchange of words. Like throw talk for one another and stuff like that. So he was passing and something she said and her boyfriend get up and try swing a blade at him. And he hold it and pull it away from his hand. All his ligaments and everything gone. He came out of the hospital about three days ago. His right hand, he can't do anything right now. He have strings and stuff on his hand trying to get it back... yeah terrible'.

The point can also work in the other direction. People congregate online and help each other with homework. But that doesn't represent the kind of commitment people make to each other in the village. Santa Ana is a place where you can spend the whole day cooking something up for a neighbour who is hosting some communal occasion. There had just recently been a wake that is celebrated on the first year's anniversary of a death, with food cooked by many neighbours and the community playing cards into the night. In a village such as this, whatever the internal quarrels, there is still the foundation for deep and sustained solidarity in relation to an external threat. When someone is ill or in crisis, you know instinctively what being in a community means, the responsibilities it gives you and the hold it has on you.

When judging the nature of Facebook as a community Alana is clear that it can only be assessed relative to offline community. She regards her situation, living in Santa Ana, as exceptional in contemporary Trinidad. When you are living in a place like that, the community is incredibly intense and her use of Facebook, however sociable, is a means to give herself some sort of break from that intensity. If people in Santa Ana turn to Facebook as a kind of milder version of community, it is to achieve some sort of distance, because the reality of living within such a close-knit community is simply too intense and invasive.

She contrasts her experience with that of a friend who lives in a much more typical settlement within Trinidad, near Tunapuna: 'it's more of a small town and you don't really see people going by each other. But she will keep in contact via Facebook'. For her friend there simply isn't enough actual community. She is frustrated at how little she knows or interacts with the people who live close to her. So her experience of Facebook does the opposite. It helps create a bit more social intensity in a situation where people have an insufficiency of direct communication and contact with each other. So Alana concludes that Facebook is used to balance out the degree of offline community.

Facebook has all the contradictions found in a community. You simply can't have both closeness and privacy. You can't have support without claustrophobia. You can't have such a degree of friendship without the risk of explosive quarrelling. Either everything is more socially intense or none of it is. This is one of the ironies of the huge emphasis on the loss of privacy that we find in journalist's accounts. It's the same public discourse that goes on and on about how we have lost neighbourhood and community and everyone is so individualistic and lonely. Well if you really do want to have more community and less isolated individualism then that means trading privacy. But popular discourse wants it both ways, they want a community that is totally private and anthropologists should be pointing out this kind of contradiction.

So the most important thing Facebook provides is a means to complement the offline version of community and to live with those same contradictions.

I found Alana's account the most plausible I have come

across and the one that accords best with the findings of my research. I don't have the space here to examine in as much detail the relationship of Facebook to other aspects of close social relations such as kinship, but my conclusions there are similar. What this means is that the best way to understand Facebook is in relation to anthropological studies of close-knit and intense society, not as part of sociology's encounter with contemporary individualism and the kind of networking envisaged by Castells (2000) Facebook seems like the end of what previously was the natural attrition of social networks. It brings all those who were once disregarded back into the frame of current regard, such as lost kin and school friends. Equally important is the ability of Facebook to bring back Diaspora populations and ameliorate the effect of their residence in different countries.

Facebook is six years old, but if it continues on its currently trajectory and a billion people use it for several hours a day mainly for actual social networking, with the resultant intensification of those social networks, then we will see a kind of shift from sociology to anthropology that we never dared expect. This is perhaps the most profound challenge to the basic presuppositions of social science for a century.

Proposition 2: Facebook is a medium for developing a relationship to god.

I have always been fascinated by the Akheda, the section in the bible where Abraham offers to sacrifice his son Isaac to god. This is when a covenant is established and we see thereby the effective institutionalisation of that monotheism that develops unto Judaism, Christianity and Islam. For theologians such as Levinas, the key moment within the Akheda is when Abraham says the word 'Here I Am'. By standing before god, he establishes humanity in the moral gaze of the divine. From a secular perspective one could turn this around and argue that this is equally the moment which establishes the divine as the projected vantage from which humanity sees itself as being seen. It is culmination of a journey a `going forth' (*lek lek'ha*) that Abraham makes from the first mythic portion of the bible which has much in common with Sumerian myths such as Noah and the Flood to the main 'historical' narrative which leads to this monotheistic trajectory.

If this is viewed, however, only as a movement from myth to history it raises the question of whether Abraham should be regarded as some kind of freakish or unique episode based on the specific latent propensity of this individual patriarch to search out such a relationship to the divine as witness and thus moral encompassment of humanity, which leads in turn to the religious conceptualisations of these three monotheistic religions and eventually to further ethical and political orders of a secular kind. Or should the story of Abraham be seen as neither myth nor history, but rather as a pointed to some broader latent propensity towards a vision of moral humanity with analogies that make it a characteristic of being human? In which case this same 'going forth' or journey towards the conditions of the Akheda is something we might expect of people generally, including those who may be polytheistic of atheist in their beleifs, in which case it could be equally prevalent in the secular conditions of the contemporary world?

When investigating Facebook, the first step is to take it at 'face-value' simply an effective means of communication to multiple audiences, that helps people keep in touch, post photos and everything else that makes up a simple description of what Facebook appears to be and do. But after a while it becomes clear that there is a sort of surplus communicative economy to Facebook, in that people seem to do all sorts of things with it, and think of it in various ways that are hard to reduce either to some kind of communicative instrumentalism or indeed to any other kind of instrumentalism.

When I first started to try and understand this surplus communicative economy, I came up with the question of whether Facebook should be considered some kind of meta-friend. What if, instead of seeing Facebook as a means to facilitate friendships between people, many of us use friendships between people in order to facilitate a relationship to Facebook itself? I had this fantasy that what most people should really be typing under the title of relationship status was: Married to Facebook lol? A common trope in modern discourse is that we feel we live in an era of materialism or fetishism, such that proper relationships between people are being replaced by relationships to things instead. This is a rather simplistic rendition of our world. As I have argued many times with regard to Mauss's *The Gift* (1990), an anthropological sensibility is surely very different from a colloquial one. We have never regarded culture as a medium constructed to facilitate friendships between persons. On the contrary, relationships and exchange between persons, for example kin relations, are usually seen as a means to grow culture, for example through exchange. So for anthropologists, a relationship to Facebook as a thing is not axiomatically morally inferior to a relationship with a person. We do not resort to such simple judgments; we try to understand these cultural processes.

Given that Facebook is a social network, perhaps the simplest idiom for conceiving of this relationship to Facebook itself is to think of it as a sort of meta-best-friend. In the popular culture of TV, on programmes such as *Sex and the City*, a best friend is the person we can turn to when we are feeling lonely, depressed or bored, when life seems to have less purpose than usual. Our best friend is the one who is least likely to mind being disturbed when having a meal, or wanting to go to sleep, because they sense our deep need to engage in long gossipy discussions about ourselves or others, just to make us feel better. One advantage of Facebook is that it is a totally reliable best friend. Even at 3 a.m., when not even our best best-friend wants to be disturbed, we can turn to Facebook and feel connected with all those other lives, and come out of it less lonely and bored. Though, of course, we may also end up being more depressed or jealous because of the revelations about all those very active other people who don't seem lonely and bored. But this can happen after face-to-face chats with actual best friends also. There are people who see themselves as irredeemably unattractive and shunned by those who, in public, don't want to be associated with them. Fieldwork suggested to me that this was not uncommon, especially for school-age children. Such people often find Facebook a lot more forgiving and benign. You can't say that the photos on someone else's Facebook site were posted specifically for you to see, but also you can't say they weren't. Once there, they are part of your social life.

Journalism is already full of extreme stories about Facebook's negative impacts. It is held responsible for people becoming jealous and murdering their lover, or for paedophilic grooming. To a lesser extent there are also positive stories about how Facebook stopped someone from committing suicide and helps those who are depressed. With 500 million users, we can be pretty sure that most stories and anecdotes about what Facebook might be capable of doing are true, however extreme. But that is a good reason to replace journalism and anecdote with more systematic research, which can demonstrate that such instances may be so exceptional as to be largely inconsequential, except for the people directly involved in those cases. It is not necessary to suggest that Facebook as a meta-best-friend necessarily cures depression or prevents suicide. We can still recognise that it is plausible, for a number of people, that it does act to complement offline friendships and to become significant as a friend in its own right.

Facebook is somewhere we can talk as much as we like, with or without responses from others. It is a site that genuinely addresses the perennial problem of boredom, especially teenage boredom, without necessarily imposing on the time of others. It has its limits; it doesn't get drunk when we do. It doesn't always comment back when we want it to. You can only 'sort of' have sex with it. But at a meta-level it may serve a purpose. Some of the most poignant examples we found were of a person who posted constantly about a baby that was born prematurely and another who posted about a parent afflicted with a terminal illness. We observed that these individuals seemed not too concerned whether or not the responses they received were from people they knew well. Facebook allowed the public sharing of suffering. It was a 'witness' to suffering that might be cathartic in its own right. The fact that Facebook is made up of actual people may give it unprecedented power and plausibility to act like a meta-person in this way. The downside to this relationship would be its potential to become so extreme that it does become appropriate to talk of fetishism or indeed pathology. One of the stories in *Tales from Facebook* is about a man who feels his partner's addiction to Facebook has become pretty much on a par with heroin addiction; at least it became fatal to their relationship. There was no evidence that this sort of thing was common, but I believe that some sort of best-friend like relationship with Facebook is.

This is a work of anthropology rather than psychology, but it is worth at least speculating about Facebook's role in facilitating the fantasy worlds of individuals. Imagine a novel in which two work colleagues have barely exchanged more than a few sentences, an occasional comment on what the other is wearing, but little more. Yet one of them dissects each word actually spoken, each glance, in copious detail. The man thereby convinces himself that he is now completely in love and in thrall to this work colleague and would surely leave his wife for her if only he didn't have children. He knows exactly which Greek island will be the site of their passionate tryst. A little molehill of conversation becomes the mountain that moves Tristan and Isolde. My evidence for the impact of Facebook in this regard is very limited. But it seems likely that people's increased ability to observe and follow another person passively gives even more licence to their internal fantasy world, where they can imagine whatever they might choose to happen between them. It is therefore possible that one of the most significant impacts of Facebook will be on internal worlds of fantasy and imagination, where many people spend much of their time.

One of the first discussions of the internet's impact that looked more deeply into its possible consequences was *The Second Self* by Sherry Turkle (1984). But much of her discussion concerned the implications of being anonymous and how people could appear to be someone quite different from their offline selves when online. Although she doesn't make explicit use of his work, her discussion leads back to Erving Goffman, the author of the most rewarding of all social science writings about the self (1956, 1974). Yet Facebook points us in the opposite direction to this concern with anonymity, indicating rather an end to anonymity. This alone should give pause for thought to anyone who thinks such digital technologies lay down a consistent path in any given direction. In either case, such debates release us from any simple or colloquial assumption that there is evidently a more true or less true self, or that these correspond to the distinction between online and offline selves. What Goffman and Turkle reveal is that all versions of the self are to some degree performative and based on frames of expectation. We play a variety of roles in life with degrees of attachment and distance.

To determine whether or how far Facebook itself makes a difference to the nature of the self or self-consciousness is extremely difficult. For example, one could argue that the sheer number of photographs a person posts online must create a new self-consciousness about their appearance. As someone commented, 'I think for teenagers Facebook is just dangerous, and seeing everybody's photos makes you so superficial. It's like constantly looking in a mirror and seeing yourself reflected. But through other people's eyes. So you have everybody's opinions coming down on you, because everyone will comment on your photos. "And, oh I love your top" or this and that and you never know, it's just constant. So I don't think it's healthy for teenagers at all or anybody who has insecurities'. There were many versions of this idea that Facebook makes us more concerned with appearances and thus more superficial. But often such arguments work by contrasting the concrete present with a mythical, more authentic past. I was conducting fieldwork in Trinidad long before the invention of the internet, and at times I would spend hours with young women who were getting changed to go out for an evening. They would try on seven different outfits to get the right image. It's hard to imagine they could be any more self-conscious about their public appearance now than they were then. At that time I argued that, in an egalitarian society such as Trinidad, the concept of the self depended less on some interior being or institutionalized position or role. The self is a more transient creation, largely formed from other people's responses to your appearance, which alone tells you who you are. So if the truth of who you are exists largely in other peoples responses to how you look, it is not that unreasonable to be obsessed about your public appearance.

Lets move this from an issue of psychology to one of anthropology. The idea that making visible relationships is far more than just a representation of those relationships has become widely accepted in anthropology largely through the writings of Marilyn Strathern. In her work a person is constituted by a network of relationships which are not just made manifest, but come to exist through becoming apparent. So in *The Gender of The Gift* the birth of a child was significant in particular because it objectified the relationships that are made evident through the existence of that child (1986) Obviously having a child is what makes people related as parents.

Scroll on a few years and it looks as though Strathern was not merely a theorist but a rather prescient prophet. Since today, when so many of us regularly use social networking sites, it seems almost common sense to see an individual on our computer screen as constituted by their network of relationships and to regard social networks as a medium of objectification that makes these not only visible, but also constitutive. A student increasingly discovers who they are by going online and checking to see in what regard they are held by how many people and how they have engaged with them and each other. Social networks also seem to generate their own compulsion to visibility. Just as people don't feel they were not actually on holiday unless they can see photographs of themselves enjoying that holiday, so today some people don't feel they have experienced an event unless they have broadcast it through Facebook or Twitter. It is as though we have all read Strathern and want to transform our lives to accord better with her understanding of the nature of social networks.

This idea that making a relationship visible also creates that relationship can extend to the self. Facebook is a place where you discover who you are by seeing a visible objectification of yourself. Central to Trinidadian cosmology, as found in Carnival, is the belief that a mask or outward appearance is not a disguise. As something you have crafted or chosen and not merely been born with, the mask is a better indication of the actual person than your unmasked face. This is why one of my informants states that the true person is the one you meet on Facebook, not the person you meet face-to-face. It follows that the truth about yourself is revealed to you by what you post on Facebook. On Facebook you find out who you are.

I believe, however, that there is a final stage in accounting for this surplus economy of communication that is Facebook. What becomes clear from studying Facebook after a while is that, whatever the reason why we first friended them, most people are well aware that there are two main layers to their network. There is the active layer they respond to and who respond to them and the inactive layer of hundreds of others who have come to represent a generic other consisting of the anyone or everyone. We may not actively engage with them, but we are well aware that they are there and the question remains what their role is in relation to our personal postings.

The idea of witnessing comes in dozens of different philosophical and theological guises. In the next section I turn to Nancy Munn on Kula; she makes considerable use of just such a concept of witnessing which she derives from Jean-Paul Sartre. There are powerful religious undercurrents to the idea that everything we do is seen, or should be seen, by another, perhaps divine force. A common trope in the various forms of Christianity found in Trinidad is the idea of an all-witnessing God from whom nothing is or should be hidden. An increasing proportion of Trinidadians follow various kinds of Pentecostal and Apostolic churches where concepts of witnessing are central. But even without any religious beliefs, there are plenty of secular equivalents. Consider, for example, Freud's concept of the superego, the introjected image of one's own parents, who see everything and again become the foundation for our moral evaluations.

This is what leads me back to my starting point when considering the Akheda and to Levinas' proposition that we are constituted as moral agents only in relation to this third observing other, which corresponds to the divine before whom Abraham can proclaim `Here I am' (Levinas 1985). It is manifested as the belief that there is a witness out there that is often the driving force behind moral action.

In Trinidad it is clear that people are increasingly aware that Facebook postings are also a form by which one sets oneself up for moral adjudication. It may be intentional presentations of ones best face or the fact that one inevitably ends up being posted while drunk and disorderly and often with the wrong partner, all of which shows why Facebook corresponds readily with a Trinidadian concept of truth. So here perhaps we reach the logical end of the search for an explanation of the surplus economy of Facebook.

These reflections imply a sort of necessity that people may feel with regard to ensuring there is a higher and wider scrutiny of their personal exchanges and self-presentations. That is, people may want an assurance that there is some higher moral evaluation and they use

Facebook to ensure that it exists. In which case, what Facebook provides is not only some particular friends who may comment on you nor even just a meta-best-friend. We have reached the point where Facebook may be regarded as providing a crucial medium of visibility and public witnessing. It gives us a moral encompassment within which we have a sense not only of who we are but of who we ought to be. Facebook is normative not just in the sense of a consensual netiquette, but also as a force for witnessing the moral order of the self. Not for all people and not necessarily. But without some kind of explanation of this ilk, it is hard to account for what often appears as a compulsion to place things under a generic public gaze rather than to post them to any particular person. Such an argument would render Facebook anything but superficial. It may be, for some, their equivalent to the presence of the divine as witness in their lives. In which case perhaps the Akheda really is a story about the latent propensity of humanity with regard to something we have in the past generally regarded as divine.

Proposition 3: Facebook, like Kula is an ideal foundation for a theory of culture, mainly because Facebook and Kula are practically the same thing.

As I have made clear in several previous publications, my all-time favourite ethnography is *The Fame of Gawa* by Nancy Munn, a book that seems to me the culmination of Malinowski's project (Munn 1986, Malinowski 1922). Social scientists are not natural scientists, but I want to suggest that, if we imagine *The Fame of Gawa* as a theorem, than Facebook would be its proof. Kula has become the ur-example of culture for anthropology. We might spend the day like animals obtaining and consuming food, mate, protect our young till they are old enough to survive for themselves and then die. By contrast, human societies such as the people of Gawa create vast arrays of custom and expectation, rituals based on spirits of good and evil, arts and artefacts, etiquettes of behaviour, all of which make for a vastly more elaborate world. This wealth of culture rests on fundamental values by which people are expected to live and are judged. In turn these values create goals in life that make it rich and complex. Not only that, thanks to the Kula ring, the cultural universe of Gawa in turn gives rise to the excitement and challenge of Malinowski's *Argonauts* within a still more expansive universe, where those who negotiate transactions with other islands make even wider possibilities and accomplishments beyond the shores of Gawa itself. *The Fame of Gawa* is so called because it rests on a series of sanctions and exhortations designed to create, maintain and increase these values. If there were not a great world out there in which we can do deeds and become known for them, there would be no possibility of fame and much less to live our lives for. Culture provides the platform that allows every person to become a player. Kula activity finally comes back as Fame; and the people who exchange the valuables become the 'celebrities' of the Kula ring. To use modern parlance, culture is what ensures that the people of Gawa 'get a life'.

Munn reasons that this activity represents an expansion of what she calls inter-subjective spacetime: the scale of the world within which people can live and gain Fame. Positive transformations expand this spacetime and negative transformations shrink it. The first chapters of *The Fame of Gawa* are mainly concerned with the establishment of positive transformations, the complex systems of exchanges based on principles of reciprocity and mutual obligation and expectation that grow spacetime: first exchanges within Gawa and then through Kula with other islands. The final chapters are more concerned with witchcraft, an aspect of these same activities that can destroy and shrink our social relationships and the field within which we can gain Fame. So culture itself can grow or shrink.

If Facebook may be regarded as a kind of social 'big bang' leading to an expanding social universe, then an analogy seems warranted with Munn's argument about culture. For this analogy to be useful, we would have to see in Facebook something equivalent to both the positive expansion and negative shrinking of spacetime. To start with expansion, in Gawa a contrast is drawn between just eating the food you grow yourself and sending it out into ever expanding networks of exchange. Similarly, in Trinidad, a person might use some experience or reflection in dyadic exchanges with someone close to them, reporting it in a personal conversation with another person. I tell you about something that happened to me and that's as far as it goes. But, with Facebook, they can harvest those same observations from the garden of their experiences and post them onto a site, where not just one other person will be able to consume them, but hundreds. Even if no direct messages are sent to and from individuals, they are made aware of aspects of others lives through textual and visual posts. As spacetime, it allows this information to carry across continents and diasporas, allowing news and information to travel vast distances with extraordinary effect. There is an unprecedented simultaneity, but also a digital inscription that lasts. As such, Facebook is a positive transformation and expansion of spacetime through social media.

Trinis are, in general, just as keen as the people of Gawa that their individual reputations should lead to enhanced respect for the island of Trinidad itself. Thanks to Facebook, the achievements of Trinidadians abroad, the degrees they pass, the children they have, are re-internalised within the local networks of Trinidad, ready for discussion and assessment. By the same token, Facebook internationalises events in Trinidad, initially to the Diaspora and then, if they are of sufficient interest, to others. Similarly, there is a consensual desire to export interest in particular aspects of Trinidadian culture, such as Steelband or Carnival. In the book, I also show how Facebook rests on reciprocal exchanges analogous to Munn's reliance on Mauss and indeed Mauss's on Malinowski. Munn, as noted above, also uses Sartre's concept of wider witnessing 'In Gawan images of kula fame, the virtual third party is the distant other who hears about, rather than directly observes the transaction......As iconic and reflexive code, fame is the virtual form of influence. Without fame a man's influence would, as it were, go nowhere: successful acts would in effect remain locked within themselves in given times and places of their occurrence or be limited to immediate transactors' (1986: 116-117). My last proposition rests on the idea that Facebook represents a realisation of this ideal as a virtual component in the construction of Fame. Again in my book I demonstrate the application of Munn's theory of the 'qualisign' to the analysis of Facebook.

The last chapters of *The Fame of Gawa* are devoted to negative transformations of spacetime. This implies that any cultural form that creates expansion has to have within itself the opposite quality which would destroy and shrink spacetime. I argue that the Trinidadian concept of Bacchanal corresponds to the Gawan concept of witchcraft because it derives from gossip and the exchange of news, which is part and parcel of what makes Facebook work. But it is equally the aspect that destroys its ability to expand spacetime positively. The very first portrait I introduce is one where viewing turns into stalking, stalking into jealousy and jealousy destroys a marriage.

There were many other stories circulating in Trinidad about inadvertent or sometimes deliberate exposure of sexual material, ranging from school girls to people's own relatives. Such as when a photographer has recorded something and tagged the photograph or, as is common with teenagers, the mere hint that one person's boyfriend was observed with another girl. These can cause an explosion of recrimination publically aired on Facebook itself. When such bacchanal occurs it often has the effect of either demolishing specific relationships or of making people in general frightened of the consequences of beinf exposed through participation in their online community. Bacchanal thereby directly contributes to the negative transformations of spacetime made possible by Facebook as. It shrinks social worlds.

The other significant impact of bacchanal is that, like

witchcraft in *The Fame of Gawa*, it also operates as an important sanction which secures normative and moral use of Facebook. In Gawa, witchcraft provides a sanction against those who would rather not bother to take part in these complex exchanges. We could call them the 'couch yams' of Gawa who just can't be bothered to help build a canoe or participate in a ritual, but come to fear witchcraft. In Trinidad, defining culture itself as bacchanal creates a fierce and continual debate about netiquette: how to determine what is proper and improper behaviour in the use of Facebook. Conversations about the immaturity of teenagers who fail to see the consequences of their desire to look more sexy than the girl next door or about how much they will regret losing their temper when they vent their spleen against a parent or best friend on Facebook are typical. Equally, many negative comments appear about people who photograph private quarrels or tag too many photos or otherwise behave inappropriately. This negative potential, the bacchanal inherent in Facebook that could destroy community, is one of the main factors that help people build consensus as to how they should behave there. At least if they want to stave off destructive acts of witchcraft.

The extended analogy can be found in the book, where it is used to demonstrate my claim that, if Munn's book were a theorem about culture, then Facebook would be its proof. The true significance of her arguments only really becomes evident when they are applied, not only to Gawa, but to an entirely different context. Her theory can work not just for a few hundred people on an island in Melanesia but helps us to comprehend the vast network that is Facebook. By the same token, this act of theorisation makes another point that is central to my decision to study Facebook from an anthropological perspective. It follows from this essay that, if Kula exemplifies what anthropologists mean by the word culture, then so does Facebook.

I would prefer to offer the evidence of the book rather than these short examples, in order to make such extreme points more plausible; but the world of publishers seems inexorably slow and the book will not be out until April. Meanwhile, I hope there is enough here at least to show why I think anthropology has the potential to appreciate aspects of Facebook that might not emerge from discussion by other disciplines. That we have have a responsibility to at least push things well beyond the incredibly superficial idea promulgated by films such as *The Social Network* that Facebook is best understood by an investigation of its invention by Mark Zukerberg. I confess that I have pushed things to extremes, partly because I get intellectual pleasure from doing so. I am sure that some of you out there will see this self-indulgence as detrimental to the larger goals of our discipline, so by all means attack.

References

Boyd, D. and Ellison, N. 2007. Social network sites: definition, history, and scholarship, *Journal of Computer-Mediated Communication*, 13(1), article 11, October.

Castells, M. 2000. *The Rise of the Network Society*. New Jersey: Wiley-Blackwell.

Goffman, E. 1974. *Frame Analysis*. New York: Harper and Row.

Goffman. E. 1956. *The Presentation of Self in Everyday Life*. Edinburgh: University of Edinburgh Social Sciences Research Centre.

Kirkpatrick, D. 2010. *The Facebook Effect*. New York: Simon and Schuster.

Levinas, E. 1985. *Ethics and Infinity*, trans. Richard Cohen. Pittsburg: Duquesne University Press.

Malinowski, B. 1922. *Argonauts of the Western Pacific*. London: Routledge, Kegan & Paul.

Mauss, M. 1990[1925] *The Gift*. London: Routledge

Miller, D. 2008. *The Comfort of Things*. Cambridge: Polity Press.

Miller, D. 2010. *Stuff*. Cambridge: Polity Press.

Miller, D. and Slater, D. 2000. *The Internet: An Ethnographic Approach*. Oxford: Berg.

Munn, N. 1986. *The Fame of Gawa*. Durham, North Carolina: Duke University Press.

Postill, J. Localising the internet beyond communities and networks, *New Media and Society* 10(3):413-431.

Putnam, R. 2001. *Bowling Alone*. New York: Simon and Schuster.

Sennett, R. 1977. *The Fall of Public Man*. New York: Alfred Knopf.

Strathern, M. 1986. *The Gender of the Gift*. Berkeley: University of California Press, 1986.

Turkle, S. 1884. *The Second Self*. Cambridge: MIT Press.

Woolgar, S. *Virtual Society? Technology, Cyperbole, Reality*. Oxford University Press, 2002.

Chapter 13

FRIENDSHIP, ANTHROPOLOGY

Liria de la Cruz and Paloma Gay y Blasco

The reflexive turn that made anthropologists protagonists of their texts did not alter the role of informants: they remain objects rather than creators of anthropological knowledge. Through their concepts, analytical frameworks, and debates, ethnographers talk to each other, not to their informants. As interlocutors, informants belong firmly in the field, not in the academy. It is as if informants were what happened to ethnographers before they started writing. And so, although ethnographies deal with the lives of informants, informants are kept out of the conversation of ethnography.

Here we collaborate, acknowledging that ethnographic knowledge is made by ethnographers and informants, and should be owned by both. We write together, an informant and an anthropologist, a Gitana (Spanish Gypsy) and a Paya (non-Gypsy), a street seller and an academic, two women born in the same city, in the same year, two mothers, two friends. We write about our worlds and about us: this text is ethnographic and biographical. We talk about being women, mothers, wives, lovers, and workers in a world shaped by inequalities to do with gender, class, ethnicity and wealth. And we talk about anthropology: not just as writing, although that too, but as a powerful presence in our lives.

By reflecting together on our lives and on how we have influenced each other through the years, we try to challenge divisions that have been fundamental to anthropology since its beginnings. These are the divisions between field and academia, between the ones who write and the ones who are written about, those who do the knowing and those who are known. We also consider other divisions: between men and women, Gitanos and Payos, people for whom everyday survival in twenty-first century Spain is easier and people for whom it is harder. These are the divisions that have moulded our lives and that underlie our friendship.

We first met in 1992, when Paloma was doing her fieldwork in a government-built Gitano ghetto in the south of Madrid where Liria had some close relatives. The two of us were twenty-three at the time, since we were born in Madrid towards the end of the Francoist dictatorship. Our lives, however, had developed in very different directions. Liria, a Gitana, had grown up in the expanding suburbs where the cheapest council housing mixed with shanty-towns. Until leaving to start university in Britain aged eighteen, Paloma, a middle-class Paya, had lived in a large apartment in an affluent district of the city. When we met, Liria was a young mother of two sharing a council flat with her husband and children near the ghetto, in an inner-city estate where Gitano families mixed with low-income working-class Payos. Paloma was working towards her anthropology PhD for Cambridge University in the UK, and was looking for a Gitano family with whom to stay. Liria and her husband, Ramón, offered their home. Quickly, we two became close friends.

Nineteen years later, Liria no longer lives with Ramón

and their children. In 2008, she met a young Moroccan immigrant, Younes, fell in love, and had to lose her whole family in order to start a new life with him. She is shunned by other Gitanos and lives instead amongst North African and Latin American immigrants. Paloma is now an academic, a wife, and a mother of two working in Scotland. On the cusp of middle-age, we are still close friends. Until recently, we have remained fixed in our roles as informant and anthropologist. Now we have decided to challenge these roles: we have things to say, and we believe we can say them best together. In this project, Liria is not the provider of raw material, of 'ethnographic data' for Paloma to analyse and argue about. We each talk, about ourselves and about each other, from our own particular standpoints, with our histories, our own interests, fears and desires as a foundation—including a deep involvement with anthropology. In these pages both of us speak, sometimes apart, sometimes together, sometimes with each other. The strength of what follows lies not only in the story we tell but also in the way we tell it. We mix voices and styles because we want to foreground our complicity and also the tensions, negotiations, agreements and disagreements involved in doing and writing anthropology.

How we work together

In order to write this article, we started by discussing what we wanted to write, and how we would do it. Since we were apart for the majority of the time, Liria in Madrid and Paloma in St Andrews, we talked on the phone and emailed each other with the kind assistance of Younes Bziz, Liria's partner. Liria wrote in Spanish, by hand, the sections where she speaks in the first person, and Paloma typed them, added punctuation and translated them into English. On her laptop Paloma wrote in English the sections where she speaks in the first person and translated them into Spanish for Liria to read and suggest changes. Paloma also wrote in English first drafts of the sections were we speak together, using the plural 'we'. She translated these drafts into Spanish, and

Liria made changes and additions, sometimes very substantial, which were then incorporated into the English text. We had Paloma's fieldnotes, and her letters from the field to her PhD supervisor in Cambridge, Stephen Hugh-Jones, but only Liria's letters to Paloma since Liria had left Paloma's letters behind when she eloped. We also had many hours of taped conversations in which we talked about our lives, past and present, and our friendship. Because Liria is unfamiliar with anthropological literature, we have not quoted other authors. We have only made a short explicit reference to anthropological debates in the introduction, and Paloma is responsible for this interpretation. We hope that readers will be able to make their own connections with other anthropological texts.

In order to make our joint and separate voices clear to readers, we use three different fonts. We use Garamond when we speak together, Cambria for Liria's sections, and Calibri for Paloma's.

Beginnings

I would like it if, with what I am going to write, people could understand how wonderful and important it was to meet my friend Paloma. No matter how much I write, it will never be enough to express *so* much gratitude towards just one friend. Because everything started with just a fieldtrip. We never thought this would reach so far into both our lives. We had barely started to live, we were both twenty, she was single and I was married with two children, Nena and Angel. We have had so much in common although we grew up in very different settings because I was Gitana and she Paya, and because we belonged to different ethnicities (*etnias*). That never pulled us apart, the very opposite. I even believe this was the interesting thing about our friendship, the desire to get to know new worlds and different people from what we were used to living with.

For this reason I remember very well the day I met Paloma. My elder sister Carmen had already talked to me about her. She had told me that she had met a Paya girl who came to the Villaverde church and who was doing a study about the Evengelical Gitanos and about all our surroundings and anything related to the Gitanos of the neighbourhood. Back then Paloma lived in Tío Basilio's house, the most respected Gitano in the area of Madrid and some provinces. He was also my father's uncle, although we have been brought up very differently in our two families, in particular we in my father's house. And so when my sister told me that a young Paya girl was staying at Tío Basilio's, I was surprised, not because they are bad people but because, as Gitanos, they still lived by rather old customs. When my sister introduced her to me, I thought she appeared ignorant and shy, but I recognise now that we were the ignorant ones, and she was also very brave to be in a neighbourhood full of Gitanos, most of them poor and with little schooling. For this reason I recognise that she was doing a very difficult job because she had started with the hardest part, and she still had a long way to go.

My first impression was that she was intelligent and a little serious. After introducing us my sister had told me that Paloma needed to live with a family in the neighbourhood but nobody was offering their house and all her studies hung on her living with a family. I hardly knew Paloma, only from seeing her in church, I had never talked to her, but my sister had said very good things about her and she told me that they couldn't have her in their house because her husband was an Evangelical pastor. They could be given a church to lead at any time, and they would have to go outside Madrid, so they wouldn't be able to pay the necessary attention to Paloma to help her do her work. But I also know they were influenced by gossip because they were a young couple, and people's tongues and their enviousness are very bad. I too was advised not to take a Paya girl into my house because she would bring problems to my marriage. But my marriage could not go to waste more than it already had, even though back then he was not so bad with me. So I felt very sorry for this girl who had so much interest in our lives and our way of life, that we would not give her the chance to realise her project and her future. It was then that my parents supported my decision to have Paloma in my house. They have always been very liberal, in particular my mother, who had friends of all ethnicities (*etnias*), not minding about race, or colour, or circumstance. She put that in our hearts, and without a doubt this helped me a lot in my decision to open my house to Paloma and to show myself the way I was. And also I acknowledge that I too was interested in knowing more about her world, because the first friends I had as a girl were Payas who went to school with me and I liked very much their way of being, so simple. For Payos live more independently in their lives, without thinking about others' opinions or gossip. And it has always bothered me, having to do things so that people will let you be and not be criticised for no matter what. For this reason I wanted to have a Payo friendship in my life, because since I married all my friends were Gitanas. I had a good group of friends, and got along with everybody, but I also wanted to make new friends, different from what I was used to.

And so, listening to my heart and my instinct, I said yes, she could come to my house to live with us and finish her research. Although in some ways I also researched her, because I was fascinated by her world and her way of life, even though I did not know what Paloma's family thought about us, the Gitanos. I admit that I have never been bothered by what her family or my family think, although I have to say that my parents behaved rather well with Paloma, and they were never negative about her work and our friendship. The truth is that Paloma earned their trust through her behaviour. She adapted very well to the Gitano world, and she knew how to get in, through the elders and then through the church, and coming to live with me was the icing on the cake.

It was an experience for both of us. In our free time we used to go to the university behind Ramón's back, because Gitanos, and in particular the men think that a woman goes to places like that because she wants to meet boys and do bad things. They do not think that two people can just be friends, without going any further. And in that they were wrong, because I met friends of Paloma, and nothing bad ever happened.

Paloma's fieldnotes, March 1993

Liria and I talked today about what it has meant for her to have me in her house, and about what other people have been asking and telling her. She told me that people have been amazed that she has a young Paya in her house, in particular because her husband is very young. Young men are easily tempted, she said, and any tiny event would make people gossip: 'you know what people's tongues are like…' For example, she said that if it was hot and Ramón took his shirt off, and I happened to be in the same room then, people would say 'Ramón is having it off with the Paya', and specially 'how stupid Liria is, they are doing it in her own house'. Even people who have known me well for a full year were, according to Liria, shocked to learn that I was living in her house. The two pastor's wives, Carmen and Emilia, who are always friendly and open with me, refused to take me in on the grounds that 'people would talk, and it would damage very much out testimony, our standing'. Today I began to understand the implications that having me in her house has for Liria, since even those who seem to accept me best and talk freely with me would not have me. According to Liria, even these people ask her if I pay her money, and if I help her in the house, and she said she feels compelled to say that I do, because it is a kind of justification. I said to Liria that, in my opinion, for them it is a question of finding out who is fooling who, who is being tricked, and who is doing the tricking, a very Gitano thing: Gitanos won't accept that ours could be a relationship on equal terms. So when her grandmother 'innocently' asked me where I was staying (she already knew) Liria told her, 'poor wee Palomi, she is very good, poor thing, she helps me a lot in the house and with the children.' Although I see that Liria could have done little else, I was rather offended at this, being made to look like a dimwit. But I didn't say anything.

Informant and anthropologist

Our friendship started with her kindness, taking me into her house although she barely knew me and even though I was bad news. I was a Paya, young, unattached, not really managing to gain acceptance in a strongly marginalised community where the dominant Payos were distrusted and despised, and where Payas were considered uniformly immoral and sexually promiscuous. It was only because Liria looked beyond the stereotypes and the conventions that dominated interactions between Payos and Gitanos, because she questioned what most around her took for granted, that we became friends. Her generosity, her compassion, and her curiosity were the foundation of our friendship. From the first time we met and throughout twenty years, she has loved, helped and supported me.

We were fascinated by each other, perhaps because we were both dissatisfied with our lives and because we embodied for the other the deep unfulfilled desire to belong somewhere else. I had had an average childhood in an upper-middle class, conservative family. I had learnt languages and travelled abroad relatively often, but had also been immersed in a world of rigid conventions regarding such things as class, upbringing, occupation, dress and accent. I looked to anthropology as an escape into imagined, alternative worlds, but all I did was exchange the inward-looking, suffocating atmosphere of the Madrid middle-class for the inward-looking, suffocating atmosphere of a Cambridge college, and I felt at ease in neither. Among the Gitanos of Villaverde I was even more out of place: by the time I met Liria I had been doing fieldwork for nine months and was increasingly frustrated and convinced that I would never 'get in'.

To start with, Liria seemed to me certain of her place and of her path in life. She was a well-respected young matron, a good street seller and money-maker, strict in her adherence to the highly elaborated Gitano code of conduct for women, always dressing modestly in long skirts, not smoking, drinking, or interacting with unrelated men. Her parents were well off by comparison with other Gitano families nearby, and they were very well liked, her father's patrilineage was large and powerful and controlled much of Gitano life in the ghetto. At fifteen, her mother had arranged her betrothal to an older relative, Ramón, and she had married well, at a wedding ceremony where her virginity was tested and displayed, rather than much less prestigiously by elopement like some of her cousins and friends. She fitted in, and yet I soon learnt that she was discontented, with her marriage to a man she did not love and who could not love her, with the routine of wifely everyday life, and with the restrictions that being a 'decent Gitana' imposed on her. Above all, she was desperately curious to know what things were like among the Payos, the Others who surrounded her but were beyond her reach. She had a deep intuitive understanding of what anthropology was about and embraced the informant role with enthusiasm.

Liria wanted to learn, about the Payos and so about me and what she called 'your world'. Together we took what seemed like huge risks, lying to Ramón and going for secret outings into Madrid so that she could see what my life was like. We dressed Payo-style, discarding our long skirts and putting on trousers, which the Gitanas never wore, and we visited museums, parks, middle-class restaurants, and the home where I grew up. Since she had opened up her house and her life to me, and she was so curious about mine, I felt I had to reciprocate and took Liria to my mother's flat, where she met not only my family but the housekeepers who worked for us, and to the university where we had lunch with my childhood friends, well-off boys and girls who studied business, law or economics. Just like fieldwork amongst the Gitanos for me, these trips into middle-class Madrid were a great adventure for Liria. Having spent all her life on the periphery of the city, she literally discovered a new Madrid. And, at the university, she talked freely with unrelated men of her own age for the first time in her life.

Our outings were interludes⬚from the strain of fieldwork for me, from the monotony of everyday life for her⬚and they made us accomplices. Aged 22, we were excited, by life itself and by our friendship. We talked endlessly, while selling in the streets, cooking, taking care of the children, and at night while Ramón watched TV. We talked about men and about sex, about our pasts and futures, about being Gitana and Paya, and about anthropology. We argued about whether, as a Paya, I really had more freedom than her, and of what kinds. I read to Liria from San Román's classic Gitano ethnography, and we discussed together the rights and wrongs of the anthropologist's account of Gitano patrilineages. I also read to her from my fieldnotes, and we laughed about things we had said only days or weeks before. Liria's friendship was a wonderful gift.

Looking back, I see that we were not preoccupied by the material inequalities between us, which now seem so blatantly important and which worry me so much. I was very aware of the large-scale hierarchies and inequalities that framed Gitano marginality, and of our relative positions within these, but in our everyday life in the ghetto I was out, wanting in. Yes, my parents were better off and I had reaped the benefits, having a comfortable life and going to study abroad. But Liria came from a Gitano family which was highly respected in Villaverde and she was secure in her role within the Gitano community, where the hierarchies and inequalities that mattered were among Gitanos, and where Payos were despised outsiders. In Villaverde Liria belonged and had status where I had none. Similarly, it did not occur to me that opening my life to Liria might be unethical. Later on, talking about our friendship to anthropological audiences in the UK, I have been criticised for not considering the impact that allowing Liria to meet my family might have on her, for not envisaging that it might make her dissatisfied with her lot as a poor Gitano woman. Back then, both of us knew that that I could not ask to be let into Liria's life whilst keeping mine out of her reach.

Friends

Paloma and I, after spending so many moments together from when she came to my house to do fieldwork until now, we have lived so many experiences together that I would not have notebooks enough to tell all the good things and the bad ones. Today I can say with all my heart that between myself and Paloma there is a relationship as if we were sisters, because friends are not just for when things go well, but for when things go badly. And throughout many years I think that both of us have realised that our relationship as friends has been very firm and sincere. Even when we were separated by a large distance because she had to work in England, nothing prevented us from staying in contact, by letters or by phone, and whenever she came to see her mother in the holidays she kept some days exclusively to share with me. Nothing has stopped our union as great friends. Even though one was Gitana and the other Paya, and even though we had such different customs, we knew very well how to share our ideas and our tastes. My whole world revolved around the Gitano environment (*entorno*), and when Paloma was living with me just seeing her was an eye-opener. I saw that a woman is not just good for marrying and having children and cleaning, even though within the Gitano world I used to go out with my sisters, to the beach in the summer, and in winter to the malls and shopping. But with Paloma I did other things, like visiting museums, or going to the university, and many more things that I loved. And above all she made me see my qualities as a woman. She always used to tell me that I was intelligent and a very good person, but in my family I was always treated as a something of a moron, and I used to be taken for a ride. One of the people who helped me see my good qualities and my worth was Paloma. In particular with Ramón, he knew how to have me all mixed up, psychologically, with the idea that I wasn't sufficiently clever, or pretty, and he told me so often that I came to believe it. Until one day a great friend turned up to tell me that this was not true, and through the years I have had other Paya friends, I had the pleasure of working with them when I was president of the parents' association in my daughter's school and they also encouraged me.

From the first time I met Paloma I opened my heart to her, as sincerely as possible, because as time went by I realised that I could tell her any secret since I knew she would keep it, and she knew she could also tell me anything, because with me it would be safe. The truth is that in this life you never know when you are going to need your friends. I think that in life, if you do good, the future can return it to you, although I never helped Paloma out of any kind of interest, and she knew it. Because when I helped Paloma I never thought that later on she would return the help to me with increase. When I decided to leave my Gitano environment (*entorno*) to find my happiness in a completely different world with a Moroccan partner (he was prepared to fight for our love against the Gitano people, Younes Bziz is his name), that is when I received all the support and the unconditional love, something never seen before, from my great friend Paloma. This is why we decided to write together. We both know we have many experiences to tell, together and apart, but our lives are always intertwined, the lives of two people, a Paya anthropologist with a great heart, and a sincere Gitana.

The middle years

Between 1993 and 2008 we wrote to each other, back and forth. We also talked on the telephone often and met whenever Paloma was in Madrid, at least once a year. As time went by, we continued to share our preoccupations – with pregnancies, children, schools, husbands, work, and our families. Liria and Ramón continued to earn their living by selling textiles at open air markets. They were resettled by the local government to a different flat, even closer to the ghetto where Paloma had carried out her fieldwork. Earning a livelihood became increasingly difficult as they became indebted and lost first one and then another permit to sell at weekly markets. Villaverde changed around them as immigration into Spain grew and more and more North Africans and Latin Americans came to the southern periphery of the city. Meanwhile,

Paloma and her husband obtained tenured academic positions, moved to Scotland and bought a house. They settled into a typically British middle-class life.

All along Paloma wrote about Liria and her relatives and neighbours, a book and articles: we were friends, but we were also anthropologist and informant. Liria helped Paloma with her anthropology because she was a friend. She had a sense of what Paloma's anthropological interests were but did not fully know what Paloma did with what she learnt, how she communicated her knowledge and to whom, and who benefitted or how. Paloma felt that she could only explain to Liria in very basic terms what her work was about, or how academic anthropology is produced. The jargon and theories through which Liria's life could be made anthropologically meaningful seemed to Paloma almost impossible to convey to her. The fact that Paloma wrote in English meant that Liria could not even read what Paloma produced.

Throughout these years our friendship continued whilst our personal lives changed. Liria's marriage deteriorated and she left Ramón several times. She took her children to her father's house, but was always persuaded by her family to return. But as her difficulties inside the home increased, Liria found satisfying rewards outside it. In 2008 she became president of the parents' association at her daughter's school. She found herself at the helm at a time of serious crisis, when the local government decided to transfer the children (mostly Gitano) to a smaller building of poorer quality, to make way for the children of a neighbouring school (mostly Payo). Liria became a key player in the campaign against the plans, making several appearances on national radio and television. Although the fight was lost, Liria discovered in herself new capacities and needs, the desire to become something else than a Gitana wife and mother. In the meantime Paloma too found herself moving in new directions. She become a mother by birth and adoption in her thirties, engaged in political activism, and let her career take second or even third place in her life. For both of us our horizons opened up throughout the 2000s: for Paloma to the world beyond anthropology and academia, for Liria beyond her family and the Gitano Evangelical Church. And then Liria met Younes, by chance, and our lives were brought closer than ever before.

Lives transformed

One morning like so many the unexpected happened. There was a young man working with some friends of mine at a stall nearby, we were separated only by some fruit sellers. I don't know how one morning I came to the stall of my friends to say hello, and to see the clothes they were selling, because often they had very pretty things and I liked to buy from them. The truth is that I had already seen that boy before, but shame and fear to fall in love, especially because he was younger than me, those things did not allow me to pay attention to him or to anybody else. But I don't know how something made me look at him that morning, and his eyes were fixed deep into mine. I felt that he talked with me through his eyes. I had never felt like that before.

One morning like so many the unexpected happened. Liria's sisters phoned me from Madrid. She had disappeared the day before, and they were desperate. They had found a small piece of paper with a man's name and a telephone number in one of Liria's handbags, and they suspected that she had eloped with him. I was to ring them immediately if she got in touch. I tried and tried Liria's phone, and texted her, 'Where are you? Everybody is worried. Is everything ok? Please get in touch, I'm dying of anguish here.' That evening she rang. She had left with Younes, her sisters had realised she was having an affair and she felt she had no option but to elope, straight away. She had tried living with Ramón for twenty years, and Younes loved her. She hadn't been able to take her young daughter along: according to Gitano customary law, which is often violently enforced, in cases of adultery children must remain with the blameless spouse. And so her family were looking for her, to bring her back and perhaps punish Liria, and Younes too. She was terrified. I was to pretend she had not been in touch, keep her secret, help her be safe.

I had no alternative but to return, because my sisters and their husbands found me, and my family threatened to kill Younes, and so I had no other option. Today I realise I allowed myself to be intimidated, and that my fear did not let me think straight. Now I see they could easily have harmed him before coming up to fetch me from the flat where I was hiding, because they were with him downstairs quite a while, but they did not. The thing is they convinced me, with threats and with kindness, they did all they could because they were desperate at that time. For me it was very painful, in two ways. First there was Younes, and being forced to leave him. I didn't know how to explain to him that my family feared that he had tricked me, or pressured me somehow to be with him, because I had never done anything like this before. And then there were my children, and when I returned my heart broke to see how much they had missed me. 'How am I going to recover my family, and my children?', that is what I was thinking back then. But it was too late, nobody trusted me, they kept me under watch all the time. They tried to make me see I was deluded, that it was all an illusion because I had never had happiness with Ramón. And so they thought I was very confused, and a little bit mad.

She had no alternative but to return and, when three weeks later I went to Madrid, all her family wanted to make sure I understood why she had done wrong. 'This is how we Gitanos do things, you know us, you understand us, you know how terrible this is for us, we are not like you Payos, this is beyond the pale, there is nothing worse than this.' I had to talk to her, they said, convince her not to elope again, help to keep her in the house, under their control. Ramón, Carmen and Liria's other sisters, her children, her daughter-in-law... they were the voice of Gitano reason. They knew how close Liria and I were, and were desperate for me to take sides. These were 'the Gitanos' of whom I had written for so many years, and what they said fitted all I had learnt about them: women's virtue and subservience to men were central to how they saw their place in the world. And yet she asked for my help, and she was Liria, my friend, a woman whose fears and desires I knew, who had shared with me her wishes and disappointments, who loved me and whom I loved. So I did not say 'leave' or 'stay', but I helped her meet Younes clandestinely, taking our young children along as cover, knowing that the family would never think we would try something like that. When she decided she would leave for good, I helped again, sorting out plans, listening to Liria's fears, anxieties, and hopes, and gving some of the money they needed to try to start again. After she and Younes went into hiding, I became the point of contact between Liria and her family, relaying her children's heart-wrenching pleas, receiving and forwarding Ramón's desperate letters.

My heart is broken in two. Every day that passes I feel worse, for my daughter. Whenever I see girls of her age in the street I die inside, it is true. Something is killing me inside. I try not to tell Younes and I go into the bathroom to cry. I tell myself, 'Be happy'. How can I be happy knowing that my daughter needs me? Then I say, 'What if I return, and I die of longing for Younes?' I can't think of anything else, I only think about her.

Her heart is broken in two. Liria spent six months of living with Younes, in flats shared with African and Latin American immigrants, working as a domestic, hiding her Gitano identity from her middle-class employers, people very similar to my own family. We talked almost every day, and I visited her in Madrid every few weeks. I could see how much she and Younes loved each other, how much fun and freedom she had in her new life, but also how deeply cutting her pain was. I saw her cry with my daughter in her arms. I raged at Ramón and her sisters, who were unwavering: so long as she stayed away, she would not see her child. And if she took the child, they told me, they would kill both her and Younes. I understood well the cultural logic that underlay their actions, and knew I could not expect them to behave in a different way, yet I did. I began to ask myself about the force of compassion and of hatred too: could Ramón and Liria's sisters not take pity on her, just because they were Gitanos? Were they so firm because they were Gitanos, or because they hurt? Liria asked for my help and from Scotland I rang women's NGOs in Madrid, government agencies, social workers, solicitors, but nobody seemed to be able or willing to give any help. They were all puzzled by the complexities of the Gitano world, unable to understand why Liria would not simply apply for a divorce, request access to her child through the usual legal routes, why she was frightened, why there were threats. We could not see a way forward and so she went back once again.

When for the second time I had to return it was much worse. I thought that after so many conversations with my sisters and my children's father, the situation was going to be better. But it was much worse. I could feel a tremendous hatred from Ramón. Earlier on, even when I was an honest and stupid woman our marriage did not go well, so imagine the situation after living six months away from home, with another man, and Ramón swallowing his pride of Gitano man, fooled by a woman who was inferior to him. So the last night I spent with my daughter I made her a promise, and I told her, 'Darling, whatever happens I want you to know I love you very much', and told her that if one day we had to be apart from each other for whatever reason, I would fight for her, until we could be together again. She looked into my eyes and said, 'Mama, you are going to leave again'. And with pain in my soul, and so as not to worry her, I said no, but that if that happened I would go back to get her. And I looked at her straight and said, 'You believe me, don't you?' So the first thing I did when I returned with Younes was find a solicitor to get custody of my child, and my divorce from Ramón. I got on with it, ready to face the world for the sake of my daughter.

When for the second time she had to return it was much worse. Ramón knew I had helped Liria with money and emotional support during her time away: although he allowed us to talk on his mobile phone, he was always nearby, listening closely to our conversations. Younes was heartbroken, thinking that she had left him for good, and would not sleep or eat. We talked often, but there was little I could do for him. Liria had managed to hide a mobile phone, and she would go into the bathroom at three of four in the morning, to ring Younes and me. In whispers, she told me about her life: she had no freedom, Ramón was in touch with a solicitor to get sole custody of her child, he wanted to have sex in spite of her reluctance, and she missed Younes desperately. When her sisters brought a Gitano Pentecostal priest to exorcise her, she thought it was the last straw, and decided to leave knowing that this time there would be no turning back.

Sharing our lives

When Liria left her home for the very first time, but also later, she and Younes were in dire need of money. Since they had to hide from Liria's family, they also lost their livelihoods. Liria could no longer sell with Ramón and Younes could no longer work for Gitano street-market sellers loading and unloading stock. As the economic crisis deepened and Spain's unemployment reached 20%, finding work became almost impossible. Without papers the only jobs Younes could find were sporadic and very badly paid. They could not afford to lose Liria's small disability pension, so she worked without contracts for two or three euros per hour, cooking in bars, as an office cleaner or as a domestic servant.

Knowing it would be difficult to provide substantial economic help on a long-term basis, Paloma applied first to her Department and then for a small grant to pay Liria for writing down her life. What began as a way to find money became a project that came to fascinate us both. We started to tape long conversations, about Liria's elopement, our earlier lives, and our families and friendship. Liria wrote, and Paloma wrote too. Liria went to Scotland, visiting Paloma abroad for the first time ever. She talked to Paloma's colleagues and students, and we gave a talk about our relationship. As Liria's and Younes' life unfolded, and as Paloma shared in it, we thought together about what it meant. Since Paloma was not just an observer, but a player in the story, it became clear that what we wrote had to include her too.

In March 2011, two years after she first eloped, Liria went to court to claim visiting rights to her child. She was the first Gitano woman to turn to the Payo courts to challenge Gitano traditional law and custom. Paloma went with her, and we came face to face with Liria's sisters, their husbands, and Ramón. In spite of repeated requests, we had not managed to be allocated police protection, and we were frightened that Ramón or Liria's brothers-in-law would manage to hurt one or both of us. All in Liria's family thought Paloma had betrayed them and had shown her true nature as a Paya, helping Liria in her transgression. They were wrong in thinking that Paloma had encouraged Liria to leave, but right in identifying the strength of our bond.

Paloma's Spanish family too have seen our friendship, and are disturbed by it. One of Paloma's sisters suggested a solicitor and a social worker who might help. Another opened her home to Liria and Younes when they needed a place to stay for a couple of nights. But their middle class, comfortable lives have very little in common with Liria's and Younes's, and they are keen to keep their distance. They have a highly developed sense of class and ethnic distinctiveness, like many other well-off, culturally conservative Madrileños. They believe firmly in their economic and moral superiority. Paloma's family see Gitanos like Liria and immigrants like Younes as unfortunate parts of Spanish society, to be blamed for their 'situation', victims of their inability to join in or 'integrate'. They perceive Younes, like other Moroccan immigrants, as one of the lowest of the low, a member of an abject tide that threatens to engulf Spain. They call him, pejoratively, 'el moro' ('the Moor'), and have been adamant that he must under no circumstance visit their homes, where Paloma stays during her visitsto Madrid. The majority of Paloma's Spanish relatives are not unlike Liria's Gitano family in the effort they make to keep themselves distinct, and in their conviction that they, and only they, live righteous and beautiful lives. But while Liria's family were the amongst the first Gitanos to open their lives and their homes to Paloma, most of Paloma's family want to have as little as possible to do with Liria or Younes. For them, Paloma's friendship with Liria is a sign of her unfortunate eccentricity. The fact that Paloma spends more time with Liria than with her own sisters or her mother, demonstrates that Paloma has failed in her responsibilities to her family.

Writing together

I learnt what anthropology was when Paloma came to live in my house. I had a vague idea of what anthropology was, but it was living together day by day, seeing Paloma's fieldwork, that I learnt its meaning. I think it is a very beautiful work that opens frontiers onto new worlds. Because it is not just writing about other people, but getting to know their lives, their customs, religions, and their ways of being. I find it fascinating, writing not only about my life, but about Paloma's life. Because I have always been the informant, but now we are breaking the mould. We know that telling our lives, together and united, is going to be something never done before. Two women, a Paya and a Gitana, but very close from youth, breaking the barriers between two different levels and ways of life, although that distance never pulled us apart. Since I started writing about anthropology I have found it wonderful to have the opportunity to express my feelings towards other people, and to understand them. As I write about Paloma, I also learn to see things in a different way, especially because we two have been brought up so differently, in our customs. I know for sure that what I am doing right now is that I would like to do for the rest of my life, because getting to know people, their customs, their experiences, their sadness and their joys, and especially having another person opening their heart to you, is wonderful.

I want people to know what the world of a Gitana is like, told by herself, and also how my life has changed so that through circumstances I find myself in the Payo world. I want to tell how I see everything, and also how my life changed, and also how things changed for Paloma and those who surround us, like Younes, and Paloma's husband and her children... All of us have come much closer together. Being able to become united while you work, that is the beauty of anthropology. For me anthropology is about complicity and union, so that we all of us can build a better world, a world with more love.

I have learnt what anthropology is alongside Liria, and my understanding has changed as we have become older and our lives have been transformed. For many years after I first did fieldwork among the Gitanos I thought that my task was to extract information, make knowledge, weave patterns with words. I wrote and I looked away from those parts of experience I could not make sense of easily, from what did not fit into the moulds I had built. And so much of Liria's life, and of the lives of her relatives and neighbours, was invisible to me. Over the last few years I have been drawn into Liria's life much deeper than ever before, and she into mine. Sharing our happiness and our difficulties, I have had to confront the nitty-gritty of experience, as a person and as an anthropologist.

The bedrock of anthropology is fieldwork, because fieldwork is what brings us into deep contact with people, with their daily miseries and joys, their fears and their hopes. And it is during fieldwork that we anthropologists open ourselves up to others. But then those others, our informants, are left behind, they do not continue the journey with us. Imagine the possibilities if the deep mutual commitment that is so often seeded in fieldwork were allowed to grow, to spread into other areas of life. I do not know how successful our experiment has been. But I know that, if I want to learn and write about Liria, I have to let her learn and write about me. We share our lives, this is why we write together.

We meet in the spaces between worlds: between Gitanos and Payos, between immigrants and middle-class Spaniards, between informants and anthropologists.

These worlds touch and interpenetrate, but they are also sealed away from each other, in many senses far apart. Anthropology is what has enabled us to come together, yet anthropology also erects barriers between us: until now Paloma has watched, investigated, looked for, written; Liria has been in a way in the dark. Our relation has been unequal, not because of Paloma's greater wealth, but because Liria was a friend above all while Paloma was always a friend and an anthropologist. For anthropology to reach its potential to change the world, barriers like these need to be not just acknowledged, but undermined. By writing together, about our lives, our friendship, and our worlds, we hope to have contributed, in a small way, towards this project.